TOLKIEN'S SACRAMENTAL VISION

Discerning the Holy in Middle Earth

Craig Bernthal

TOLKIEN'S SACRAMENTAL VISION

Discerning the Holy in Middle Earth

First published
by Second Spring, 2014
www.secondspring.co.uk
an imprint of Angelico Press
© Craig Bernthal 2014

For information, address:
Angelico Press
4709 Briar Knoll Dr.
Kettering, OH 45429
angelicopress.com

978-1-62138-053-5

Cover design: Michael Schrauzer

CONTENTS

For Sarah and Luke

ACKNOWLEDGMENTS

Most of what we have has been given to us, and this is no less true in the writing of books than in any other endeavor. Not only do we inherit a language, but the "story soup" of all mankind.

Although I take sole responsibility for the contents of his book, many people helped me to produce it. I want to thank Dean Vida Samiian and the College of Arts and Humanities at Fresno State for a sabbatical, during academic year 2012–2013, that gave me the time to do the writing and for financial aid in paying for copyright permissions; and to the Hoover Institution, where I was a W. Glenn Campbell and Rita Ricardo-Campbell National Fellow in 2012–2013. Victor Davis Hanson and Bruce Thornton were constant in their encouragement and stimulation. The Rev. Canon Keith Brown read the entire book and parts of it twice, checking my theology and offering his own insights. Loren Palsgaard also read portions and gave valuable advice. I want to thank my wife Gail, and my children, Sarah and Luke, for their reading, comments, and steadfast encouragement. Finally, my deep appreciation goes to John Riess and Angelico Press for publishing *Tolkien's Sacramental Vision* and to Mark Sebanc for his copy-editing skills.

In going through the process of obtaining copyright permissions, I had the gracious help of Clare Posner (Houghton Mifflin Harcourt) and Imogen Plouviez (HarperCollins UK). Thanks to the publishers of Tolkien's work and to the Tolkien Estate for allowing me to quote from the following books:

Acknowledgments

Excerpts from the following books are reprinted by permission of HarperCollins Publishers Ltd.:

The Lord of the Rings © Fourth Age Limited 1954, 1955, 1966.

The Silmarillion © The J.R.R. Tolkien Estate Limited and C.R. Tolkien 1977.

The Hobbit © The J.R.R. Tolkien Estate Limited 1937, 1965.

On Fairy Stories © The Tolkien Trust 1964.

Morgoth's Ring © The J.R.R. Tolkien Copyright Trust and C.R. Tolkien 1993.

Letters of J.R.R. Tolkien © The J.R.R. Tolkien Copyright Trust 1981.

Leaf by Niggle © The Tolkien Trust 1964.

Mythopoeia © The J.R.R. Tolkien Copyright Trust 1988.

"I believe that legends and myths are largely made of 'truth', and indeed present aspects of it that can only be received in this mode."
J.R.R. Tolkien[1]

---

1 J. R. R. Tolkien, *The Letters of J. R. R. Tolkien,* ed., Humphrey Carpenter with Christopher Tolkien (New York: Houghton Mifflin, 2000), 147.

INTRODUCTION
Light From an Invisible Lamp

The Lord of the Rings, though panned by many academics and intellectuals, has for half a century been one of the most popular books in the history of English literature.[1] Wikipedia lists it as the second best-selling novel of all time, at 150 million copies, behind *A Tale of Two Cities*. *The Hobbit* ranks as number 4 with 135 million sales.[2] Those who dislike Tolkien's work tend to dislike both it and him intensely. Some associate Tolkien with an atavistic and authoritarian Catholicism and all the baggage they assume goes with it. Others see him, usually in addition, as the constructor of an infantile and escapist fairy-story, naively patriarchal, and misogynistic.[3] Harold Bloom condescendingly says about "Tolkien's trilogy," that, "Its style is quaint, pseudobiblical, overly melodramatic, and its personages are so much cardboard.

---

1 Tom Shippey, *J.R.R. Tolkien, Author of the Century* (Boston: Houghton, Mifflin, 2000). Shippey's "Foreword" has an excellent summary of Tolkien's popularity and the vitriolic intellectual response.

2 Https://en.wikipedia.org/wiki/List_of_best-selling_books, accessed April 1, 2013.

3 Edmund Wilson was one of the first detractors in "Oo, Those Awful Orcs," *The Nation* (April 14, 1956). For more current examples, see Jenny Turner's ironically titled "Reasons for Liking Tolkien," *London Review* 23, no. 22 (15 November 2001), in which she credits Tolkien and his work with paranoia, soggy-sentimentality, and male supremacy. My favorite detractor is Germaine Greer: "it has been my nightmare that Tolkien would turn out to be the most influential writer of the twentieth century. The bad dream has materialized [in] 'the book of the century.'" *W: The Waterstone's Magazine* (Winter/Spring 1997) 8: 2–9; W.H. Auden, on the other hand, hardly a sentimentalist, loved the book. See his two reviews, "The Hero is a Hobbit," *The New York Times* (October 31, 1954), on *The Fellowship of the Ring*; "At the End of the Quest, Victory," *The New York Times* (January 22, 1956), on *The Return of the King*.

But then, I am aware that my standards are literary-critical, and many now find them archaic in our age of pop culture."[4] Thus Bloom manages to preen while his scholarship fails. Tolkien never meant *The Lord of the Rings* to be published as anything but one book and only accepted a tripartite split at the insistence of his publisher, Allen & Unwin.[5] Bloom's rejection of Tolkien's style is finally a rejection of epic register, but to reject that is to deny the possibility of writing a heroic romance in the 20th century. Tolkien writes in many registers, from the psalm-like proclamations of eagles to the mundane and novelistic speech of Hobbits, and he needs them all to create the multi-layered world of Middle-earth.[6] What might strike Bloom as "quaint" in all of this is not just Tolkien's prose, but what it dramatizes: a pre-modern sense of self that understands its source of meaning to be located, not within an expressive and experimental self that is essentially private, but from without, in allegiance to neighborhood, friends, kingdoms, and however hidden, to angelic powers and ultimately to God.[7] This, I hope to show, is part of what it means to have a "sacramental imagination."

Tolkien stated that death was the central concern of *The Lord*

4 Harold Bloom, ed. *Bloom's Modern Critical Interpretations: J. R. R. Tolkien's 'The Lord of the Rings'* (NY: Infobase Publishing, 2008). Bloom has not gotten past his distaste for Tolkien's fiction into any significant reading of biographical background or publication history. In addition to the goof about Tolkien's "trilogy," he also asserts that at the Western Front Tolkien "was wounded," whereas he was evacuated with trench fever.

5 *Letters*, 163–65; Tolkien did not want *The Lord of the Rings* split into three parts. Also see, on this topic, Humphrey Carpenter, *J. R. R. Tolkien, A Biography* (NY: Houghton Mifflin, 1977), 213.

6 For an argument that Tolkien writes beautiful prose, see Steve Walker's meticulous study, *The Power of Tolkien's Prose: Middle-Earth's Magical Style* (NY: Palgrave MacMillan, 2009).

7 For a history of the development of the modern self, two good starting points are Michael Gillespie, *The Theological Origins of Modernity* (Chicago: University of Chicago Press, 2009) and Charles Taylor, *The Secular Age* (Cambridge, MA: Belknap Press of Harvard University, 2007); a good overview is provided in Ron Highfield, *God, Freedom & Human Dignity: Embracing a God-Centered Identity in a Me-Centered Culture* (Downers Grove: InterVarsity Press, 2013).

of the Rings, but Michael Moorcock, who calls the book "Epic Pooh," claims its central fault is that it ignores death. He then indicts Tolkien for being plagued by nostalgia for a lost countryside and failure to "derive any pleasure from the realities of urban industrial life."[8] Tolkien was outspoken about his distaste for the modern urban world, and, I believe, would have admitted nostalgia for the countryside of his youth. But he certainly would not have thought love of the countryside "infantile," and neither would a line of England's best poets from Thomas Traherne through Wordsworth, Coleridge, and Hopkins. Tolkien's greatest villains hate the countryside and try to destroy it, as they do all of creation. They mean to desacralize the world and, therefore, desacramentalize it.

Even readers who love *The Lord of the Rings* are sometimes allergic to the idea that a specifically Catholic vision is part of the work. "After speaking on Tolkien in San Francisco and New York City, critic Joseph Pearce witnessed some members of the audience leaving the room 'upon hearing that Tolkien's Catholicism was an integral and crucial part of *The Lord of the Rings*.'"[9] This reaction can also be found among some critics who screen out Christian influence or reject the idea that Catholic Christianity is displayed in Tolkien's work in any significant way. Philip Pullman, who had a moment of notoriety with the book, *His Dark Materials*, dismisses Tolkien simply on the basis of his Catholicism: "Tolkien was a Catholic, for whom the basic issues of life were not in question, because the Church had all the answers. So nowhere in 'The Lord of the Rings' is there a moment's doubt about those big questions. No one is in any doubt about what's

---

8 Michael Moorcock, "Epic Pooh," *Bloom's Modern Critical Interpretations: J.R.R. Tolkien's 'The Lord of the Rings'*, 3–18. Moorcock indicts orthodox Catholic writers and their imagined public, the petit bourgeoisie, *en masse*: "Like Chesterton, and other Orthodox Christian writers who substituted faith for artistic rigor he [Tolkien] sees the petit bourgeoisie, the honest artisans and peasants, as the bulwark against Chaos," 5–6.

9 Paul E. Kerry, "Tracking Catholic Influence in *The Lord of the Rings*," in *The Ring and The Cross*, ed. Paul E. Kerry (Kent, OH: Kent State University Press, 2012), 239, quoting Joseph Pearce, "Tolkien Revisited," *Saint Austin Review* (January–February 2003): 1.

good or bad; everyone knows where the good is, and what to do about the bad. Enormous as it is, TLOTR is consequently trivial."[10] But Pullman's ignorance of the Catholic Church is abysmal. It has always understood that God and his Creation are mysterious, beyond human understanding, and has maintained a lively debate about the conjunction of moral rules, happiness, and the demands of love since its foundation.[11] One might rather say, with a more profound writer than Pullman, Walker Percy, that it is the materialists who look for the pat explanations:

> This life is too much trouble, far too strange, to arrive at the end of it and then to be asked what you make of it and have to answer "Scientific humanism." That won't do. A poor show. Life is a mystery, love is a delight. Therefore I take it as axiomatic that one should settle for nothing less than the infinite mystery and the infinite delight, i.e., God. In fact I demand it. I refuse to settle for anything less. I don't see why anyone should settle for less than Jacob, who actually grabbed ahold of God and would not let go until God identified himself and blessed him.[12]

Tolkien, with Percy, does not settle for less. And it is not true that Tolkien fails to present his characters with moral dilemmas, including the most important one in human politics, whether the end ever justifies the means. Tolkien's characters have clear-cut moral decisions and face the pervasive problem of finding the will to deny self-interest and pursue the right, which is the human dilemma most of the time. We do not usually dwell in some ambiguous moral twilight, however much such border-zones are loved by modern philosophers and fiction writers.

10 Email interview with Peter T. Chattaway, November 28, 2007, in *Patheos*, http://www.patheos.com/blogs/filmchat/2007/11/philip-pullman-the-extended-e-mail-interview.html, accessed October 17, 2013.

11 For an excellent introduction to that discussion, see Paul J. Wadell, *Happiness and the Christian Moral Life* 2nd ed. (Plymouth, UK: Rowman and Littlefield, 2012).

12 Walker Percy, "Questions They Never Asked Me," from *Esquire* 88 (December 1977) in Lewis A. Lawson and Victor A. Kramer, eds. *Conversations with Walker Percy* (Jackson, MS: University Press of Mississippi, 1985), 175. [Author's note: Percy goes on to point out that *ahold* is a Louisiana expression.]

There is something to be said for dealing with the main problem of our lives: finding the will to do what we know is right. If this provides a trivial topic for literary exploration, then *Crime and Punishment* too would have to be marked down as "trivial."

I find among my students that those who enjoy Tolkien are initially drawn in by an exciting adventure with Hobbits, Elves, Wizards, and Orcs, but there is something more in Tolkien that attracts his huge audience: his creation of a world that is both mysterious and meaningful all the way down. As students delve into the religious and metaphysical underpinning of Middle-earth, they become even more attracted to it. There is a good reason for this. They come to the humanities looking for meaning—they want to understand what a good life is and how to live it, whether there is "truth" and what it might be; they look for beauty and sublimity in literature and an enlarged understanding of who they are.

Many of them are attracted by Tolkien's vision of the holy. *The Lord of the Rings* has a numinous quality. It comes in part from Tolkien's unique ability to suggest great depths of time, which he does through the creation of ancient languages, the continual suggestion of providential depth, and the display of immense and psychologically productive landscapes. Tolkien uses landscape in the same way as Tennyson, "not as a decorative adjunct to character but as the mythopoetic soil in which character is rooted and takes its being."[13] The Shire, Rivendell, Lothlórien, Gondor, and Rohan tell us much about their inhabitants. By knowing geography, we come to know people whose selves grow organically from their native soil. In addition, Tolkien's panoramic vistas, by which his travelers orient themselves, display a broad range of moral and psychic potential. The continual question for the heroes of *The Lord of the Rings* is, "Which way do we go?" This is both a practical question and a spiritual one: stay on the Great

---

13 John D. Rosenberg, *The Fall of Camelot: A Study of Tennyson's "Idylls of the King"* (Cambridge, MA: Harvard University Press, 1973), 67–68; quoted by Andrew Lynch, "Archaism, Nostalgia, and Tennysonian War in *The Lord of the Rings,*" in Jane Chance and Alfred K. Siewers, eds. *Tolkien's Modern Middle Ages* (New York: Palgrave Macmillan, 2009), 77–92.

Road or get off it? Caradheras or Moria? Gondor or Mordor? The Black Gate or Cirith Ungol? Each landscape presents a moral choice and actualizes a spiritual condition, from comfort to desolation. Tolkien's most lyric descriptions of the world his characters pass through are founded in a deep gratitude for creation, the foundation of his spiritual and ethical vision.

Finally, like all great works of art, *The Lord of the Rings* has a taste all its own that defies restatement in critical analysis. One "tastes" its particular enchantment or one does not. For those who can taste it, Tolkien alerts them to a deep hollow in contemporary life and a way it might be filled. It is a hollow many nineteenth- and twentieth-century English writers felt and resisted: Samuel Taylor Coleridge, John Henry Newman, Gerard Manley Hopkins, and G.K. Chesterton, as well as Eliot, Auden, Waugh, Lewis and their immediate predecessors, all of whom held out for a universe which was both meaningful and beyond human comprehension, in which God and the three transcendentals were assumed to exist, objectively, not according to taste. These men, with Flannery O'Connor and Walker Percy on the American side, were either Roman Catholics or "Catholic" in the broad sense of the word. They believed in a Christian reality that just *was* reality.[14] A secularized literature, by excluding God, was a maimed literature; it could only present a maimed and distorted view of the world, for it had sliced away the most real thing in it.

---

14 This group of artists and thinkers was mainly powered by Catholic converts such as Newman, Hopkins, Chesterton, Waugh, Graham Greene, and, at a very young age, through his mother, Tolkien himself. Christopher Dawson, the historian, was one of the most influential. On the American side, converts included Orestes Brownson, Dorothy Day, and Thomas Merton. Books about this efflorescence of Catholic thought, which passes unnoticed by the big literary anthologies or departments of English, include: Paul Elie, *The Life You Save May Be Your Own: An American Pilgrimage* (NY: Farrar, Strauss, Giroux, 2003) and Patrick Allitt, *Catholic Converts: British and American Intellectuals Turn to Rome* (Ithaca: Cornell University Press, 1997). Other English and American converts with influence in the world of letters and art include Oscar Wilde, Muriel Spark, Alec Guinness, Avery Cardinal Dulles, G.E.M. Anscombe, and, oddly enough, Buffalo Bill Cody.

Tolkien's main contribution to the "recovery" of reality in art was, he claimed, to write not a novel, but a heroic romance, "a much older and quite different variety of literature,"[15] of which *Sir Gawain and the Green Knight*, which Tolkien edited, and *Morte D'Arthur* are examples. *The Lord of the Rings* is in many ways a novel—the Hobbits of necessity bring in the level of mundane, which is the novel's hallmark—but it is also full of the elements of chivalric romance: great martial deeds, fiercely loyal lovers, wizards, strange creatures, the irruption of the supernatural into the natural. Tolkien creates with a pre-modern sense of reality— a mythopoetic sense—and Middle-earth, though under attack by evil forces and deathly assumptions, is so alive that trees talk and even mountains have malevolent dispositions. "Mythopoeia," refers to the entire process of myth-making throughout history; in Tolkien's use of the word "mythopoesis," however, he also includes the deliberate construction of myth, the process by which one author sets forth the numinous dimension of reality in story. Tolkien gives us a world, 6000 years before the birth of Christ, placed roughly in Northwest Europe, which he positions theologically between man's fall and ultimate redemption[16]—a world which has not yet been "disenchanted,"[17] which is uninformed by Christian revelation and yet informed *by* it as an underlying providential rhythm.

Whether his readers realize it or not, Tolkien's meaningful world is specifically embedded in a Roman Catholic account of what reason is and, more importantly, what is real. This account combines Hellenic and Judaic thought to give an explanation of why we assume the world can be rationally understood in the same way, day after day. Andrew Davison gives a thumbnail description of the genealogy of Western rationality that might

15 *Letters*, 414.

16 *Letters*, 387: "The Fall of Man is in the past and off stage; the Redemption of Man in the far future."

17 The famous phrase is Max Weber's, adapted from Frederich Schiller. See H.H. Gerth and C. Wright Mills, "Bureaucracy and Charisma: A Philosophy of History," in *Charisma, History and Social Structure*, Ronald Glassman and William H. Swatos, Jr. eds. (Westport, CT: Greenwood Press, 1986), 11.

make even atheists like Richard Dawkins and Daniel Dennett feel uncomfortably Christian:

> As Einstein is said to have put it: 'what is most incomprehensi-
> ble about the world is that it is comprehensible.' In other
> words, why does the world make sense? What right have we to
> assume that it should? Christians can make sense of the uni-
> verse's sense, saying that it is God's creation, made after the
> pattern of the Son, who is Word, Reason, or Logos. There is
> logic because there is Logos; the world is open to reason
> because there is Reason in God. . . . It is part of the Christian
> faith that we have an account of why it is so.[18]

Tolkien places the Logos in his universe through the Music of Ilúvatar, and this makes it not only meaningful, but grace-full. A universe created by the Logos runs on an economy of grace and graceful transactions—sacramental transactions—which fill *The Lord of the Rings* from beginning to end.

In this book, I will argue for four general propositions in order of increasing specificity: 1) *The Lord of the Rings* is a "Catholic Novel," written by a Catholic author; 2) The idea of the Logos, as set forth in the prologue of the Gospel of John and developed in patristic and medieval theology, is largely incorporated into Tolk-ien's creation myth, *The Ainulindalë*; 3) Tolkien is influenced by wide biblical understanding and imagery throughout his work, particularly the Gospel of John, letters attributed to John, and Catholic sacramental theology; and 4) Tolkien's Logos-centric universe in the *Ainulindalë* becomes the foundation for his por-trayal of Arda (Earth) from a sacramental perspective in *The Lord of the Rings*.

My last three claims rest upon Tolkien's understanding of the relationship of Truth to myth, including the myths that people deliberately make up. Specifically, it is about the relationship of his own works, such as *The Hobbit*, *The Lord of the Rings*, and *The Silmarillion* to Truth. I capitalize Truth, because for Tolkien, a devout Catholic Christian, God was the Truth, and the Logos of

---

18 *"Christian Reason and Christian Community,"* in Andrew Davison, ed. *Imaginative Apologetics: Theology, Philosophy, and the Catholic Tradition* (Grand Rapids: Baker Academic, 2012); Kindle Location 680–97.

John's Gospel—the Incarnate Word—its most humanly powerful expression. Tolkien believed, with John, that "the true Light" of Christ enlightened "every man" (John 1:9), though the closer to the Logos people stood, the more light their minds received.

If we imagine a solar system, with the Divine Logos, "the Word" of St. John's prologue, at the center like a blazing sun, and world mythologies swirling like planets around it, we have a good picture of Tolkien's basic idea. At the closest orbit to the Son/Sun we have salvation history, the "true myth," the Word which Tolkien believed God himself was inscribing in human events, the most important chapter being the life, death, and resurrection of Christ. Orbiting very closely to the Truth as inscribed in history is the recording of that truth in the Bible, especially the four gospels. At farther removes, and with more or less eccentric orbits, were other world mythologies. The ones which came in closest, perhaps more like comets than planets, were the rising and dying god myths attached to Near East, Eastern, Greek, and Germanic deities such as Baal, Melqart, Ishtar, Adonis, Eshmun, Tammuz, Ra, Dionysius, Persephone, Odin and Baldur. That there were many such myths was not, for Tolkien, to suggest that Christianity was just another dying and rising god myth, but rather a confirmation of Christian belief: not so much the worse for Christianity, but so much the better for the pagans that so many of them in so many places and times had seen part of the Truth. Closely akin to myth, and gravitating toward it were fairy stories, whose miraculous, happy endings, achieved after hope is lost, catch an Easter-like joy.

For Tolkien, the supreme true myth of the gospels was one in which the Logos, Art, and History had fused:

> There is no tale ever told that men would rather find was true, and none which so many skeptical men have accepted as true on its own merits. For the Art of it has the supremely convincing tone of Primary Art, that is, of Creation. To reject it leads either to sadness or to wrath.[19]

---

19 J.R.R. Tolkien, "On Fairy Stories," in *Tree and Leaf* (New York: Harper Collins, 1988), 72.

This was the supremely centripetal tale that drew men in, whether they wanted or not, whether they realized it or not.

Within Tolkien's Logos-centric system we also can place deliberately constructed myths, which also take a position with respect to Truth, such as Virgil's *Aeneid,* Dante's *Commedia,* Milton's *Paradise Lost,* and Tolkien's own legendarium. In love with Germanic myth, Tolkien placed the orbit of his work somewhere between the biblical account of Truth and those myths and sagas, which included not only Norse and Celtic mythology, but Anglo-Saxon literature such as *Beowulf,* "The Wanderer," and *The Battle of Maldon.* The Greek and Roman gods have a place in his myth as well. One of Tolkien's correspondents told him that, "you create a world in which some sort of faith seems to be everywhere without a visible source, like light from an invisible lamp."[20] That invisible lamp is the Logos, shining through Germanic myth. My purpose is to examine the sacramental Christian reality at the foundation of the Germanic mythos that forms *The Lord of the Rings,* which Tolkien described as a "fundamentally religious and Catholic work."[21]

✠

Tolkien's life could also be described by this Logos-centric model. For the orphaned Tolkien, the Catholic Church became his home and a priest his foster-father. This formed the core of this character. His love of languages and Germanic mythology followed shortly thereafter, so much so, that he first began to create his own languages and then realized he needed a mythic world to put them in, for languages themselves were essentially mythic.

Tolkien was not Catholic by birth, but his early life put him inside Catholic spirituality, liturgy, and thought to an unusual degree, at a time when English Catholics still had a sense of themselves as a persecuted minority. Tolkien literally lived *within* the Catholic Church as a boy, in the Birmingham Oratory, where he inhaled that inflection of Catholicism associated with Cardinal John Henry Newman: the English love of nature, commonsense,

20 *Letters*, 413.
21 Ibid., 172.

and the sacraments. Add to this a playful acceptance of eccentricity, an appreciation of tobacco and beer, a seemingly unquenchable thirst for languages, and a fascination with "Northernness," the myths and sagas of Germanic legend, and one gets a good sense of Tolkien's imaginative world.

His father died in South Africa, when Tolkien was three, after he, his brother Hillary, and his mother, Mabel, had moved back to England. She became a Catholic convert in 1900. She had been raised in the Anglican Church, but, when Tolkien was eight, she was received into the Church of Rome together with her sister, May. Conversion not only isolated Mabel both from her family, the Suffields, and from the Tolkiens, but subjected her to their anger and outrage. She was virtually disowned and had to find a way to survive on her own with her two young sons, John Ronald Reuel and Hilary. Mabel remained true to her faith and began instructing her sons in it.

When Tolkien was ten, Mabel moved her family from the Sussex countryside to Birmingham, into a house next to the Grammar School of St. Philip, which was very close to the Birmingham Oratory and staffed by its clergy. The Oratory had been founded by Newman, who died within its walls during the year of Mabel's conversion. It had been home to Newman's pupil, Gerard Manley Hopkins, during the first months of Hopkins's conversion.

At St. Philip, Mabel's sons received a Catholic education, and Mabel became friends with Father Francis Xavier Morgan, who would become a foster-father to John Ronald and Hilary. Humphrey Carpenter gives this sketch of Fr. Morgan:

> Francis Morgan ... had an immense fund of kindness and humour and a flamboyance that was often attributed to his Spanish connections. Indeed he was a very noisy man, loud and affectionate, embarrassing to small children at first but hugely lovable when they got to know him. He soon became an indispensable part of the Tolkien household.
>
> Without his friendship, life for Mabel and her sons would have shown scant improvement on the previous two years.[22]

22 Humphrey Carpenter, *J. R. R. Tolkien, A Biography* (Boston: Houghton Mifflin, 2000), 35.

11

Mabel Tolkien died in 1904 in a cottage on the grounds of a country house built by Cardinal Newman as a retreat for Oratory clergy. She had diabetes, and she was exhausted. Nine years after her death, Tolkien wrote in a letter, "My own dear mother was a martyr indeed, and it is not to everybody that God grants so easy a way to his great gifts as he did to Hilary and myself, giving us a mother who killed herself with labour and trouble to ensure us keeping the faith."[23]

Mabel's death, like baptism and confirmation, sealed Tolkien as a Catholic. Tolkien remembered his mother as one who had lived a life of self-sacrificing love, fulfilling her baptismal vocation by participating in Christ's self-sacrificing love. She was buried in the Catholic cemetery at Bromsgrove and, on her grave, Fr. Morgan placed a cross of the same design used for Oratory clergy. Mabel had appointed him guardian of her two sons, probably to prevent relatives from taking them out of the Catholic Church. Morgan not only supported the boys with the little money that Mabel had left, but with his own. The boys went to live with an aunt, Beatrice Suffield, who gave them little affection and a rather miserable home, but the Oratory was near and became their real home. Humphrey Carpenter describes the brothers' routine:

> Early in the morning they would hurry round to serve mass for Father Francis at his favourite side-altar in the Oratory church. Afterwards they would eat breakfast in the plain refectory, and then, when they had played their usual game of spinning the kitchen cat around in the revolving food-hatch, they would set off for school.[24]

If we had access to the conversations between Fr. Morgan and the Tolkien boys, before and after mass, we might understand a lot about how Tolkien's sacramental vision was formed. Perhaps Tolkien's fullest and most personal statement of belief is contained in a long letter to his son Michael, written on 1 November 1963, only a few weeks before the death of C. S. Lewis. In it we see

23 Carpenter, 39.
24 Ibid., 41.

a characteristic reliance on the Gospel of St. John and its implicit Logos-centered sacramental theology:

> It takes a fantastic will to unbelief to suppose that Jesus never really 'happened', and more to suppose that he did not say the things recorded of him—so incapable of being 'invented' by anyone in the world at that time: such as 'before Abraham came to be I am' (John viii). . . or the promulgation of the Blessed Sacrament in John v: 'He that eateth my flesh and drinketh my blood hath eternal life.' We must therefore believe in Him and in what he said and take the consequences; or reject him and take the consequences. . . .
>
> The only cure for sagging of fainting faith is Communion. Though always Itself, perfect and complete and inviolate, the Blessed Sacrament does not operate completely and once for all in any of us. Like the act of Faith it must be continuous and grow by exercise. Frequency is of the highest effect. Seven times a week is more nourishing than seven times at intervals.[25]

The sacraments were bone-deep in Tolkien. They were established in him during his boyhood, as love for the English countryside and the sacrament of communion grew together.

One might ask at this point just how a Catholic sacramental vision differs from a Protestant one, for even Calvinists like Jonathan Edwards saw a powerful sacramental dimension in the world about them,[26] and many of the English Romantic poets, Unitarian or Anglican (a progression that Coleridge went through), saw it as well, and Anglicans, from Thomas Traherne to Evelyn Underhill, have valued mysticism and the sacramental aspect of nature. But I would argue there is a difference in degree and in kind. There is a pronounced Catholic habit of seeing a sacramental dimension to all of creation. Andrew Greeley recognizes it as a fundamental characteristic of the Catholic imagination: "It sees created reality as a 'sacrament,' that is, a revelation of the presence of God."[27] Flannery O'Connor sees what her fiction

25 *Letters*, 338–339.

26 See Michael J. McClymond and Gerald R. McDermott, *The Theology of Jonathan Edwards* (Oxford: Oxford University Press, 2012), especially 105.

27 Andrew Greeley, *The Catholic Imagination* (Berkeley: University of California Press, 2000), 1.

depicts, the sacramental character of life as a whole: "The Catholic sacramental view of life is one that sustains and supports at every turn the vision that the storyteller must have if he is going to write fiction of any depth."[28] In addition to this mental habit of seeing the world as sacramental, Catholic participation in at least two specific sacraments, communion and penance, is continuous. Tolkien's experience as an altar boy immersed him in the sacrament of communion daily, and, with the exception of one period in his life, Tolkien took Holy Communion daily. This practice is unavailable to Protestants, except in a few high Anglican churches, but Catholic belief and practice foster daily communion, and Tolkien's belief that frequency makes a difference is Catholic orthodoxy.

Perhaps even more distinctively, Roman Catholics are comfortable with the belief that even human productions can be mediators of God's grace. The stained glass windows and colorful murals that Puritans smashed and white-washed as idolatrous did not represent idols to Catholics, but doorways to a larger world of grace which they both symbolized and participated in. The distinction between Catholic and Anglican can be found in Lewis's disapproval, when Tolkien mentioned he had a special devotion to St. John (see chapter 3). No longer would Tolkien be able to talk to Lewis about the things he loved in Catholicism, "the rood screen" through which Catholics viewed "the holy of holies." That rood screen was a very human one, fully participating in human production: saints' lives, relics, painting, music, and statuary, represented at their most extreme in the baroque chapel of Evelyn Waugh's *Brideshead Revisited* and the Cathedral of Santiago in Spain. We see this sensibility in Tolkien's "Leaf by Niggle," in which Niggle's single painted leaf mediates the enormous reality of an entire landscape, later made real by God. Tolkien's work has a sacramental dimension that we can think of as broadly Christian, but the tendency to see the numinous in the world is prevalently Catholic and manifests itself in *The Lord of the Rings* in specifically Catholic ways.

28 Flannery O'Connor, *Mystery and Manners* (NY: Farrar, Strauss, and Giroux, 1957), 152

Tolkien's mother began teaching him Latin, French, and German, before he entered King Edward's School in 1900 at the age of eight, and she saw that he had a talent for languages. In 1902, Tolkien had to leave King Edward's because of the expense, and he went to St. Philip's. But it was not as good a school as King Edward's, and a scholarship enabled Tolkien to return there the following year, where he stayed until entering Oxford in 1911.

Tolkien became proficient in Latin and Greek and virtually taught himself Old English, Middle English, including the dialect used in *Sir Gawain and the Green Knight*, Old Norse, Gothic, and Spanish. He also picked up some Welsh and made Finnish a goal, when he discovered the *Kalevala,* the collection of poems that formed the mythology of Finland.

How good at these languages was Tolkien before leaving the English equivalent of an excellent private high school? Humphrey Carpenter offers this anecdote:

> There was a custom at King Edward's of holding a debate entirely in Latin, but that was almost too easy for Tolkien, and in one debate when taking the role of Greek Ambassador to the Senate he spoke entirely in Greek. On another occasion he astonished his schoolfellows when, in the character of a barbarian envoy, he broke into fluent Gothic; and on a third occasion he spoke in Anglo-Saxon.[29]

One of Tolkien's teachers at King Edward's, Robert Cray Gilson, was also an excellent linguist and helped Tolkien develop an interest in the general principles and structure of language. This led to Tolkien's hobby of inventing languages. His first encounter with a made-up language was "Animalic," an invention of his cousins, Mary and Margaret Incledon. He learned this language and collaborated with Mary on the invention of another, "Nevbosh," or "The New Nonsense."[30] Altogether Tolkien constructed more than twenty languages, including fifteen

---

29 Humphrey Carpenter, *J. R. R. Tolkien, A Biography* (Boston: Houghton Mifflin, 2000), 56.

30 Ibid., 43–44.

Elvish languages and dialects from three different eras, including Quenya, Noldorin, and Sindarin. Tolkien's Dwarves speak Khuzdul; his Ents Entish; the Powers of Valar Valarin; and Sauron the Black Speech of Mordor. Tolkien worked on his Elvish languages from 1910 to his death in 1973. He acknowledged that his occupation with made-up languages and story writing might be considered eccentric in a university professor whose subject was supposed to be real languages, but he maintained it was an important part of what he did:

> It is not a 'hobby', in the sense of something quite different from one's work, taken up as a relief-outlet. The invention of languages is the foundation. The 'stories' were made rather to provide a world for the languages than the reverse. To me a name comes first and the story follows. (I once scribbled 'hobbit' on a blank page of some boring school exam. paper in the early 1930's. It was some time before I discovered what it referred to!) I should have preferred to write in 'Elvish'.[31]

In Tolkien's life, we can see, Christianity and "the Word" in its broadest sense grow up together, followed by a love of fairy tales and especially Northern myth. Among the first stories he liked were those in the *Red Fairy Book* of Andrew Lang, especially that of Sigurd and the dragon, Fafnir. He loved George MacDonald's "Curdie" books, and a stage presentation of *Peter Pan* made a great impression on him. At King Edward's, he discovered *Beowulf, Sir Gawain,* the *Pearl,* and the whole complex of northern European myth.

Tolkien began composing his legendarium in 1913 with a poem about Earendel, based on two lines from *Crist* [Christ], by the Anglo-Saxon poet Cynewulf: "Lux fulgebat super nos. Eala Earendel engla beorhtast / ofer middangeard monnum sended," which translates as "Hail Earendel, brightest of angels / above the middle-earth sent unto men." Tolkien told the American professor Clyde Kilby that these were "the rapturous words from which ultimately sprang the whole of my mythology."[32] It is significant

---

31 *Letters,* 219–220.

32 Bradley J. Birzer, "The 'Last Battle' as Johannine Ragnarök: Tolkien and the Universal," in *The Cross and Ring,* 262. Birzer's source is footnoted "Tolkien

that the beginning of Tolkien's mythology finds its origin in a poem about Christ, whose connections to Johannine light would not have been lost on Tolkien.

> I was struck by the great beauty of the word [Earendel] (or name) . . . euphonic to a peculiar degree in that pleasing but not 'delectable' language. . . . To my mind, the Anglo-Saxon uses seem plainly to indicate that it was a star presaging the dawn . . . that is what we now call Venus: the morning-star as it may be seen shining brilliantly in the dawn, before the actual rising of the Sun. That is at any rate how I took it. Before 1914 I wrote a 'poem' upon Earendel who launched his ship like a bright spark from the havens of the Sun. I adopted him into my mythology—in which he became a prime figure as a mariner, and eventually as a herald star, and a sign of hope to men.[33]

In the poem by Cynewulf, Tolkien interpreted Earendel to be John the Baptist,[34] a herald of the Son, as Venus, the morning star, is the herald of the Sun. We get a clue here as to how Tolkien will construct a Germanic mythology with Christian depth. When Eärendil appears in *The Silmarillion* as one of the redeemers of Middle-earth, there will be no obvious connection to either Christ or John the Baptist. But he has some of the functions of both and the imagery of light and glory that the Bible shares with Germanic myth. There is a sacramental dimension to Eärendil, who fills men's hearts with the grace of hope, a Christian virtue. Thus Tolkien's intellectual development is a rough companion to my picture of Tolkien's intellectual solar system relating truth to myth. Tolkien begins with language and Christianity and soon begins to love mythology and create his own myth out of Northern materials in the light of Christianity.

to Clyde Kilby, December 18, 1965, in WCWC, Folder "JRRT to Miscellaneous Correspondents."

33 *Letters*, 385.

34 Carpenter, 72.

35 A small sample: Bradley Birzer, *J.R.R. Tolkien's Sanctifying Myth: Understanding Middle-earth* (Wilmington, DE: ISI Books, 2002); Stratford Caldecott, *The Power of the Ring: The Spiritual Vision Behind the Lord of the Rings* (NY: Crossroad, 2005); Matthew Dickerson, *Following Gandalf: Epic Battle and Moral Victory*

Although many people have written books on the Christian content and orientation of J. R. R. Tolkien's *The Lord of the Rings*,[35] it is not a universally accepted way of approaching his work. A recent collection of essays, *The Ring and the Cross*,[36] takes up the issue of whether Christianity in general and Catholicism in particular have a substantial presence in the book. No one challenges the fact that Tolkien was a devout Catholic, but Tolkien's love of Anglo-Saxon literature and Northern legend is a massive presence in the book, and those who reject a Catholic dimension hold that his myth is grounded in those sources to the exclusion of others. To me, this initially seemed the kind of issue which academics devise to generate conference papers. I recognized the presence of Christianity, when I first read *The Lord of the Rings*: Gandalf's resurrection, Frodo and Sam's trip up Mt. Doom, the Ring as something like the Edenic apple—all seemed to have easy biblical connections.

The books which have most energized my own thinking about Tolkien and Catholicism are Bradley Birzer's *J.R.R. Tolkien's Sanctifying Myth*, Stratford Caldecott's *The Power of the Ring: The Spiritual Vision Behind the Lord of the Rings*, Alison Milbank's *Chesterton and*

---

in The Lord of the Rings (Grand Rapids: Brazos Press, 2003); Matthew Dickerson, *A Hobbit Journey: Discovering the Enchantment of J. R. R. Tolkien's Middle-earth* (Grand Rapids: Brazos Press, 2012); Peter Kreeft, *The Philosophy of Tolkien: The Worldview Behind* The Lord of the Rings (San Francisco: Ignatius Press, 2005); Louis Markos, *On the Shoulders of Hobbits: The Road to Virtue with Tolkien and Lewis* (Chicago: Moody, 2012); Alison Milbank, *Chesterton and Tolkien as Theologians* (London: T & T Clark, 2009); Joseph Pearce, *Tolkien, Man and Myth: A Literary Life* (San Francisco: Ignatius Press, 1998); Joseph Pearce, ed., *Tolkien, A Celebration: Collected Writings on a Literary Legacy* (San Francisco: Ignatius Press, 1999); Richard Purtill, *J.R.R. Tolkien: Myth, Morality and Religion* (San Francisco: Ignatius Press, 1984); Fleming Rutledge, *The Battle for Middle-earth* (Grand Rapids: Eerdmans, 2004); Ralph C. Wood, *The Gospel According to Tolkien: Visions of the Kingdom in Middle-earth* (London: Westminster John Knox Press, 2003).

36 Paul E. Kerry, ed., *The Ring and the Cross: Christianity and 'The Lord of the Rings'* (Teaneck: Farleigh Dickinson University Press, 2011), also see the companion collection edited by Kerry, *Light Beyond All Shadow* (Teaneck: Farleigh Dickinson University Press, 2011).

Tolkien as Theologians, and Ralph C. Wood's *The Gospel According to Tolkien*. There is now a lot of Tolkien criticism, much of it excellent, so I do not aspire to offer a completely new book on Tolkien and Christianity. My debts throughout are great and too numerous to mention without overwhelming the reader with footnotes. I do believe that no one has offered a reading of Tolkien's work as being fundamentally and thoroughly grounded in Catholic sacramentality—that will be the contribution of this book.

For me, this book has been as much a theological meditation as literary explication. My theological inspiration starts with three books: David L. Schindler's *Ordering Love: Liberal Societies and the Memory of God*, which renewed my vision of a Logos-centric cosmos and made me see Tolkien in this light; and two books on sacraments: Alexander Schmemann's *For the Life of the World* and Herbert McCabe's, *The New Creation*.[37] Schindler's book inspired me to examine Tolkien's work within the framework of the Johannine Logos and Catholic sacramentality and Schmemann's and McCabe's confirmed that as a productive approach and led me back to patristic theologians, who never lost sight of the sacramental dimension of the cosmos.

Late in my revision process, I began to realize, largely due to the books of J. Robert Barth, S.J.,[38] that Tolkien's debt to the Romantic poets, especially Samuel Taylor Coleridge, was far greater than I had realized. Some of that understanding will peep into this book, but it is a topic for a book by itself. Coleridge's understanding of the imagination and its symbol-making ability is accepted in the main by Tolkien and explains, among other things, his aversion to allegory. More importantly for my purposes, a sacrament is a specific kind of symbol, referring to a real-

---

37 David L. Schindler, *Ordering Love: Liberal Societies and the Memory of God* (Grand Rapids: Eerdmans, 2011); Alexander Schmemann, *For the Life of the World* (Crestwood, NY: St. Vladimir's Seminary Press, 2000); Herbert McCabe, *The New Creation* (London: Continuum, 2010).

38 *The Symbolic Imagination: Coleridge and the Romantic Tradition*, 2nd ed. (NY: Fordham University Press, 2001), *Romanticism and Transcendence: Wordsworth, Coleridge, and the Religious Imagination* (Columbia: University of Missouri Press, 2003), and *Coleridge and Christian Doctrine*, rev. ed. (NY: Fordham University Press, 1987).

ity greater than itself and in which it participates. Tolkien wrote with this understanding.

Because I want this book to be accessible to all readers of Tolkien, especially students and those not familiar with other criticism, I offer information and support that an academic audience may sometimes find unnecessary. When I envision my audience, I see a class of undergraduate students who have enjoyed reading *The Lord of the Rings* and are eager to read it again and learn more. Still, I hope the greater audience of Tolkien readers and professors as well will find something here that is new and of value.

None of the four main propositions I will argue for leads an existence independent of the others. The first, that Tolkien was a "Catholic novelist" will be the main burden of Chapter 1. What it means to be a "Catholic novelist" as opposed to any other kind of novelist is perhaps not readily apparent, but it is grounded in the Catholic sacramental view of the world, and so is important to my argument.

The second proposition, that the Logos of John's Gospel is woven into the spiritual foundation of Middle-earth will be discussed in the second chapter on *The Ainulindalë*. The third and fourth propositions that biblical imagery and sacramentality are interwoven with the Germanic mythos of Middle-earth will be the matter for part of the third chapter and the rest of the book. Tolkien had strong ideas about the relation of truth to myth, and it is necessary to understand these in order to understand the relation of the "true myth" of Christianity to his mythopoetic works, *The Silmarillion* and *The Lord of the Rings*. Tolkien is amazingly forthright about his own work (though he can also be cagey at times). His letters, his essays on *Beowulf* and fairy-stories, his short story "Leaf by Niggle," and his poem to C. S. Lewis, "Mythopoeia," set out a remarkably consistent and thorough explanation of his own artistic agenda and the relation of Art to Logos. As a result, he gives us the general direction in terms of which he wants *The Lord of the Rings* to be read. I set forth his ideas about myth and story and their relation to truth in the third chapter.

1

J. R. R. TOLKIEN, CATHOLIC NOVELIST

"I take my models, like anyone else—from such 'life' as I know."
J. R. R. TOLKIEN, 1956, letter to Michael Straight.[1]

"The subject of my fiction is the action of grace in territory held largely by the devil." FLANNERY O'CONNOR[2]

"[T]he monsters do not depart whether the gods go or come. A Christian was (and is) still, like his forefathers, a mortal hemmed in a hostile world." J. R. R. TOLKIEN[3]

BEFORE ARGUING Tolkien's status as a Catholic novelist, it makes sense to define the category. What might a Catholic novelist be? For my purposes, Flannery O'Connor provides guidance in two essays from *Mystery and Manners*. A Catholic novelist is not an apologist, because an apologist is not a novelist. A Catholic writer is not an evangelist, because novels are not concerned with evangelization, and a Catholic novelist is not necessarily one who tells Christian tales in allegorical form. A Catholic novelist is a writer who sees the world from a Catholic perspective:

> What we roughly call the Catholic novel is not necessarily about a Christianized or Catholicized world, but simply that it

1 *Letters*, 235.
2 Flannery O'Connor, "On Her Own Work," in *Mystery and Manners*, eds. Sally and Robert Fitzgerald (NY: Farrar, Straus, and Giroux, 1961), 118.
3 *The Monsters and the Critics and Other Essays* (NY: Harper Collins, 2006), 22.

is one in which truth as Christians know it has been used as a light to see the world by.[4]

The novelist is required to create the illusion of a whole world with believable people in it, and the chief difference between the novelist who is an orthodox Christian and the novelist who is merely a naturalist is that the Christian novelist lives in a larger universe. He believes that the natural world contains the supernatural. And this doesn't mean that his obligation to portray the natural is less; it means it is greater.[5]

O'Connor's point is that, unless the natural world is portrayed exactly, the supernatural's part in it will be all the more obscure. Nature and super-nature are not opposed to each other, neither is there a distinct boundary between them; rather, they are different aspects of a unified whole. If, as Psalm 19 proclaims, the heavens declare the glory of God, then that glory can only be obscured by a sloppy portrayal. The Catholic universe is not Gnostic, but incarnational, and God is not only transcendent, but immanent.

Tolkien often demonstrates this immanence in painstakingly detailed landscape description, and his work must be read at a walking pace to appreciate its beauty. One of his most illustrative passages occurs at the end of "Journey to the Cross-Roads," where Frodo and Sam see the beheaded statue of the king:

Standing there for a moment filled with dread Frodo became aware that a light was shining; he saw it glowing on Sam's face beside him. Turning towards it, he saw, beyond an arch of boughs, the road to Osgiliath running almost as straight as a stretched ribbon down, down, into the West. . . .

Frodo and Sam then see the statue, its head knocked off and a rough-hewn stone with the Eye of Sauron painted on, set on the king's shoulders in mockery. Yet, as the light continues to shine from the setting sun, they find the real head of the statue:

Suddenly, caught by the level beams, Frodo saw the old king's head: it was lying rolled away by the roadside. 'Look, Sam!' he

---

4 O'Connor, "Catholic Novelists," in *Mystery and Manners*, 173.
5 Ibid., 175.

cried, startled into speech. 'Look! The king has got a crown again!'

The eyes were hollow and the carven beard was broken, but about the high stern forehead there was a coronal of silver and gold. A trailing plant with flowers like small white stars had bound itself across the brows as if in reverence for the fallen king, and in the crevices of his stony hair yellow stonecrop gleamed.

'They cannot conquer for ever!' said Frodo. And then suddenly the brief glimpse was gone. (702)[6]

Tolkien has captured a fleeting epiphany on the doorstep of Mordor: grace in territory held largely by the devil. The Orcs' mockery of the king echoes the mockery of Christ during his passion, while the coronal of flowers suggests Easter hope replacing the crown of thorns. It is also a prophetic indicator of Aragorn's return as King. The vision of light on the flowered king stirs Frodo. Grace gives him courage. Sauron cannot conquer forever. There is no Christian table-thumping in this description, but a vision of reality rich with Christian association and one that encourages Christian reflection.

The obligation to portray the natural vividly is greater for a Catholic novelist, as O'Connor says, because it is through the natural that the action of grace—divine aid—is discerned; and it is in nature that the supernatural comfortably resides. Tolkien is scrupulous in his portrayal of nature; he makes the reader feel that the soil of the Shire and the trees of Lothlórien are full of grace. This understanding that the supernatural and natural are bound-up and in harmony with each other grounds the Catholic understanding that the world is sacramental—a fount of grace. O'Connor explains:

> The Catholic sacramental view of life is one that sustains and supports at every turn the vision that the storyteller must have if he is going to write fiction of any depth.[7]

---

6 J.R.R. Tolkien, *The Lord of the Rings: 50th Anniversary, One Vol. Edition* (Boston: Houghton Mifflin Co., 2005). All page references, usually indicated in parenthesis, are from this source.

7 O'Connor, "The Church and the Fiction Writer," *Mystery and Manners*, 152.

Every mystery that reaches the human mind, except in the final stages of contemplative prayer, does so by way of the senses.[8]

Open and free observation is founded on our ultimate faith that the universe is meaningful, as the Church teaches.[9]

The Catholic vision is that the holy is not located outside a material universe that is corrupt, but within a material universe that is mainly good, though fallen, and this means that holiness can enter through the senses and that the world at large has a sacramental quality. Christianity makes spiritual goods out of the most mundane material: bread, water, wine, oil; everything is meaningful. O'Connor says this way of seeing is so *habitual* a part of the Catholic mind-set, that it works unconsciously:

> The tensions of being a Catholic novelist are probably never balanced for the writer until the Church becomes so much a part of his personality that he can forget about her—in the sense that, when he writes, he forgets about himself.[10]

O'Connor's main point, that a Catholic novelist sees a world illuminated by the light of Catholic culture and thought—more specifically, by commitment to Christ—is the important one, but, although this illumination may touch everything, it may not establish itself in symbols or action readily identifiable as Christian. A Catholic novel, like Graham Greene's *Brighton Rock* or O'Connor's *Wise Blood*, may not look Catholic on its face. One deals with a small time thug in Brighton, the other with an atheist evangelist in the Protestant South. Both, however, bring a supernatural reality into the novel by assuming a universe meaningful in Catholic terms. O'Connor has one important addition in her essay, "The Nature and Aim of Fiction": *all* fiction writers need an anagogical vision, "the kind of vision that is able to see different levels of reality in one image or situation."[11]

---

8 O'Connor, "Catholic Novelists," 176.
9 Ibid., 178.
10 Ibid., 181.
11 Ibid., 72.

Anagogical vision goes hand in hand with having a "sacramental view" of life, for the sacramentality of the world is apprehended through such vision. Fr. Andrew Greeley describes a general Catholic imagination, into which O'Connor's view of Catholic novelists neatly fits:

> Catholics live in an enchanted world, a world of statues and holy water, stained glass and votive candles, saints and religious medals, rosary beads and holy pictures. But these Catholic paraphernalia are mere hints of a deeper and more pervasive religious sensibility which inclines Catholics to see the Holy lurking in creation. As Catholics, we find our houses and our world haunted by a sense that the objects, events, and persons of daily life are revelations of grace. . . .
>
> This special Catholic imagination can appropriately be called sacramental. It sees created reality as a "sacrament," that is, a revelation of the presence of God. The workings of this imagination are most obvious in the Church's seven sacraments, but the seven are both a result and a reinforcement of a much broader Catholic view of reality.[12]

The sources in patristic and medieval literature for this sacramental view of Creation are so extensive that they defy any complete listing. The understanding of the created world as in itself sacramental was a pervasive one, biblically based on Romans 1:20, Wisdom 13:1–9, Psalm 148 and Daniel 3:57–81. Among the people who explicate it are Clement of Alexandria, Athanasius, Ephrem, Basil of Caesarea, Augustine, John Scotus Eriugena, Pseudo-Dionysius, Hildegard of Bingen, Alan of Lille, Hugh of St. Victor, St. Francis, Bonaventure, Thomas Aquinas, Saint Gregory of Palmas, and as a group, Celtic monastics and the desert fathers.[13] This tradition continues to this day through the works

---

12 Andrew Greeley, *The Catholic Imagination* (Berkeley: University of California Press, 2000), 1–2.

13 See, for a sampling, Saint Clement of Alexandria, *Stromateis,* trans. John Ferguson (Washington, DC: Catholic University Press, 1991), 2.2.5. 1–5, 160; Saint Athanasius, *Contra gentes,* ed. and trans. Robert W. Thomson (Oxford: Clarendon Press, 1971), 35, 95–97; Saint Syrus Ephrem, *Hymns on Virginity and the Symbols of the Lord,* in *Ephrem the Syrian: Hymns,* trans. Kathleen E. McVey (NY: Paulist Press, 1989) and Ephrem's *Hymns on Paradise,* trans. Sebastian Brock

of spiritual writers such as John of the Cross, Thomas Traherne, and, as already cited, Gerard Manley Hopkins;[14] I am not the first to see its connection to Tolkien.[15]

Che Logos and the Sacramental Universe in Colkien's Life and Writing

T. S. Eliot asserted that one of the characteristics of being human in the modern world was the "dissociation of sensibility," i.e., the separation of thought from feeling. This dissociation produces "the wasteland" of modernity, where thinking, turned loose on

(Crestwood, NY: St. Vladimir's Seminary Press, 1998); Basil of Caesarea, *On the Hexaemeron,* in *Exegetic Homilies,* trans. Sister Agnes Clare Way, Fathers of the Church 46 (Washington, DC: Catholic University of America Press, 1963), 3–150, esp. homily 1.7, 112; Saint Augustine, *The Trinity,* trans. Stephen McKenna (Washington, DC: Catholic University of America Press, 1963), 81–82, 105; John Scotus Eriugena, *Periphyseon* (The Division of Nature), trans. I. P. Sheldon-Williams; rev. John J. O'Meara (Washington DC: Dumbarton Oaks, 1987); Pseudo-Dionysius, *The Divine Names,* in *The Complete Works,* trans. Colm Luibheid; notes and trans. collaboration by Paul Rorem; introduction by Jaroslav Pelikan, Jean LeClerq, and Karlfried Froehlich (NY: Paulist Press, 1987), 4.1–10, 71–80; Hildegard of Bingen, *Book of Divine Works,* ed. Matthew Fox and trans. Robert Cunningham (Santa Fe: Bear & Co, 1987) vision 1.2.8, 10–11, and 2:15, 36; Wanda Cizewski, "Reading the World as Scripture: Hugh of St. Victor's *De Tribus Diebus,*" *Florilegium* 9 (1987): 65–88; Adam of Lille, *The Plaint of Nature,* trans. James J. Sheridan (Toronto: Pontifical Institute of Mediaeval Studies, 1980); Saint Bonaventure, *The Soul's Journey into God (Itinerarium mentis in Deum), Classics of Western Spirituality,* trans. Ewert Cousins (NY: Paulist Press, 1978), 59–68; Thomas Aquinas, *Summa contra Gentiles,* 1.92, 2.1–3, 2.39, 3.112, 3.113, 3.64, 3.69, 3.144.10, 3.145, and *Summa Theologiae* 1.15.2, 1.47.1, 22.1–2, 3.60. 2, 3.60.4; St. Gregory of Palmas, *The Triads,* ed. John Meyendorff; trans. Nicholas Gendle (NY: Paulist Press, 1983).

14 Saint John of the Cross, "The Spiritual Canticle," in *The Collected Works of St. John of the Cross,* trans. Kieran Kavanaugh, OCD and Otilio Rodrigues, OCD (Washington, DC: ICS Publications, 1973), par. 25, 472–73; Thomas Traherne, *Centuries of Meditation* (Cosimo Classics, 2007); virtually all of Hopkins's poetry. For additional sources, see Jame Schaefer, *Theological Foundations for Environmental Ethics: Reconstructing Patristic & Medieval Concepts* (Washington DC: Georgetown University Press, 2009).

15 For instance, Joseph Pearce, in *Tolkien, Man and Myth,* argues that "Tolkien succeeds in synthesizing the physical with the metaphysical in a way which

its own, runs an insane course, without brake from feeling or intuition or faith, and where feeling is likewise unguided by reason.[16] Tolkien understood this problem very well; indeed, Saruman is its exemplar and Mordor its terminus. The sacraments, in which the natural and spiritual world become one, are the antithesis of modern dissociation.

There are seven established sacraments of the Catholic Church; in addition, the Church itself is considered a sacrament. Surrounding these is the larger sacramentality of life in a universe that speaks of God, because it was made by God. The current *Catechism of the Catholic Church* defines "sacraments" as "efficacious signs of grace, instituted by Christ, by which divine life is dispensed to us." The sacraments are celebrated in "visible rites" that "make present the graces proper to each sacrament" and, "They bear fruit in those who receive them with the

---

marks him as a mystic" (97); Bradley Birzer, in *J.R.R. Tolkien's Sanctifying Myth*, writes that, for Tolkien, the world of fairy "offered a glimpse of the way in which sacrament and liturgy infuse the natural law and the natural order" (xx); Kath Filmer, "An Allegory Unveiled: A Reading of *The Lord of the Rings*," *Mythlore* 13.4, 50 (1987): 19–21; Robert Murray, "A Tribute of Tolkien," *Tablet*, September 15, 1973, reprinted in Ian Boyd and Stratford Caldecott, eds. *A Hidden Presence: The Catholic Imagination of J.R.R. Tolkien* (Seton Hall, NJ: Chesterton Press, 2003); C.N. Sue Abromaitis, "The Distant Mirror of Middle-Earth: The Sacramental Vision of J.R.R. Tolkien," in *The Catholic Imagination*, ed. Kenneth D. Whitehead (Southbend, IN: St. Augustine's Press, 2003), 56–73. In "J.R.R Tolkien: Lover of the Logos," *Communio* 20 (Spring, 1993) 85–106, Mark Sebanc recognizes the central importance of the Logos in *The Lord of the Rings*, noting "the eternal Maker is incarnately manifest in Tolkien's work through his sub-creator's own deeply informed Christian piety, which evinces a humble outlook on a universe irradiated by an indwelling *lumen increatum*. LOTR is distinctive in its minute and sacramental regard for mundane particulars" (95).

16 Walker Percy presents an amusing look at the divide between "angelism" and "bestialism" in his novel, *Love in the Ruins*, in which the hero psychiatrist, Tom Moore, measures the extent of this modern schizoid condition with his "lapsometer." On the problems of disconnecting faith from reason, see Joseph Cardinal Ratzinger, *Truth and Tolerance: Christian Belief and World Religions* (San Francisco: Ignatius Press, 2003), especially Chapter 2, "Faith, Religion, and Culture."

required dispositions."[17] The seven distinct sacraments recognized by the Church are baptism, confirmation, the Eucharist, penance, ordination, anointing of the sick, and marriage. The graces conveyed by each sacrament, no matter how specific to an occasion, all serve the same function of uniting the partaker in a living and transformative union with Christ.

We almost[18] never see anything like a religion in Middle-earth, let alone explicitly celebrated sacraments, so how do sacraments get into Tolkien's ancient world? The most basic fact of a created universe is that, as an artifact, it directs our attention back to its Creator and, in so doing, becomes an "efficacious" dispenser of grace.[19] Made by God, the universe cannot avoid being sacramental; it *must* refer to the glory of its Maker. De Caussade eloquently sets forth the principle:

> By our senses we can see only the action of the creature, but faith sees the creator acting in all things. Faith sees that Jesus Christ lives in everything and works through all history to the end of time, that every fraction of a second, every atom of matter, contains a fragment of his hidden life and his secret activity. The actions of created beings are veils which hide the profound mysteries of the working of God.[20]

Tolkien's vision of Middle-earth, as his letters testify, was faith-filled. He was enough of a Romantic—particularly of a Coleridgean temper—to accept the inspirational power of nature, and his fiction is steeped in it. Tolkien read Hopkins, who presents the point neatly: "The world is charged with the grandeur

17 *Catechism of the Catholic Church*, 2nd Ed (Washington, DC: United States Catholic Conference, 1994), no. 1131, 293.

18 The exception is the prayer-like ceremony of Faramir and his men in "The Window on the West," *The Lord of the Rings*, 676.

19 The literature on the sacramental nature of the world is vast, and, as the current revival of interest in the early church fathers gains ground, it will grow. Good places to begin reading are Hans Boersma, *Heavenly Participation: The Weaving of a Sacramental Tapestry* (Grand Rapids: Eerdmans, 2009) and Stratford Caldecott, *Beauty for Truth's Sake: On the Re-enchantment of Education* (Grand Rapids: Brazos Press, 2009).

20 Jean Pierre de Caussade, *Abandonment to Divine Providence* (NY: Image, Books, 1975), 36.

of God. / It will flame out, like shining from shook foil; / It grows to a greatness, like the ooze of oil crushed."[21] The world, Hopkins proclaims, oozes sacramental oil and has the potential to anoint us. Even if we lose sight of this reality, the fact is, "nature is never spent; / There lives the dearest freshness deep down things," and the Holy Ghost continues its creative brooding over the world "with warm breast and with ah! bright wings." One merely has to pay attention to it, as do the Elves, and some Men and Hobbits, to get the benefit of that grace.

The assumption of sacramentality is everywhere in Tolkien's descriptions of nature. The Shire, Rivendell, and Lothlórien, the caves of Helmsdeep, and Fangorn Forest ooze sacramental oil. Tolkien's ecological models are medieval, based on a well-organized and hierarchical structure in the universe in which all creatures have both an inherent value, in that they are divine artifacts that tell us something about the Creator, and have an instrumental value in serving the rest of creation. There is nothing wrong with the food chain, and Tolkien's characters are not vegans—Sam likes his fish and chips and stewed rabbit—but his good characters respect the world rather than seeing it as a "standing reserve" to be mined for their own pleasure. Aragorn tells Frodo he has some skill as a hunter "at need" (190), but first he mentions berries, roots, and herbs. Each individual component of the world has sacramental value, since it mediates the presence of God, and all the components working together make a powerful statement. The world must be respected as God's text.

Tolkien's sacramental orientation can be discerned in a passage that even critics who appreciate Tolkien have found to be generically out of place, more suited for children's fiction than *The Lord of the Rings*. In this passage, early in the book, we see Frodo, Sam and Pippin under observation by a curious fox with a full agenda:

> A fox passing through the wood on business of his own stopped several minutes and sniffed.
> 'Hobbits!' he thought. 'Well, what next? . . . There's some-

21 Gerard Manley Hopkins, "God's Grandeur," in *Poems and Prose of Gerard Manley Hopkins*, ed. W.H. Gardner (London: Penguin Books, 1953), 27.

thing mighty queer behind this.' He was quite right, but he never found out any more about it. (72)

What is Tolkien's point? Simply that the fox was *on business of his own*. Not everything in the world is centered on the problem of the Ring. Though creatures are interdependent, they are also independent. They have their own value and their own agendas. It is just on this basis that the Rangers, unknown to the residents of the Shire, have been protecting the Hobbits for years. The fox's dignity and independence as a creature suggest an entire ethic of stewardship.

Allegory, Symbol, and Sacrament

Tolkien does not merely present a generally sacramental Middle-earth, but gives us a world in which many of the seven sacraments are replicated as a continuing pattern in the lives of his characters. Tolkien believes in a reality designed to bring these sacraments forth—to "ooze oil"—even in a pre-Christian society. Events very much like baptisms occur; life for the heroes assumes a Eucharistic pattern; there are penance, confirmation, healing, and marriage. Sacraments flowing out of the natural courses of human life move the souls of Tolkien's characters toward Eru Ilúvatar—God.

This does not mean that Tolkien ever presents Church sacraments as sacraments proper or in thinly disguised allegories. Tolkien sees the imposition of allegory as an infringement of the reader's interpretive freedom, explicitly recognizing this in his "Foreword to the Second Edition" of *The Lord of the Rings*:

> I cordially dislike allegory in all its manifestations, and always have done so since I grew old and wary enough to detect its presence. I much prefer history, true or feigned, with its varied applicability to the thought and experience of readers. I think that many confuse 'applicability' with 'allegory'; but *the one resides in the freedom of the reader*, and the other in the purposed domination of the author. (emphasis added; xxiv)

Here, the freedom of the reader comes into play, accommodating an applicability that can be sustained by the text, even if not mandated by it. Tolkien's intention, in part, is to give the reader this freedom, and, as he says in his prologue, it is not his intention to determine outcomes. "If you want to apply Sauron and the Ring to the Cold War and see Stalin and the H-Bomb, more power to you," Tolkien might say. "Just don't imagine that I want you to limit the meaning of my book to that association. I'm not Edmund Spenser." (By the way, Tolkien would have thought an exclusively Cold War reading an impoverished production.)

Yet, the word "allegory" cannot be so neatly dismissed, despite Tolkien's proclamation of distaste for it, for he is not nearly so dismissive in his letters. Tolkien tells Milton Waldman, probably in 1951:

> I dislike Allegory—the conscious and intentional allegory—yet any attempt to explain the purport of my myth or fairytale must use allegorical language. (And of course, the more 'life' a story has, the more readily will it be susceptible of allegorical interpretations: while the better a deliberate allegory is made, the more nearly will it be acceptable just as a story.)[22]

The word, "life," in this quotation refers to more than verisimilitude, though it certainly means that. Tolkien is acknowledging a good story's potential to generate multiple interpretations which can only be set forth in allegorical language. A story with "life" is, for its readers, continually suggestive, a fountain of meanings. The point for the writer is not to get in the way of larger significance by forcing an artificially restrictive allegory on the reader.

In a 1947 letter to Stanley Unwin, Tolkien provides more nuance:

> There is a 'moral,' I suppose, in any tale worth telling. . . . Allegory and story converge, meeting somewhere in Truth. So that the only perfectly consistent allegory is a real life; and the only fully intelligible story is an allegory. And one finds, even in imperfect human 'literature', that the better and more consistent an allegory is, the more easily can it be read 'just as a story'; and the better and more closely woven a story is, the more easily can *those so minded* find allegory in it.[23] (my italics)

22 *Letters*, 145.
23 Ibid., 121.

To understand this from a generic perspective, we can say that Tolkien firmly moves us away from allegorical interpretation toward the symbolic. Here, his predecessors are the Romantic poets, especially Coleridge and the late Victorian, Hopkins, but also Modernists, like Eliot and Waugh. Tolkien acknowledges, in his pre-publication letter to Robert Murray that *The Lord of the Rings* contains symbolism with Catholic content (p. 43). A symbol refers to a reality greater than itself, but participates as a constituent of that reality; it does not have neat boundaries, but points toward what cannot be expressed in language. As J. Robert Barth explains, allegory and metaphor lead to a literature of reference, while symbol leads to a literature of encounter.[24] A sacrament is a particular kind of symbol, referring to and participating in a divine reality greater than itself. Tolkien's work, like that of Coleridge and Hopkins, aspires not just to symbolic, but to specifically sacramental meaning and, hence, to encounter with a pre-modern, God-filled world.

At the risk of putting words in Tolkien's mouth, I believe he is saying that symbolic writing yields a range of allegorical interpretation. While a deliberately constructed allegory ought to yield just one explicit decoding by a knowledgeable reader, a symbol, by its very nature, cannot be so restricted. Yet, the interpretation of a symbol must use the language of allegory; it must say this means that—among other things. Tolkien's friend, C.S. Lewis, lucidly explains the distinction, and relationship, between allegory and symbol in his book, *The Allegory of Love*:

> It is of the very nature of thought and language to represent what is immaterial in picturable terms. . . . This fundamental equivalence between the immaterial and the material may be used by the mind in two ways. . . . On the one hand you can start with an immaterial fact, such as the passions which you actually experience, and can then invent *visibilia* to express them. If you are hesitating between an angry retort and a soft answer, you can express your state of mind by inventing a person called Ira with a torch and letting her contend with

24 J. Robert Barth, S.J., *The Symbolic Imagination: Coleridge & The Romantic Tradition* 2nd Ed. (NY: Fordham University Press, 2001).

another invented person called Patientia. This is allegory. . . .
But there is another way of using the equivalence, which is
almost the opposite of allegory, and which I would call sacramentalism or symbolism. If our passions, being immaterial,
can be copied by material inventions, then it is possible that
our material world in its turn is the copy of an invisible
world. . . . The attempt to read that something else through
sensible imitations, to see the archetype in the copy, is what I
mean by symbolism or sacramentalism.[25]

Now, the symbolic or sacramental text is certainly what Tolkien wants to create—a text with "life," which he acknowledges
can only be discussed in "allegorical language," but is not itself
allegorical, because it refers to and participates in a reality greater
than itself. It does not take an idea and then invent a material
reality to express it, but works through the material to represent
a greater truth. "Real life" is allegorical to Tolkien, because, in
the Augustinian tradition, real life has a meaning beyond itself.
The objects of creation point to their creator: the physical universe itself is a collection of signs which have meaning.[26] As a narrative, the ordinary human life figures forth the master-narrative
of salvation history. Augustine's autobiography, *The Confessions*,
shows him reading the meaning of his own life in exactly this
way.

Tolkien does not offer allegories of sacraments—but rather a
novel which contains and illustrates sacramental truth. By recon-
textualizing the sacraments in a romantic quest, Tolkien helps us
to *recover* their meaning, recovery being one of the functions of
fairy-story. Tolkien will use character, plot, and scene to get at
the truth that underlies sacraments, by showing how such truth
manifests itself in Middle-earth. Now, of course, sacraments
themselves are symbols that point at a deep, underlying truth.
Moreover, they are sufficient symbols, instituted by Christ himself, using the right signs (bread, wine, water, oil) not only to convey a spiritual reality, but to confer grace. Tolkien does not try to

25 C.S. Lewis, *The Allegory of Love: A Study in Medieval Tradition* (NY: 1958),
44–45.

26 The locus classicus is St. Augustine, *De Doctrina Christiana*.

trump Christ with substitutes. Events with baptismal significance (see chapter 5), while not baptisms, will contain enough of the elements of baptism to indicate the connection. *Lembas*, while not having the communion significance of Christ's body, will have some of the efficacy of a communion wafer by empowering Frodo and Sam and nearly choking Gollum, who is in a state of mortal sin (see Chapter 10). The signs will be the similar and the effects will be similar, because Tolkien's intention is to create a sacramental world, interpretable as such. He does this to tell us the truth about our own world.

✠

Critics who dismiss the Christian influence in Tolkien's work seem to believe it can only occur as crude allegory. But this is absent. As Verlyn Flieger notes, "there is in Tolkien's mythology no explicit Christ episode (though the reappearance of Gandalf comes close) such as the sacrificial death and resurrection of Aslan in Lewis's *The Lion, the Witch, and the Wardrobe*."[27] In his long letter to Milton Waldman, Tolkien explains that his work reflects and contains "in solution . . . elements of moral and religious truth (or error), but not explicit, not in the known form of the primary 'real' world."[28] But Tolkien's "solution" becomes so super-saturated with the Catholic vision that, at times, crystals begin to form, and a certain quality we might call "grace" enters the page. It is with this less strident quality of Christian influence that this book is concerned.

By keeping Christian truth "in solution," Tolkien conveyed truth in the manner of all myth, not in a ham-fisted or transparently allegorical statement, but "incarnate" in events and their surroundings. As he explains in his essay on *Beowulf*: "The significance of myth is not to be pinned on paper by analytical reasoning. It is at its best when it is presented by a poet who *feels* rather than makes explicit what the theme portends, who presents it

---

27 Verlyn Flieger, *Splintered Light: Logos and Language in Tolkien's World* (Kent, OH: Kent State University Press, 2002), xxi.

28 *Letters*, 144.

incarnate in a world of history and geography."[29] If Tolkien has done his job well, his work will not shout out "sacramental influence," but will yet contain it in suggestion, nuance, and a particular kind of energy that a sacramental sensibility apprehends or, as Tolkien says, "feels." Tolkien said, "myth is alive at once and in all its parts, and dies before it can be dissected." Reading Tolkien well requires not dissection, but sensitivity to symbol and allusion.

Some of the critical skepticism about Christian influence in Tolkien's work arises from simple ignorance of Christianity. For instance, Patrick Curry, in *Defending Middle-earth*, argues that Tolkien was better than his Catholicism in embracing a pagan, "grace-filled" view of the world. Paganism, he maintains, in contrast to Catholicism, is an ecological spirituality,[30] and so Tolkien provides us just what we need, as the world confronts the problems of industrial pollution. It is not modernity that has "disenchanted the world," but Christianity, which underlies the current "social, ecological, and spiritual crisis."[31] Whereas "the principal thrust of institutionalized Christian tradition is the license to exploit nature,"[32] based on belief in a God who is outside of nature, Tolkien's paganism recovers nature. To theologize this, Curry argues that Catholicism desacralizes the world, and so Tolkien must have looked to paganism for succor. This gets everything backwards. Catholicism has always recognized an immanent God as well as a transcendent one, as St. Francis, Gerard Manley Hopkins, G.K. Chesterton, and Hilaire Belloc were well aware. Curry simply is unaware of, or has ignored, the immense patristic and medieval part of the Catholic tradition and the way it continued. Flannery O'Connor, who saw the world from inside the Church, sees the consciousness of sacramentality in the world as the very mark of a Catholic novelist. That some

---

29 *The Monsters and the Critics and Other Essays* (NY: Harper Collins, 2006), 15, my emphasis.

30 Patrick Curry, *Defending Middle-Earth. Tolkien: Myth and Modernity* (Boston: Houghton Mifflin, 2004), 108

31 Ibid., 109.

32 Ibid., 109. Even Curry acknowledges the existence of St. Francis, but seems to see him as an aberration.

pagan beliefs about God's close relation to the world would line up with Catholic beliefs was no surprise to Tolkien, who would have been horrified, nonetheless, to have *The Lord of the Rings* enlisted as part of the New Age bromide about why traditional Christianity needs to be replaced by an ecologically sensitive paganism.[33]

There are few critics who hold Tolkien can be purged of Christianity entirely. Ronald Hutton, in his essay, "The Pagan Tolkien,"[34] comes close, but even his argument is mainly limited to Tolkien's work in the 1920s on his legendarium. Initially, Hutton cites Flieger in support of the proposition that Tolkien was severely split between belief and unbelief in his own Catholic life, implying that this diminishes the influence of Catholicism in his work, but this distorts Tolkien's biography, and Flieger is not a strong ally. In *Splintered Light*, Flieger initially portrays Tolkien as a man of great contradictions, split between Christian hope and the pessimism of Germanic myth. Yet Christianity doesn't expect a heaven on earth—not until God brings history to an end and recreates the world. Until then, looking forward to "the long defeat" within history was typical Catholic thinking in Tolkien's day;[35] his Christianity and his use of Germanic myth support each other powerfully with regard to man's lot in this world.

Flieger quotes two of Tolkien's letters[36] in opposition to each other, to illustrate the religiously-conflicted Tolkien. The first (quoted at length near the end of this chapter) is to Christopher Tolkien. It is a mystical vision that Tolkien had himself, comparing guardian angels to beams of God's attention. In contrast, Flieger cites a short phrase from a letter to Michael Tolkien: "[if] there is a God. . . ." I have not been able to find this sentence fragment in Tolkien's letters, and Flieger provides no citation. My

---

33 See *Letters*, 412, in which he worries that *The Lord of the Rings* will become "a soil in which the fungus-growth of cults is likely to arise," for Americans with ecological concerns. The letter is written in 1972.

34 Ronald Hutton, "The Pagan Tolkien," in *The Ring and the Cross*, 57–70.

35 *Letters*, 255. "I am a Christian, and indeed a Roman Catholic, so that I do not expect 'history' to be anything but a 'long defeat.'"

36 Flieger, *Splintered Light*, 1.

best guess is that she is paraphrasing part of the letter to Michael Tolkien that addresses Michael's disappointments with the Catholic Church and the importance of taking Holy Communion. Let us consider a fuller citation:

> *If He is a fraud* and the Gospels fraudulent—that is: garbled accounts of a demented megalomaniac (which is the only alternative), then of course the spectacle exhibited by the Church . . . in history and today is simply evidence of a gigantic fraud. If not, however, then this spectacle is alas! only what was to be expected: it began before the first Easter, and it does not affect faith at all. . . . (my emphasis)[37]

Tolkien then spends the rest of the letter counseling his son as a pastor would, defending the Catholic faith while acknowledging its very imperfect Church, often an unfortunate "spectacle," which began in Peter's denials of Christ and Jesus' disciples running for their lives. Tolkien only put up the "if" clause to reject it. Even Flieger finally acknowledges that her split between Tolkien's "optimism" and "pessimism" can be explained in terms of standard Christian theology, making one wonder why she bothered asserting an antithesis: "But a Christian acceptance of the Fall leads inevitably to the idea that imperfection is the state of things in this world and that human actions, however hopeful, cannot rise above that imperfection."[38] (We shall see in the next chapter how despair and hope are resolved in Tolkien's thoroughly Christian concept of *eucatastrophe*.)

On the basis of this one letter to Michael, Hutton argues that Tolkien's "religious faith was not a robust and untroubled one, but subject to doubt and losses of confidence."[39] In another part of the letter to Michael, Tolkien says, "Out of wickedness and sloth I *almost* ceased to practice my religion—especially at Leeds,

---

37 *Letters*, 338.

38 Flieger, *Splintered Light*, 4.

39 Hutton, 59. Of course, the condition of faith in a secular age is that it will always be held amid doubt, as Charles Taylor argues. See *A Secular Age* (Cambridge, MA: Harvard University Press, 2007), 1–22. Doubt is not the antithesis of faith, but one of its modern components. Faith, as Tolkien recognized in his letter to Michael, is mainly fidelity despite doubt.

and at 22 Northmoor Road" (my emphasis).[40] What "almost" means to a man who, at the time of writing this letter, went to communion daily is not so easy to say. Only going twice a week? Hutton has nothing to offer but Tolkien's own assessment of his faith at this point, and this from a man who for most of his life had a very high commitment and was likely to be hard on himself. It is the flimsiest of evidence for lack of a "robust" religious life. But even if Tolkien had stopped going to mass for an entire decade and then come back, it would not mean much. Ups and downs were part of Mother Teresa's religious life as well. They are the bread and butter of the Catholic life and are to be expected, as Tolkien also explains in the letter:

> [T]he act of will of faith is not a single moment of final decision: it is a permanent indefinitely repeated act › state which must go on—so we pray for 'final perseverance'. The temptation to unbelief (which really means rejection of Our Lord and His claims) is always there within us.[41]

Even Hutton acknowledges that this lapse seems only to have affected Tolkien's initial work on his legendarium, but not the final product, which had nearly forty more years of work to go before *The Silmarillion* was published. (And needless to say, one could be quite a wavering Catholic and still have significant Catholic influence in one's writing, Graham Greene being an example.)

Hutton's tone deafness about Catholic practice and belief is striking. Despite the importance of Frodo's attempts to forgive Gollum and the great reward of that forgiveness at the end, when Gollum takes the Ring (albeit along with Frodo's finger) into the volcanic fire, Hutton argues that the emphasis on forgiveness in *The Lord of the Rings* does not support Christian influence, because in Tolkien's story forgiveness does not work: i.e., "Gollum . . . fits the usual dismal pattern of repaying mercy with ultimate treachery—and so reinforces the argument that forgiving enemies never redeems them."[42] But what Catholic theologian ever said that

40 *Letters*, 340.
41 Ibid., 338.
42 Hutton, 67.

human forgiveness *did* redeem the forgiven? In this instance, Hutton simply displays his unfamiliarity with basic Christian dogma. If I do forgive a man who has destroyed something or someone I love, it may have much more to do with my sanctification than his, just as Bilbo's decision not to take Gollum's life makes his custody of the Ring less spiritually damaging. Forgiveness is good for the forgiver, as it is for Frodo, who is saved by Gollum from captivity to the Ring; it may also be very good for the forgiven, as in the cases of Boromir and Galadriel. But a person who is forgiven by another is not magically transformed or redeemed according to any Catholic theology.

Hutton looks for explicit disavowals of Catholic influence in Tolkien's letters and paraphrases his 1958 letter to Rhona Beare as follows: "he . . . suggested . . . that his Catholicism could not in fact be deduced from his books."[43] But here is the verbatim quotation from the letter: "I am a Christian (which can be deduced from my stories), and in fact a Roman Catholic. The latter 'fact' *perhaps* cannot be deduced. . . ."[44] Tolkien actually embraces Beare's deduction of Christian influence, and that "perhaps" certainly does not rule out a deduction of Roman Catholicism—to my ear, it does rather the reverse, suggesting Catholicism is in the book, easily deducible or not. Finally, Hutton himself admits Christian content in Tolkien's work: "Tolkien's supreme being, Ilúvatar . . . is in personality very much a Christian God."[45] Speaking of *The Silmarillion*, Hutton notes, "The result is a coherent and harmonious Christian Neoplatonism."[46]

Again, the problem seems to be that Hutton is looking for precise allegorical representations of Christian stories, practices, or beliefs. We will not find anything that crude. But, I believe, we will see the sacramental understanding of the world which Flannery O'Connor identifies as the most distinctive quality of the Catholic novelist. This is part of the distinct flavor in the *The Lord of the Rings* and *The Silmarillion* which makes them what they are.

43 Ibid., 59.
44 *Letters*, 288, my emphasis.
45 Hutton, 62.
46 Ibid., 65.

A sensitive reader tastes it, even if she cannot put a name to the taste.

✠

The temptation to interpret one's work, especially when readers are not "getting it" and are asking for help, must have been intense for a literature professor whose *raison d'être* is furthering the understanding of literary texts. When people wrote letters to Tolkien, expressing an interpretation that delighted him, he had no compunctions about ruling it in bounds, sometimes with enthusiasm and sometimes with restraint. When they wrote letters to him, and he clearly believed they had gone wrong or needed a suggestion to go right, he also responded, sometimes with restraint and sometimes with amazingly lengthy and forthcoming letters. This may seem to contradict his "Foreword to the Second Edition," where he also says of *The Lord of the Rings,* "As for any inner meaning or 'message', it has in the intention of the author none" (xxiii). Now, in one sense, this is true of all good novels. The message is not "inner," as if the novel were a nut that needed cracking—the message is the entire novel itself. "Inner" is the problem word for Tolkien, but that he had a message is made quite explicit in his letters. Let us see what some of them have to say about Catholicism's impact on his imagination and *The Lord of the Rings.*

Tolkien's letters reveal a writer who used Christian concepts not only as commonplaces for the construction of fictional reality, but as ideas through which he understood his own life. The most direct letter authorizing a Catholic reading of *The Lord of Rings* is to Robert Murray, S. J., in which Tolkien simply declares the work to be fundamentally Catholic. Murray, I suspect, has brought up the question of Marian influence on Tolkien's creation of Galadriel and perhaps an association of Galadriel with grace. Tolkien replies:

> I think I know exactly what you mean by the order of Grace; and of course by your references to Our Lady, upon which all my own small perception of beauty both in majesty and simplicity is founded. *The Lord of the Rings* is of course a fundamentally religious and Catholic work; unconsciously so at

first, but consciously in the revision. That is why I have not put in, or have cut out, practically all references to anything like 'religion', to cults or practices, in the imaginary world. For the religious element is absorbed into the story and the symbolism.[47]

This is perhaps enough to establish that looking for a Christian and more specifically Catholic subtext in *The Lord of the Rings* is not only legitimate, but the very thing which Tolkien's letters, if not Tolkien himself, would goad a reader to do.

Tolkien's response to Murray raises many questions: "A fundamentally religious and Catholic work"? What does "fundamentally" mean to Tolkien? How is the Catholic element "absorbed into the story itself and the symbolism"? When he says that the book was unconsciously Catholic at first, but consciously so in revision, what does that imply? (Remember O'Connor's comment that, for a Catholic writer, the Church becomes "so much a part of his personality" that he forgets about her in the writing.) In what sense does cutting out "religion" as an element of his imaginary world allow its fundamental Catholicism more potency?

We get some clues as to how this "Catholic imagination" might inform *The Lord of the Rings* in a 1958 letter to Deborah Webster, who inquired about Tolkien's life and its relevance to the book. Tolkien first says that he doesn't like biographical criticism, because it only distracts attention from the author's works and because "only one's guardian Angel, or indeed God Himself, could unravel the real relationship between personal facts and an author's works." Yet, a distinction can be made between biographical facts and *beliefs*, especially those that might provide models, as the rest of the letter suggests:

> [M]ore important, I am a Christian (which can be deduced from my stories), and in fact a Roman Catholic. The later 'fact' perhaps cannot be deduced; though one critic (by letter) asserted that the invocations of Elbereth, and the character of Galadriel as directly described (or through the words of Gimli and Sam) were clearly related to Catholic devotion to Mary. Another saw in waybread (*lembas*) = viaticum and the reference

to its feeding the *will* (vol. III, 213) and being more potent when fasting, a derivation from the Eucharist. (That is: far greater things may colour the mind in dealing with the lesser things of a fairy-story.)[48]

Tolkien clearly believes that Christianity is in his stories to be deduced, and, although he says Roman Catholicism "perhaps" cannot be deduced, he cites two correspondents who have deduced it. The letter writer who found Marian influence in Elbereth and Galadriel may be Fr. Murray, of the previous letter. Tolkien provides us with interpretive clues about how to read him, when he discusses *lembas* as being like a communion wafer because of its Eucharistic associations: it feeds the will and is more potent on an empty stomach. Tolkien does not say that *lembas is* a communion wafer or that it *allegorizes* the communion wafer, but that *lembas* has a spiritual reality which is Eucharistic in a broad sense. Like a communion wafer, *lembas* gives one the power to stay on the journey. It communicates grace. Tolkien never gives a catalog of specific characters, items, or scenes that could be deduced as products of a Catholic imagination at work. One would never expect him to. But what this letter reveals is a facet of how his imagination operates—that he creates with a Catholic mind. In addition, it is the Catholic "colour" of the author's mind that transfers to the text, which becomes clear in scenes such as that of the flower-crowned but beheaded king.

How does a Catholic understanding of reality affect Tolkien as the creator of plot? He gives a very detailed discussion of this in a 1956 letter to Michael Straight, in which he discusses Frodo's "catastrophe," the moment in which Frodo decides not to destroy the Ring, but keep it for himself. The plot, Tolkien says, can be understood as exemplifying (a word he italicizes) two petitions from the Lord's Prayer: "Forgive us our trespasses as we forgive them that trespass against us. Lead us not into temptation, but deliver us from evil." Tolkien says, the Quest is "the story of humble Frodo's development to the 'noble', his *sanctification*" (my emphasis). He explains that the prayer not to be led into temptation is a prayer that one retain the power to resist

48 Ibid., 288.

temptation, but finally, at the end, Frodo's will is completely overborne. Using Eucharistic language, Tolkien describes how Frodo has been confronted with a "sacrificial situation":

> [T]here are abnormal situations in which one may be placed. 'Sacrificial situations' I should call them: sc. Positions in which the 'good' of the world depends on the behaviour of an individual in circumstances which demand of him suffering and endurance far beyond the normal—even, it may happen (or seem, humanly speaking), demand a strength of body and mind which he does not possess: he is in a sense doomed to failure, doomed to fall to temptation or be broken by pressure against his 'will': that is against any choice he could make or would make unfettered, not under duress.
>
> Frodo was in such a position: an apparently complete trap.[49]

What is striking about this passage is how thoroughly theologized it is. Tolkien is not saying Frodo is a "Christ-figure," but he is saying that Frodo acts very much like a disciple who takes up his cross to follow Christ. Frodo's trek into Mordor *sanctifies* him, sanctification being a specifically Christian term referring to one's growth in grace as a result of commitment to Christ, a commitment that always has a sacrificial aspect. To carry Frodo's imitation of Christ further, his sacrifice brings about the salvation of the world, if not from sin, at least from Sauron.

Another petition of the Lord's Prayer brings Frodo's plot-line to conclusion: "Forgive us our trespasses as we forgive those who trespass against us." It is Frodo's forgiveness of Gollum which finally saves the day, when Frodo's will gives out and Gollum has to bite off Frodo's finger to get the Ring. Tolkien explains:

> [A]t this point the 'salvation' of the world and Frodo's own 'salvation' is achieved by his previous *pity* and forgiveness of injury. At any point any prudent person would have told Frodo that Gollum would certainly betray him, and could rob him in the end. To 'pity' him, to forbear to kill him, was a piece of folly, or a mystical belief in the ultimate value-in-itself of pity and generosity even if disastrous in the world of time. He did rob him and injure him in the end—but by a 'grace', that last

49 Ibid., 233.

betrayal was at a precise juncture when the final evil deed was the most beneficial thing any one cd. have done for Frodo! By a situation created by his 'forgiveness', he was saved himself and relieved of his burden.[50]

Here, Tolkien gives us the theological scaffolding of the central plot line of the *Lord of the Rings,* which extends from the beginning of the book, when Frodo wishes that Bilbo had killed Gollum, to the point where Frodo's pity for Gollum loses him a finger and saves the world. Pity, forgiveness, self-sacrifice, grace, salvation, the Lord's Prayer: these are all part of the Christian lens through which Tolkien envisions his story. He does very little to foreground or "flag" characters, scenes, objects, events, plot lines, or places as having a Christian valence. But he clearly believes that Christian categories of all kinds are tools that he is using in the construction of Middle-earth, and the product is a sub-creation that is "fundamentally religious and Catholic."

The moral compass that Tolkien describes in this letter is definitively Christian, separating it from the morality of classical Greece or Rome in the single most important way: on the basis of loving not for the good of oneself, but for the good of the other. Classical thought was no stranger to pity or compassion or forgiveness, but never without a utilitarian aspect. But, as Tolkien says, in Christianity, forgiveness and mercy are values in themselves, regardless of their earthly consequences. They are a divine imperative, and Christians, like Frodo, have "a mystical belief in [their] ultimate value."

In several letters Tolkien simply declares the Christian orientation of *The Lord of the Rings.* In his private notes on W. H. Auden's review of the book, Tolkien noted, "In *The Lord of the Rings* the conflict is basically not about 'freedom', though that is naturally involved. It is about God, and His sole right to divine honour."[51] In a subsequent letter to Auden, Tolkien wrote: "I don't feel under an obligation to make my story fit with formalized Christian theology, though I actually intended it to be consonant with Christian thought and belief, which is asserted somewhere . . .

50 Ibid., 234.
51 Ibid., 243.

where Frodo asserts that the orcs are not evil in origin."[52] Frodo in that scene tells Sam that Mordor can create nothing, only mar what is already created—a thumbnail description of the Augustinian idea that evil has no positive existence, but is an absence, a deformation of creation by subtraction.

✠

Let us look at two of the most personal of Tolkien's letters to get a sense of where the Catholic apparitions in Tolkien's story may reside. These letters deal with religious experiences of Tolkien that border on the mystical. The first, a draft letter to Carole Batten-Phelps in 1971, deals with the origin of *The Lord of the Rings* and spiritual power in the book itself:

> A few years ago I was visited in Oxford by a man whose name I have forgotten (though I believe he was well-known). He had been much struck by the curious way in which many old pictures seemed to him to have been designed to illustrate *The Lord of the Rings* long before its time. He brought one or two reproductions. I think he wanted at first simply to discover whether my imagination had fed on pictures, as it clearly had been by certain kinds of literature and language. When it became obvious that, unless I was a liar, I had never seen the pictures before and was not well acquainted with pictorial Art, he fell silent. I became aware that he was looking fixedly at me. Suddenly he said: 'of course you don't suppose, do you, that you wrote all that book yourself?'[53]

This rather jolted Tolkien, who relates in previous letters that he had long felt he wasn't making up his story about Middle-earth but discovering it.[54]

> Pure Gandalf! I was too well acquainted with G. to expose myself rashly, or to ask what he meant. I think I said: 'No, I don't suppose so any longer.' I have never since been able to

52 Ibid., 355.
53 Ibid., 413.
54 Ibid., 145 and 231. Tolkien says the stories "arose in my mind as given things," and "I have long ceased to *invent*. . . . I wait until I seem to know what really happened. Or till it writes itself."

suppose so. An alarming conclusion for an old philologist to draw concerning his private amusement. But not one that should puff any one up who considers the imperfections of 'chosen instruments', and indeed what sometimes seems their lamentable unfitness for the purpose.[55]

Imperfections indeed! But look what Tolkien is considering: that he is writing with inspiration, perhaps even divine inspiration. This implies that he has produced a book that contains "divinity," at least in the less exalted sense that it is about divine truth. But where does that truth reside? For his visitor, especially in Tolkien's landscapes. But even in Tolkien, rivers and mountains do not announce their doctrinal preoccupations or allegiances. Yet I, and perhaps millions of others, have felt what Tolkien's visitor felt. Tolkien goes further yet, to address his correspondent's sense of "sanctity" in the book:

> You speak of a 'sanity and sanctity' in the L.R. 'which is a power in itself.' I was deeply moved. Nothing of the kind had been said to me before. But by a strange chance, just as I was beginning this letter, I had one from a man, who classified himself as 'an unbeliever, or at best a man of belatedly and dimly dawning religious feeling . . . but you,' he said, 'create a world in which some sort of faith seems to be everywhere without a visible source, like light from an invisible lamp.' I can only answer: 'Of his own sanity no man can securely judge. If sanctity inhabits his work or as a pervading light illumines it then it does not come from him. And neither of you would perceive it in these terms unless it was with you also. Otherwise you would see and feel nothing, or (if some other spirit was present) you would be filled with contempt, nausea, hatred. "Leaves out of the elf-country, gah!" "Lembas—dust and ashes, we don't eat that."'

This correspondence concerns itself with the taste of *The Lord of the Rings*, the overall impression that it gives Batten-Phelps and the two people Tolkien writes about. "Sanctity" and "grace" and "light" are the words they apply. Tolkien doesn't refuse them, and I don't think it is an act of pomposity on his part. He also

---

55 Ibid., 413.

feels *The Lord of the Rings* has been given to him as a gift. Moreover, to react to the book with violent disgust, as Gollum does to the communion wafer-like *lembas*, is to refuse grace. (The phrase "if some other spirit was present" is probably derived straight from the language of Ignatian meditation—"discernment of spirits.") These are speculations verging on enormous Christian claims, and a critic who wants a full understanding of *The Lord of the Rings* must account on the basis of the text for this reader's response, which I doubt is unusual.

Critics who want to discount Tolkien's letters as evidence for Catholic content in *The Lord of the Rings* have a tough chore in getting around them. Robert Hutton attempts to accomplish it by asserting that Tolkien felt embarrassment in the pagan sources of his work and wanted to impose a Catholic interpretation after the fact. Tolkien's letters, thus, are "targeted at particular recipients for specific ends" and have "a defensive air."[56] This is psychologically speculative and very weak. The last volume of *The Lord of the Rings* was published in 1955. The seminal works in which Tolkien establishes his Christian artistic agenda are all published before *The Lord of the Rings* is finished. These are "The Monsters and the Critics" (1936), "On Fairy-Stories" (1939, with particular emphasis), "Mythopoeia" (1931), and "Leaf by Niggle" (1938–39), these last three to be discussed in the next chapter. The letters are more specific adumbrations of what might be expected to follow from his more general intentions and beliefs. The letter to Robert Murray was written in response to Murray's comments on the prepublication galleys of *The Lord of the Rings,* and most of the other letters I have cited occur in the 1950s, shortly after publication. What is remarkable is the consistency of Tolkien's thought about the relationship of myth (including his own) to Christian truth, from "Mythopoeia" in 1931 to the end of his life in 1973.

The last letter to consider of relevance to Tolkien's sacramental view of the world is independent of *The Lord of the Rings* or any of his writings, but sheds light on the kind of mind he possessed—acutely visual, symbolic, attentive to detail, and mystically inclined. The letter is to his son Christopher, in the RAF,

---

56 Hutton, "The Pagan Tolkien," 58; Hutton's argument goes from 57–59.

who has written about his guardian angel. The date is November 1944.

> I had [a sudden vision] not long ago when spending half an hour in St. Gregory's before the Blessed Sacrament when the Quarant' Ore was being held there. I perceived or thought of the Light of God and in it suspended one small mote (or millions of motes to only one of which was my small mind directed), glittering white because of the individual ray from the Light which both held and lit it. (Not that there were individual rays issuing from the Light, but the mere existence of the mote and its position in relation to the Light was in itself a line, and the line was Light). And the ray was the Guardian Angel of the mote: not a thing interposed between God and the creature, but God's very attention itself, personalized. And I do not mean 'personified', by a mere figure of speech according to the tendencies of human language, but a real (finite) person. Thinking of it since—for the whole thing was very immediate, and not recapturable in clumsy language, certainly not the great sense of joy that accompanied it and the realization that the shining poised mote was myself (or any other human person that I might think of with love)—it occurred to me that . . . this is a finite parallel to the Infinite. As the love of the Father and the Son (who are infinite and equal) is a Person [the Holy Spirit], so the love and attention of the Light to the Mote is a person (that is both with us and in Heaven): finite but divine: i.e., angelic.[57]

This mystical Johannine experience of Trinitarian love and light may well have something to teach us about scenes in *The Lord of the Rings*. Tolkien describes its demonic reversal in the scene on Amon Hen, where the fiery eye of Sauron searches for Frodo, attempting to connect to him, and then does connect. The gaze of Sauron is like a beam of demonic light, moving across the landscape. Its angelic opposite is the opening of the dawn sunlight on the Rohirrim before Théoden leads the charge against the Orcs at the Fields of Pelennor, the beams of the setting sun falling on the broken-off head of the statue-king at the end of "Journey to the Crossroads," the blazing light around the

---

57 *Letters*, 99.

White Rider in Fangorn Forest, the beams of sunrise shining off Éowyn's golden hair as she confronts the Nazgûl King, and Frodo's felt inclusion in the tableau of Elrond, Aragorn, and Arwen at the feast in his honor in Rivendell, as Arwen gazes at him. These scenes do not didactically speak of grace or its reverse, but Tolkien's letters provide a warrant for thinking about them, and the rest of *The Lord of the Rings*, in the context of Catholic spirituality. In fact, Tolkien seems to guarantee it is there to find.

2

TOLKIEN'S
MYTHOPOETIC AGENDA

And she saw two angels in white, sitting, one at the head, And the other at the feet, where the body of Jesus had been laid. They say to her: Woman, why weepest thou? She saith to them: Because they have taken away my Lord; and I know not where they have laid him. When she had thus said, she turned herself back, and saw Jesus standing; and she knew not that it was Jesus. Jesus saith to her: Woman, why weepest thou? Whom seekest thou? She, thinking that it was the gardener, saith to him: Sir, if thou hast taken him hence, tell me where thou hast laid him, and I will take him away. Jesus said to her: Mary. She turning, said to him: Rabboni (which is to say Master). JOHN 20:13–16[1]*

And they drew nigh to the town, whither they were going: and he made as though he would go farther. But they constrained him; saying: Stay with us, because it is towards evening, and the day is now far spent. And he went in with them. And it came to pass, whilst he was at table with them, he took bread, and blessed, and brake, and gave to them. And their eyes were opened, and they knew him: and he vanished out of their sight. LUKE 24:28–31*

TOLKIEN IS VERY FORTHCOMING about how he understands truth, its relation to myth, and how one might create a truthful account of the world through mythopoesis—the creation of one's own myth. He sets forth the essentials in "Mythopoeia,"

---

1 All quotations from the bible are taken from the Douay-Rheims Bible, which was the most influential English translation for English Catholics during most of Tolkien's life.

"On Fairy-Stories," and "Leaf by Niggle." Following Augustine, he believed that the world was a text, written by God, and that the myths of mankind were sub-creative attempts to understand the truth of God's text—of "the Logos," which not only refers to the second person of the Trinity, but God's foundational design of Creation, the underlying truth of the world as manifest in nature and human history. (By "sub-creation," Tolkien meant humanity's capacity to truly create in imitation of its own Creator, using God-given gifts in a God-given creation. He especially uses the word in reference to the creation of imaginary or "secondary" worlds and myth.) Tolkien believed the gospels were a record of God's "true myth," the death and resurrection of Jesus, the one historical event on which the truth of other pagan myths of dying and reborn gods converged.

The gospel stories that are the epigrams of this chapter, about the sudden recognition of Jesus after his resurrection, are two of the most powerful examples of what Tolkien calls "eucatastrophe" in the New Testament. "Eucatastrophe" is the word Tolkien coined from two Greek words, "eu," meaning "well," and "catastrophe," meaning "overturning or undoing." We generally think of catastrophes as undoing what is good in a surprising and disastrous way. Tolkien wanted a word that meant the unexpected overturning of evil by good. As in tragedy, the turning point is a recognition and reversal, but of unexpected good overturning what had been seen as the sure triumph of evil. Caravaggio's painting, *The Supper at Emmaus* captures the eucastrophic turn in the Gospel of Luke, when the Emmaus disciples recognize the stranger who has been teaching them is Jesus. In 1683, when Prince Jan of Poland and his cavalry lifted the siege of Vienna; when the prince kisses Sleeping Beauty and the Fairy Godmother appears to help Cinderella; when at the end of his life Jean Valjean is led by Fantine into the next world; when a deadly cancer mysteriously disappears[2]—this is eucatastrophe. And just as fear

---

2 For two interesting studies of medical miracles, see Nancy Lusignan Schultz, *Mrs. Mattingly's Miracle: The Prince, The Widow, and the Cure that Shocked Washington City* (New Haven: Yale University Press, 2011) and Craig S.

and pity are the appropriate emotions to tragedy, the catch in the throat, wonder, and joyful tears are appropriate to eucatastrophe. Thus Shakespeare, in *The Winter's Tale* describes the reunion of King Leonidas, after 16 years, with the daughter he thought he had lost. "There might you have beheld one joy crown another, so in such manner that it seemed sorrow wept to take leave of them; for their joy waded in tears."

In "On Fairy Stories,"[3] Tolkien argued that eucatastrophe was at the foundation of both fairy-story and human reality. Death would not be the end. The ultimate eucatastrophe would be the defeat of death itself, which the Christian enters as through a gate, following his leader, Christ, into new life. Tolkien wrote that the main subject of *The Lord of the Rings* was "Death and Immortality,"[4] but it is death within a sacramental and eucatastrophic frame. Without C. S. Lewis's goading, Tolkien might never have given us his eucatastrophic epic, and without Tolkien's argument about truth, myth, and eucatastrophe, Lewis might not have become a Christian. This exchange took place, at least in part, in the middle of the night, on Addison's Walk, in Oxford.

✠

Lewis had invited Tolkien and Henry Victor ("Hugo") Dyson to dinner in Magdalen College, after which they went for a long walk through the Magdalen grounds and on Addison's Walk. In the early morning hours of Sunday, September 14, 1931, they discussed the relationship of Christianity and myth, and Lewis, who had been thinking about the problem for a long time, came to see it in a new way, as he listened to Tolkien describe Christianity

Keener, *Miracles: The Credibility of the New Testament Accounts,* 2 vols. (Grand Rapids: Baker Academic, 2011), which also addresses contemporary miracles.

3 J. R. R. Tolkien, "On Fairy-Stories," in *Tree and Leaf* (London: HarperCollins, 2001).

4 Tolkien says this explicitly in four letters. See *Letters,* 246, 262, 267, 284. In the letter to C. Ouboter, 267, Tolkien writes: "But certainly Death is not the enemy! I said, or meant to say, that the 'message' was the hideous peril of confusing true 'immortality' with limitless serial longevity."

as a "true myth." Lewis later wrote to his childhood friend Arthur Greeves that, as the three walked, there was a "rush of wind which came so suddenly on the still warm evening and sent so many leaves pattering down that we thought it was raining. We all held our breath, the other two appreciating the ecstasy of such a thing almost as you would."[5] The discussion certainly had gotten Lewis thinking, but the wind and the rustle of leaves was a moment that for all three men had a Pentecostal weight.

Lewis recognized almost immediately that the evening was a turning point in his life, a critical moment in his conversion to Christianity. Two important accounts came out of that night: Lewis's record of the conversation (in two letters to Arthur Greeves) and Tolkien's commemoration of what they talked about in "Mythopoeia,"[6] an epistolary poem he dedicated to Lewis. In it, Tolkien explained his understanding of myth and its relation to the Logos, which he later extended and more directly explained in "On Fairy-Stories."

The fullest description of the conversation between the three men is given in Lewis's letter to Greeves, dated October 18, 1931, in which Lewis explains that the power of resurrection myths derive from their imperfect reflection of the "true myth" of Christ's death and resurrection:

> The story of Christ is simply a true myth: a myth working on us in the same way as the others, but with this tremendous difference, that it really happened: and one must be content to accept it in the same way, remembering that it is God's myth where the others are men's myths: i.e., the Pagan stories are God expressing Himself through the minds of poets, using such images as he found there, while Christianity is God expressing Himself through what we call 'real things'.[7]

5 C.S. Lewis, *The Collected Letters of C. S. Lewis*, ed. Walter Hooper (San Francisco: Harper, 2004), 1: 970. The letter is dated September 22, 1931.

6 J.R.R. Tolkien, "Mythopoeia," in *Tree and Leaf* (London: Harper Collins, 2001), 85–90.

7 C.S. Lewis, *The Collected Letters of C. S. Lewis*, 1: 976–977. The primary sources for the discussion on Addison's Walk and his ride to Whipsnade with Warnie are Lewis's two letters to Greeves, just quoted, and Lewis's description

Tolkien had argued to Lewis that myth was an attempt, and not an unsuccessful one, to tell the truth of the world. Myths were not just enjoyable stories that modern science had debunked as primitive mistakes about the origins and working of the cosmos (the principal 19th century theory about myth[8]), but rather insights, however clouded and incomplete, into truth, into, in fact, the Logos. God created us to see the world mythically and communicates the truth to us mythically through our total apprehension. Such truths can be experienced and suggested in poetry, but cannot be fully captured in any abstract argument.[9] The Christian "myth" was God's own myth, and, if it was similar to preceding myths of dying gods, sacrifice, and renewal, so much the better. Rather than invalidating the gospel account of Christ's

in *Surprised by Joy: The Shape of My Early Life* (NY: Harcourt Brace & Co., 1955), 237–38. There are many biographical accounts of Lewis's conversation with Tolkien and Dyson, the ride to Whipsnade, and how these incidents played into Lewis's conversion. They include: George Sayer, "The Pilgrim's Regress," in *Jack: A Life of C. S. Lewis* (Wheaton, Illinois: Crossway Books, 1988), 217–231; Sayer writes, "Jack's conversion to Christianity occurred over a period of several years—from 1926, the year *Dymer* was published, when he began to believe in a nebulous power outside himself, to 1931, when he became a believer in Christ," 217; Humphrey Carpenter, "Mythopoeia," in *The Inklings: C. S. Lewis, J. R. R. Tolkien, Charles Williams and Their Friends* (London: Harper Collins Publishers, 1997), 33–45; Colin Duriez, *Tolkien and Lewis: The Gift of Friendship* (Mahwah, N J: Hidden Spring, 2003), 53–59; David C. Downing, *The Most Reluctant Convert: C. S. Lewis's Journey to Faith* (Downers Grove, Ill.: Inter-Varsity Press, 2002) 145–154; Bradley Birzer, *J. R. R. Tolkien's Sanctifying Myth* (Wilmington, DE: ISI Books, 2002), 7–8; Alan Jacobs gives a fine account of the influence of Tolkien's ideas about myth, and so provides a good summary of the issues Lewis, Dyson, and Tolkien were concerned with on their walk, in *The Narnian* (San Francisco: Harper Collins, 2005), 136–150; Michael White, *Tolkien: A Biography* (NY: New American Library, 2001), 133–8.

8 E.B. Tylor and J.G. Frazer were the principal English exponents of this view, and Frazer certainly still had influence in the educations of Lewis and Tolkien. For a short summary of their views, see Robert A. Segal, *Myth: A Very Short Introduction* (Oxford: Oxford University Press, 2004), 11–24.

9 In a different context, see Bernadette Waterman Ward's wonderful book on Hopkins, *The World as Word* (Washington, DC: Catholic University of America, 2002), especially Chapter 6, "Sacraments and Poetry."

death and resurrection as just another dying god story,[10] the previous myths, as genuine insights into the nature of reality, supported it. If not 100% true, they contained a measure of truth.[11] God had revealed the truth to us in the most complete and compelling way: the true myth of the death and resurrection of his Son. The implications for Tolkien's own mythopoesis are obvious: one could construct a myth, very close to the Christian true myth, out of non-Christian material, that was, in its own terms, fundamentally Christian. This is what Tolkien did in his mythology, constructing it of Celtic, Anglo-Saxon, and Norse myth, with biblical elements as well, and giving them a Christian moral and spiritual shape, the way a magnetic field lines up iron filings.

Tolkien argues that even the mythographers of a fallen world had some of that Pentecostal flame upon their heads—enough to perceive some of the truth of the Logos, however incomplete or garbled. Their fingers may not have been "faultless," being fallen men with fallen capacities to see and convey the truth. Still, they were closer to the truth than modern man. In contrast, salvation history is God's "myth," and therefore faultless. In his perfected state as sub-creator and story-teller, restored man shall be able to "choose forever from the all," making art that is beautiful, true, and undistorted.

Understood mythopoetically, the wind that mysteriously arose on Addison's Walk and stirred the September leaves is more than just wind, but Breath, Spirit, and Life. The three men felt themselves joined by another presence, when that took place, and all of

10 Fairly typical of such viewpoints is W. T. Jones', in *The Medieval Mind*, vol. 2 of *A History of Western Philosophy*, 2nd ed. (NY: Harcourt, Brace, Jovanovich, 1969), 20: "That Christianity should have survived, whereas the other cults gradually disappeared, is not so much evidence of the objective truth or moral superiority of the Christian beliefs, as it is testimony to the energy, the ingenuity, and the polemical ability, and the administrative skill—not to mention the good luck—of the early Christian fathers." One can imagine Gandalf replying, "if luck it was."

11 See Michael Ward's excellent essay, "Good Serves the Better, and Both the Best: C.S. Lewis on Imagination and Reason in Apologetics," in *Imaginative Apologetics: Theology, Philosophy, and the Catholic Tradition* (Grand Rapids: Baker Academic, 2012).

them clearly understood its significance. It was a transformational moment for Lewis. In a secular society, we might wonder if a particular instance of wind was a sign of the Holy Spirit or just an approaching high pressure system. But in a mythopoetic society, those two ideas would never be divorced. The wind just *does* give physical embodiment to the idea of spirit—that's what wind is.

"Mythopoeia," Tolkien's Epistolary Poem, September 1931

Tolkien must have realized the importance of that night for Lewis, for he was inspired to put his argument into an epistolary poem, "Mythopoeia." He begins by addressing the materialist understanding of the world that Lewis, as a former atheist,[12] had felt compelled to accept: "You look at trees and label them just so . . . a star's a star, some matter in a ball, / compelled to courses mathematical / amid the regimented, cold Inane, / where destined atoms are each moment slain." The material and spiritual dimensions of the universe are split at the beginning of the Enlightenment, and the spiritual is progressively marginalized and diminished to such an extent that it plays little part in our apprehension of the world. What is left is just material, decipherable in mechanical terms only, the beauty of the rainbow reduced to water vapor and formulas of refraction. The world is rendered "inane," "disenchanted." Somehow, atoms come and go out of being, with no creator, ironically "destined" to be slain in mystery the modern world has pushed to the margins of its consciousness.

Any teleological sense of history is also lost, as history, in Toynbee's words, becomes "just one damn thing after another"; or in Tolkien's words, "Time unrolls / from dark beginnings to uncertain goals; / and as one page o'erwritten without clue." But one age of history did not simply overwrite another as if the preceding years were not there. Tolkien, who had been reading the Catholic historian Christopher Dawson, would have found modern, materialist assumptions about history to be blind to its basic

12 At the time of this conversation, Lewis had accepted theism, but not Christianity.

nature—it had a beginning and would have an end. History was going somewhere. The view Tolkien expresses is grounded in St. Augustine's *De Doctrina Christiana,* which argues that the world is a text, meant to be read, and pointing to God.[13] This was true of history as well as nature.

In contrast with logical positivism or scientism, Tolkien offers a mythic account of reality that starts with the origin of language:

> Yet trees are not 'trees', until so named and seen—
> and never were so named, till those had been
> who speech's involuted breath unfurled,
> faint echo and dim picture of the world,
> but neither record nor photograph,
> being divination, judgement, and a laugh. . . .

Language isn't merely the arbitrary assignment of a complicated human noise to a tree or beast or star, not a "record" or a "photograph," but an exclamation of wonder, a "divination, judgement, and a laugh," a total human response to the way reality presents itself. Words are a response of wonder, joy, and exclamation to the sacramental reality of Creation. Until speech's "involuted breath" is "unfurled," like a triumphant flag, even a "faint, dim picture" of the world fails to exist for us. But with speech, we mythologize, we are, paradoxically, "free captives," limited by our sensory apparatus, but set free by "the word," so that we can undermine the "shadowy bars" of sensate experience in a complex process of apprehension and verbal reaction. Here no distance lies between Hopkins and Tolkien. The world speaks itself into language, announcing its very nature: "Each hung bell's bow swung finds tongue to fling out broad its name."[14] The soul of man, therefore,

13 For a lucid introduction to this subject, with emphasis on Gregory the Great and Augustine, see R.A. Markus, *Signs and Meanings* (Liverpool: Liverpool University Press, 1996).

14 Gerard Manley Hopkins, "As kingfishers catch fire, dragonflies draw flame," in *Poems and Prose of Gerard Manley Hopkins,* ed. W.H. Gardner (London: Penguin, 1953), 51. In a beautiful explication of the triple connection of Logos to human words, to nature, Hopkins proclaims: "Each mortal thing does one thing and the same: / Deals out that being indoors each one dwells; / Selves—goes itself; myself it speak and spells, / Crying What I do is me: for that I came."

is not so much a private, internal entity as something public, communal, and contained in speech—the symbol-sharing that makes the human polity possible and human being possible.

An example of what Tolkien has in mind is given by the origin of Elvish speech in *The Silmarillion,* when the Elves are created and awake on the shore of Cuiviénen. The first thing they see is stars, and their first word is *el,* which is initially an exclamation, but quickly signifies "star" (and by no coincidence, I think, it is one of the names for God in Hebrew). "Long they dwelt in their first home by the water under stars, and they walked the Earth in wonder; and they began to make speech and to give names to all things that they perceived."[15] The Elves go through the process of naming depicted of Adam in Genesis, and Tolkien tells us of Men doing the same thing.[16] The first language is inherently mythic, a response to wonder, as the Creative Word elicits the words which are spoken in rapturous response to Creation.

Tolkien continues in a Platonic vein by implying that our search for truth is like a recollection—we are trying to get at something we already know, "digging the foreknown from experience."[17] Unlike Plato, however, we do not contact spiritual truth on the other side of the material, but, rather, we contact it *in* the material: "panning the vein of spirit out of sense." Tolkien's point is not Plato's, that matter is a skein over spirit that we ought to reject and break through, but that matter or "sense," despite the fall, is good and has a spiritual "vein" that we mine

15 *J.R.R. Tolkien, The Silmarillion* (Boston: Houghton Mifflin Co., 1977), 49. All subsequent page references, indicated in parenthesis, are from this source.

16 J.R.R. Tolkien, "Athrabeth Finrod ah Andreth" in *Morgoth's Ring,* vol. 10 of *A History of Middle Earth,* ed. Christopher Tolkien (NY: Houghton Mifflin, 1993), 345: "Then the desire for words awoke in us, and we began to make them."

17 Verlyn Flieger in her interesting book *A Question of Time: J.R.R. Tolkien's Road to "Faërie"* (Kent, OH: Kent State University Press, 1997) considers many contemporary sources for Tolkien's interest in time, including J.M. Barrie, George du Maurier, H.G. Wells, and Henry James, and also occult writers, following it through *The Notion Papers* to *The Lord of the Rings*; oddly, she does not consider the more obvious influence of classical texts and Catholic theology, such as Thomas Aquinas.

through language. Tolkien here is much closer to Aristotle and Aquinas. Speech, the "involuted breath" that "unfurls like a flag," is spirit—it is life giving because it makes the world come alive out of what otherwise might be a sensible chaos. The breath of speech has organizing, creative power.

According to Tolkien, we do not really see anything, if we don't see it mythopoetically, and, in a mythopoetic world, the division between natural and supernatural has not occurred. Matter is laden with meaning—not a meaning we create, but which is given to us through the Logos. Tolkien said that he did not create Middle-earth, but that he discovered it. Life, in a mythopoetic world, is mainly the discovery of meaning, and these discoveries are given to those open to the gift. The "jeweled tent" of heaven already presents man with a spectacle more beautiful and awesome than jewels themselves.

Tolkien asserts that God is present to us in a manner analogous to recollection: "The heart of man is not compound of lies, / but draws some wisdom from the only Wise, / and still recalls him."[18] God as "the only Wise" from whom the heart of man draws wisdom, not lies, is both an allusion to Wisdom as depicted in the Proverbs and other wisdom books and to the Logos as Wisdom immanent in creation. The mythopoetic world is a fully sacramental world, in which matter and spirit have not been divorced. The meaning of the logos-centric universe is apparent in its beauty, which bursts in human language like "after-song," echoing a far more ancient song, which Tolkien will offer in his creation myth, "The Ainulindalë," as the Music of the Ainur, God's Holy Ones. Our hearts, which we can trust, resonate with the world—and the ancient song of the Logos—and lead us to truth.

Tolkien acknowledges that the triple jointure of spirit, language, and nature is no longer easily discerned, as it was for his Elves or Adam. We are "long estranged" from ourselves, the world, and God, but, although we are "dis-graced" and "dethroned," we are not "wholly changed." Tolkien's understanding of the fall is like that of the Orthodox theologian, Alexander Schmemann, who argues the original sin of Adam and Eve, sym-

18 "Mythopoeia," 87.

bolized by taking the forbidden fruit, was a failure to accept the things of the world as a means of communion with God. Adam and Eve's eating of the fruit was an image of the world loved for itself alone, an end in itself, without reference to its Creator. This desacralization of the world is the Fall: "The world is fallen because it has fallen away from the awareness that God is all in all. The accumulation of this disregard for God is the original sin that blights the world."[19]

Despite the original sin of splitting material from spiritual for the purpose of taking possession and seizing power, we can recover something of our innocent apprehension through myth and mythmaking. Through mythopoesis, we attempt to recon-nect through language that which the fall sundered. Man as sub-creator both reflects and refracts the Word by which he is made; through imagination, man can reconnect the spiritual to the material. Man is:

> the refracted light
> through whom is splintered from a single White
> to many hues, and endlessly combined
> in living shapes that move from mind to mind.[20]

Filling the nooks and crannies of the world with Orcs, Trolls, dragons, and Hobbits is partly what people were made to do, to create myth according to the way they were created, to refract the Logos with the individual and cultural imagination, "panning the vein of spirit out of sense" and inscribing it in story. What is waiting to be panned out is eucatastrophe—mankind's destiny to go beyond death into new life. However unconscious or dimly visible, this truth emerges in myth and fairy-tale.

Tolkien realizes that mythmaking is not only subject to abuse, but can be put into the service of horrendous mistakes and lies. Myth, like Faërie, is a perilous realm. For instance, understanding that sacrifice is somehow important gets at part of the truth, but it is finally self-sacrificial love that God values, the sacrifice of the

19 Alexander Schmemann, *For the Life of the World* (Crestwood, NY: St. Vladimir's Seminary Press, 1973), 16.
20 "Mythopoeia," 87.

Son to raise mankind, not the Mayan sacrifice of mankind to keep the sun coming up. If the Logos is at the foundation of the world, we still occupy a stratum that is "fallen," and this too affects myth. Tolkien makes the point explicit in "On Fairy-Stories":

> [Fantasy] can be ill done. It can be put to evil uses. But of what human thing in this fallen world is that not true? Men have conceived not only of Elves, but they have imagined gods, and worshipped them, even worshipped those most deformed by their authors' own evil. But they have made false gods out of other materials: their nations, their banner, their monies; even their sciences and their social and economic theories have demanded human sacrifice. *Abusus non tollit usum.* Fantasy remains a human right: we make in our measure and in our derivative mode, because we are made: and not only made, but made in the image and likeness of a Maker.[21]

Because we are basically myth-making and myth-hearing creatures, we are made of myth, whether we realize it or not. It is one of the myths of modernity, Tolkien implies, to believe we have grown beyond myth, when we are still enmeshed in it. Our false sophistication makes us pushovers for the propagandists. The Nazis took the Germanic myth Tolkien loved and bent it to their own purposes. Tolkien watched, as this terrible perversion took Europe and his sons into a second world war.[22] He was appalled at the myth of progress, backed by the immense concentration of capital, which he believed was ruining England and had already nearly destroyed the United States.[23] One of the charms of Tolk-

21 "On Fairy-Stories," 55–6.

22 "That ruddy little ignoramus Adolf Hitler . . . Ruining, perverting, misapplying, and making for ever accursed, that noble northern spirit, a supreme contribution to Europe, which I have ever loved, and tried to present in its true light." Tolkien to his son Michael in 1941. See *Letters*, 55–56. For an interesting speculation on how World War II affected Tolkien's views on the power of myth, see Christine Chism, "Middle-earth, the Middle Ages, and the Aryan Nation," in *Tolkien the Medievalist*, ed. Jane Chance (London: Routledge, 2004), 63–92.

23 Tolkien's social thought seems to be fully in line with Chesterton and Belloc's distributism, which itself is consistent with Pope Leo XIII's encyclical, *Rerum Novarum*, which rejected both socialism and unrestricted capitalism.

ien's Hobbits is that, though "down to earth" to a fault, they are blessedly free of nationalism. Modernism and the consumerism it promotes do not hold the truth; rather, Tolkien says, the frail "ark-builders" of the past provide it, the legend makers, who send their truth-bearing messages into the future. These forswear the "organized bliss" offered by that cheaper modern myth, advertising.[24]

To embrace modernity is to see everything in terms of material causation. Man not only gets rid of God, but meaning as well, "forswearing" his own soul and, following Sartre's line, accepting himself as "a useless passion." Tolkien says, moderns have "forgot the Night," the darkness from which creation came, by giving themselves to frantic amusement and consumption—"organized delight" for profit. We cooperate in being "twice-seduced." We forget the Logos-centric meaning of the world and then replace it with lesser goods, which themselves are symbolically replaced by consumer goods; this process is a "Circe-kiss" that bereaves us of our spiritual birthright and turns us into swine. We want love, settle for a cheap kiss, and, at the end of the line, we settle for the shaving cream that symbolizes the cheap kiss! Thus, we are seduced and swindled by the modern mythology of consumption and desire.

The mythic ark-builder knows death and ultimate defeat and can still sing joyfully of victory, "with light of suns as yet by no man seen." Here Tolkien makes a familiar medieval pun on "sun" and "Son" and a mythopoetic point as well, for the light of the sun, in a mythopoetic world, ought to entail, in its meaning, the Johannine light of the world.

Tolkien ends with a series of forceful rejections, very reminiscent of Thomas Wyatt's ending to "Mine Own John Poyns." Like Wyatt, he refuses to accept the corrupt beliefs and practices of his days, declaring, "I will not. . . . I will not. . . . I will not." Tolkien will not accept the way the modern cult of mass consumption corrupts and deadens human creativity. He will not walk with

---

24 For a good historical view on the opponents of "mythical thinking," see Peter Gay, *The Enlightenment: An Interpretation, The Rise of Modern Paganism* (NY: Norton, 1966), 72–126, in which Gay reviews ancient opponents of myth, such as Lucretius, as a foundation of Enlightenment criticism.

progressive apes toward a dark abyss, he will not walk the path that declares the universe and therefore human life to be meaningless. He says, "I bow not yet before the Iron Crown / nor cast my own small golden scepter down."[25] Here, the Iron Crown is the prison of the modern mind, trapped in its self-imposed mythos of central control and buying power, and the gold scepter the God-given imagination of man, the myth-maker.

That dark abyss to which progress tends is apocalyptic destruction of all kinds: industrial warfare, environmental catastrophe. But Tolkien's main point is that, for "progressive apes," what has been lost is the soul: man renders himself a progressive ape by leaching meaning from the world and, consequently, diminishing his life. The "ceaselessly revolving" course of the naturalistic philosophy of Enlightenment is to make discovery after discovery about a world which is immutable because dead. This is a world in which the "little maker" has no part with "maker's art," because he is disconnected from Christ, the Logos, the Big Maker, from whose creation the sub-creations of little makers derive beauty and meaning. Also, as we will see in Tolkien's creation myth, the *Ainulindalë,* the split of matter from meaning describes the fall, time after time. The "Iron Crown" which Tolkien refuses to bow before (and which is worn by Morgoth[26]), is the materialistic determinism that nullifies free will, making truth impossible. Michel Foucault, in arguing that such materialism does in fact control artistic production, asks the logical question: "What is an Author?"[27] His answer is that he is nothing more than a nexus in which different cultural and material forces

---

25 "Mythopoeia," 89.

26 In *The Silmarillion,* Morgoth wears a crown of iron in which the Silmarils are set (166). Morgoth in his fortress is like Dante's Satan, in Hell, frozen with sin and regret: "All his court were cast down in slumber, and all the fires faded and were quenched; but the Silmarils in the crown on Morgoth's head blazed forth suddenly with a radiance of white flame; and the burden of that crown and of the jewels bowed down his head, as though the world were set upon it. Laden with a weight of care, of fear, and of desire, that even the will of Morgoth could not support" (181).

27 Michel Foucault, "What is an Author," in *The Foucault Reader,* ed. Paul Rabinow (NY: Pantheon, 1984).

are given voice—a kind of ventriloquist's dummy. It is this dead-
ness that Tolkien believed the modern world had embraced.

The final stanza of the poem affirms that cosmos is ordered by
truth. The order and beauty of Paradise and that of the renewed
world to come mirrors Christ, the Logos, and frees its inhabitants
from the stain of sin, giving them the capacity to add to creation—and to play. Tolkien imagines that in Paradise the
redeemed eye may blamelessly stray from the source of Light,
Christ, to what it illumines, the world, and there fully appreciate
the way in which the world mirrors its Creator.[28] But what is
more, the image of Christ reflected in creation may "renew" the
direct vision of Christ. For Tolkien, one of the three functions of
fairy story and, by extension, myth, is to "recover" a true vision
of the world by de-familiarizing it. To understand dragons is to
see, once again, what a horse or wolf is. The "Blessed Land" is
what it is—not how we mistakenly see it through sin-distorted
vision. Salvation takes us out of the world of fun-house mirrors
and gives us the real thing, but allows us to garden and to play—
to join in the ongoing work of creation.

Tolkien suggests a theodicy in which the origins of evil begin
in the act of "crooked" perception, which then leads to crooked
choices. A saved and transformed humanity will finally see the
world aright:

> Evil it will not see, for evil lies
> not in God's picture but in crooked eyes,
> not in the source but in malicious choice,
> and not in sound, but in the tuneless voice.
> In Paradise they look no more awry;
> And though they make anew, they make no lie.
> Be sure they will still make, not being dead,
> and poets shall have flames upon their head
> and harps whereon their faultless fingers fall:
> there each shall choose forever from the all.[29]

Tolkien echoes William Blake, who is himself, in *The Marriage of
Heaven and Hell*, amending Plato: "If the doors of perception were

28 "Mythopoeia," 90.
29 Ibid.

cleansed, every thing would appear to man as it is, Infinite. For man has closed himself up, till he sees all things thro' narrow chinks of his cavern." For Blake, the world is not a less real copy of some ideal Platonic realm; rather, our imprisoned senses are caught in a Cave that makes it impossible to apprehend the full glory of the world as it is. Worse, rather than struggling for adequate perception, we cooperate in its decay. For Tolkien, our voluntary and mistaken move into this box is our fall, from which all our woes follow. The tuneless voice is the voice that cannot make music, because it cannot hear music. To see the world as only material, or to see it as material split away from the spiritual, is to force fallenness on the world and oneself. One can chase "zest" in such a world, but it won't be available.[30] Tolkien's characters fall, time after time, as do Milton's Adam and Eve, in the quest for power. A restored humanity, Tolkien asserts, will not experience heaven as perpetual vacation, but finally realize its true vocation as sub-creator. The mythographers of heaven will have Pentecostal fire on their heads, as they become in-Spirited singers of a new creation. We see their like in the Elves of Rivendell.

To see the relation of the world to the Logos is to experience it as a sacrament, a palpable sign of God's grace. Once this connection is made, Alexander Schmemann says, we

> live in the world, seeing *everything* in it as a revelation of God, a sign of His presence, the joy of His coming, the call of communion with Him, the hope of fulfillment in Him. Since the Day of Pentecost there is a seal, a ray, a sign of the Holy Spirit on everything for those who believe in Christ and know that he is the life of the world—and that the world in its totality has become a *liturgy,* a *communion,* and *ascension.*[31]

Tolkien's argument in "Mythopoeia" is fully consistent with Schmemann's understanding of sacramentality and constitutes the theological and metaphysical basis for Tolkien's fiction.

---

30 Bertrand Russell, *The Conquest of Happiness* (NY: Liveright, 1972).
31 Schmemann, *For the Life of the World*, 112.

"On fairy-Stories,"
The Andrew Lang Lecture, 1939

In "On Fairy Stories," Tolkien takes the ideas he set forth in "Mythopoeia," and shows how they are realized in one literary genre, the fairy tale. Tolkien wrote few academic essays, yet, when he did write them, they had enormous influence. His essay on *Beowulf*, "The Monsters and the Critics," set the criticism of that poem on a new course, in which its artistic merit was considered rather than just its value as a source of historical data. His essay, "On Fairy-Stories," sets forth Tolkien's understanding of where fairy tales come from and what they are for. He wants to take the field in a new direction, rejecting contemporary ideas that fairy tales derive from actual persons or events. Rather, he says, they come out of the "story soup," the narrative inheritance of mankind, whose ingredients have many points of origin.

Romantic ideas about perception, the imagination, and truth all lie at the foundation of Tolkien's theory. Like Coleridge and Hopkins, Tolkien believed that the individual mind had a significant part in the "creation" of the world. The simple viewing of any object depends on the point of the observer, the purpose of the observation, and the memories the observer brings. At nineteen, Hopkins wrote a poem on the problem, imagining many people observing a rainbow in a waterfall from different positions, none of them seeing the same rainbow.[32] Everyone created a slightly different rainbow, making them, in Tolkien's terminology, all sub-creators perforce, because perception itself is sub-creative, "a repetition in the finite mind of the eternal act of creation in the infinite I AM."[33]

Tolkien asserts that reading fairy stories is a way to "recover"

---

32 "It was a hard thing to undo this knot. / The rainbow shines, but only in the thought / Of him that looks. Yet not in that alone, / For who makes rainbows by invention? / And many standing round a waterfall / See one bow each, yet not the same at all, / But each a hand's breadth further than the next. / The sun on falling waters writes the text / Which yet is in the eye or in the thought. / It was a hard thing to undo this knot." From *The Poetical Works of Gerard Manley Hopkins* (Oxford: Oxford University Press, 1990), 31.

33 S. T. Coleridge's famous declaration from *Biographia Literaria*.

the world. To see centaurs and dragons is to see afresh shepherds, sheep, dogs and horses; to see dragons is to see wolves again. Especially for modern man, whose world has long been "disenchanted," entering Faërie opens the senses to new possibilities, to "arresting strangeness."[34] "Recovery" entails regaining a clear vision of the world as something different and wondrous. A person open to the possibilities of Faërie is likely to be open to the possibilities of sacramentality—and hence, fairy stories can help us recover the world as sacrament.

Thus, the relation of fairy-story to the truth is based partly on its capacity to de-familiarize the world, to recover our sense of the world as strange, to recapture "the queerness of things that have become trite."[35] Here Tolkien recognizes his debt to G.K. Chesterton. The route to Catholicism and sacramental vision for G.K. Chesterton lay through fairyland:

> When we are asked why eggs turn to birds or fruits fall in autumn, we must answer exactly as the fairy godmother would answer if Cinderella asked her why mice turned to horses or her clothes fell from her at twelve o'clock. We must answer that it is magic. It is not a "law," for we do not understand its general formula. It is not a necessity, for though we can count on it happening practically, we have no right to say that is must always happen. It is no argument for unalterable law (as Huxley fancied) that we count on the ordinary course of things. We do not count on it. . . . We bet on it. . . . The only words that ever satisfied me as describing Nature are the terms used in fairy books, "charm," "spell," "enchantment." They express the arbitrariness of the fact and its mystery.[36]

Tolkien recognizes that all fantasies are "neither beautiful nor even wholesome, not at any rate the fantasies of fallen Man." Man often stains what he touches, Tolkien says, echoing Hopkins' lines that all "wears man's smudge and shares man's smell." Yet, myth and its lesser cousin fairy-story can also take us in the direction of the Holy: "Something really 'higher' is occasionally

34 Tolkien, "On Fairy-Stories," 48.
35 Ibid., 58.
36 G.K. Chesterton, *Orthodoxy* (San Francisco: Ignatius Press, 1995), 57–8.

glimpsed in mythology: Divinity, the right to power (as distinct from its possession), the due of worship; in fact 'religion.'"[37]

Fairy-story and myth focus our attention on aspects of reality that our modern habits obscure. In Hopkins' terms, they are an aid to "instress." Hopkins believed that every object in the world, natural or manmade, had an "inscape," by which he meant layers of structured meaning. He also believed that the "inscape" of anything could be accessed, though not without effort, and perhaps not completely, by a concentration of morally directed attention that he called "instress." (Satan, Hopkins speculated, directed his instress to his own inscape and became the premier of all narcissists.) The Elves in Tolkien's work might all be followers of Hopkins, for they effortlessly practice instress and incorporate their perceptions in poetry and song. Hopkins believed that Christ, as Logos, was somewhat apprehensible in the inscapes of the world. By Hopkins' reasoning, fairytales also have their own inscapes, as do all objects made by artists and artisans. In the last few pages of "On Fairy-Stories," Tolkien's reading of fairy tales reveals some of their "inscape" in their three functions: recovery, escape, and consolation.

"Recovery" means "to see things as we were meant to see them"—to recover that sacramental perception which sees the world as created and ordered by the love of God. And this means to see things apart from our desires, having their own value:

> We need . . . to clean our windows; so that the things seen clearly may be freed from the drab blur of triteness or familiarity—from possessiveness. . . . This triteness is really the penalty of 'appropriation': the things that are trite . . . are the things that we have appropriated, legally or mentally. We say we know them . . . we laid hands on them, and then locked them in our hoard, acquired them, and acquiring ceased to look at them.[38]

Once again echoing Blake, Tolkien accuses us of being percep-

---

37 Tolkien, "On Fairy-Stories," 26.

38 Ibid., 58. Fairy stories try to put us in touch with the world as completely as we were meant to be. The similarity between Tolkien's language and that of Alexander Schmemann, linking appropriation to the fall, is striking, especially given that Schmemann is writing after Tolkien.

tual dragons, who sleep on a treasure of material that has essentially become trash, because we don't see or understand what we have—we just have it. To recover this dragon's hoard, which would mean letting go of it, would be to *really* have it as treasure.

Recovery brings generosity and gratitude, the realization that the entire world is God's gift. Though it invites our use, it does not exist just to be utilized, but to be contemplated and appreciated in its own right. To recover the world is to recover its plenitude, to recognize we can't just control it. Ents and foxes have objectives of their own. When Tolkien describes the land of Faërie as the Perilous Realm, it is just the aspect of uncontrollability and otherness that he has in mind. Faërie cannot be appropriated and demands we give up appropriation and control.

The second function, escape, is one that Tolkien acknowledges is usually denigrated, but Tolkien's rejoinder is that the desire to escape is understandable and can be morally commendable, depending on what you want to escape from and to. Escape from the twentieth century did not seem a bad idea to Tolkien, who believed we lived in "an age of 'improved means to deteriorated ends.'"[39] In comparison with what he saw taking place around him, Tolkien, a veteran of the Somme, believed that fairy tales offered entry to a *more* real world.

Finally, the purpose of the fairy-story is consolation, and, in discussing this, Tolkien directly identifies the story of the death and resurrection of Christ as the Logos at the center of fantasy. Unlike drama, which he believes to be most suited to tragedy, the fairy-story must end with *eucatastrophe*, the happy ending, the redemptive resurrection of those on the verge of defeat or seemingly lost. All complete fairy-stories must have it. This joy of happy ending is *not* essentially escapist:

> In its fairy-tale—or otherworld—setting, it is a sudden and miraculous grace: never to be counted on to recur. It does not

---

[39] Ibid., 65, quoting Aldous Huxley, *Brave New World*. Here is Huxley's full sentence: "We are living now, not in the delicious intoxication induced by the early successes of science, but in a rather grisly morning-after, when it has become apparent that what triumphant science has done hitherto is to improve the means for achieving unimproved or actually deteriorated ends."

deny the existence of dycatastrophe, of sorrow and failure: the possibility of these is necessary to the joy of deliverance; it denies (in the face of much evidence, if you will) universal final defeat and in so far is *evangelium*, giving a fleeting glimpse of Joy, Joy beyond the walls of the world, poignant as grief.

It is the mark of a good fairy-story, of the higher or more complete kind, that however wild its events, however fantastic or terrible the adventures, it can give to child or man that hears it, when the 'turn' comes, a catch of the breath, a beat and lifting of the heart, near to (or indeed accompanied by) tears, as keen as that given by any form of literary art. . . .[40]

Tolkien connects all of fairy-story to the master-narrative of Christianity: fall and redemption through the impossible *eucatastrophe* of resurrection. This is the Christo-centric passion of the Logos as we see played out in the death and resurrection of Gandalf, Aragorn's journey into and return from the land of the dead, Éowyn's rescue of Théoden from the King of the Wraiths and her healing by Aragorn, the charge of the Rohirrim, and Frodo's trudge up the Golgotha of Mt. Doom to be saved, finally, by Gollum. Eucatastrophe is the main feature of the inscape of *The Lord of the Rings,* and it is why Tolkien said its main topic was Death, not as final dissolution or end, but as the beginning of new creation. What Tolkien sees as the essence of fairy-story is what modern sensibilities tend to be most cynical about: the miraculous happy ending.[41]

In "On Fairy-Stories," Tolkien doesn't just hint at the connec-

---

40 Ibid., 69.

41 In his comedies, Shakespeare provides such an ending more often than not. *The Winter's Tale* is perhaps the most stunning example, but *Comedy of Errors, As You Like It, The Merchant of Venice, Twelfth Night,* and *A Midsummer Night's Dream* show that Shakespeare deeply understood the human desire for *eucatastrophe;* I can never shake the sense, when I read critics who detest Tolkien, that what they really hate is *eucatastrophe,* which implies not only the final helplessness of man, but faith in ultimate rescue by God; that this should be so popular is a galling confirmation of the defects of the multitude. For the genesis of this attitude in literary modernism and the English department that came out of it, see John Carey's illuminating *The Intellectuals and the Masses: Pride & Prejudice Among the Literary Intelligentsia,* 1880–1939 (Chicago: Academy Chicago Publishers, 2002).

tion of fairy-story to the gospels, but makes it explicit. The true sub-creator wants to be a real maker, and so draws on reality:

> The Gospels contain a fairy-story, or a story of a larger kind which embraces all the essence of fairy-stories. They contain many marvels . . . and among the marvels is the greatest and most complete conceivable eucatastrophe. But this story has entered history and the primary world; the desire and aspiration of sub-creation has been raised to the fulfillment of Creation. The Birth of Christ is the eucatastrophe of Man's history. The Resurrection is the eucatastrophe of the story of the Incarnation. . . . There is no tale ever told that men would rather find was true, . . . For the Art of it has the supremely convincing tone of Primary Art, that is of Creation. To reject it leads either to sadness or to wrath.[42]

In the story of Christ, Tolkien proclaimed to Lewis, we have "true myth," art verified, and the fusion of Legend and History, and it becomes manifest in the world even in the humble fairytale. The makers of story and myth can present some of this truth, even if not perfectly: "The Christian has still to work, with mind as well as body, to suffer, hope, and die; but he may now perceive that all his bents and faculties have a purpose, which can be redeemed."[43]

"Leaf By niggle,"
a Eucatastrophe about Sub-creation, 1938–1939

Tolkien composed two fictional explorations of sub-creation and its relationship to love: "Leaf by Niggle," an allegorical short story written from 1938 to 1939, but published in 1945, and his creation myth, the *Ainulindalë*, which dates from the mid-1930s.[44] Both "Leaf by Niggle" and the *Ainulindalë* are fully consistent with "Mythopoeia" and "On Fairy-Stories" in asserting that the ongo-

---

42 Tolkien, "On Fairy-Stories," 72.

43 Ibid., 73.

44 Christina Skull and Wayne G. Hammond, *The J. R. R. Tolkien Companion and Guide: Reader's Guide* (NY: Houghton Mifflin, 2006), 29. Tolkien made major revisions in 1946 and 1951.

ing work of creation is natural to human beings—and, in the *Ainulindalë*, even to angels—but also that it is perilous, for it contains within itself the seeds of the Fall: selfishness, pride, envy, and the hunger for power. While the *Ainulindalë* (which we will explore in the next chapter) is Tolkien's myth of the world's creation and the beginnings of evil, "Niggle" is about a very ordinary post-lapsarian man who was "never intended" to be very important and his frustration at having so little time to paint. "Leaf by Niggle" is Tolkien's *Everyman*. It presents the problem, perhaps felt acutely by Tolkien himself, that the demands of living a decent human life could make artistic production impossible. "Leaf by Niggle" precedes Tolkien's beginning of *The Lord of the Rings,* which would take fifteen years to complete, by only a few months.

Tolkien's life as husband, father of four children, and professor, as many have remarked, was very busy apart from writing fiction. He had the full round of lectures, meetings with students, faculty meetings, administrative chores, and, in addition, he took on extra work grading "School Certificate papers." He devotion to his family is obvious in his letters and especially his *Letters from Father Christmas,* which he wrote and illustrated for his children and lavished time upon. *The Hobbit* itself was composed initially for the entertainment of his own children. When he wrote fiction, Tolkien typically did not begin until ten in the evening; he would continue, while his family slept, until one or two. After a few hours sleep, he'd begin another day. At times, perhaps, he felt Niggle's exasperation at the way duty imposed on art. A sense of this comes through Tolkien's letter to W.H. Auden about writing the first sentence of *The Hobbit*:

> All I remember about the start of *The Hobbit* is sitting correcting School Certificate papers in the everlasting weariness of that annual task forced on impecunious academics with children. On a blank leaf I scrawled: 'In a hole in the ground there lived a hobbit.' I did not and do not know why. I did nothing about it, for a long time, and for some years I got no further than the production of Thror's Map.[45]

We can assume that *The Hobbit* was incubating in Tolkien's mind

45 *Letters*, 215, dated 7 June 1955.

and being tried orally on his children, for, when he came to write it down, out it flowed with little need for backtracking or revision. This was unusual for him. The writing of *The Lord of the Rings* was far more difficult.

"Leaf by Niggle" provides a wry catalog of the kinds of distractions, internal and external, that an artist must overcome to create. Niggle's main external difficulty is that his neighbors, Parish (a fine gardener) and Mrs. Parish, his mean-spirited wife, often make demands on him which he finds exasperating. Also, Parish sees Niggle's painting as a waste of time and Niggle as a neglector of what is important: gardening. Niggle helps Parish when he is asked for help, but resents it. He wants time alone to work, yet he invites company—and then resents it when company comes. He is, in a small way, ungenerous, though he struggles against his attitude, worrying at the same time that he can get nothing done on his painting.

His external problems are nothing compared to the internal drag on his productive use of time. He is a "niggler," trying to paint a tree, leaf by leaf, but hung-up on getting the first leaf exactly right. He doesn't organize his time well and, sometimes, he just wastes it, day-dreaming about his picture. One can't help but get the impression that Tolkien is satirizing himself, as his own writing process was often laborious and focused on detail to an obsessive degree.

Like Everyman, Niggle has the journey of death to prepare for. (The story begins with the sentence: "There once was a little man named Niggle who had a long journey to make.") One day Niggle gets a fever, as he bicycles through the rain to get help for Mrs. Parish, who is ill. It turns out that she is not so ill, but, out in the rain, Niggle literally catches his death and, a few days later, dies of fever. The "Driver" comes, taking him away from his picture. Niggle has packed nothing for his journey but a box of paints and some sketches, and he even loses those on the train, which takes him through a "dark tunnel" and leaves him in an institution both like a hospital and a prison. Tolkien makes his allegory crystalline, and we are clearly meant to see this place as purgatory, with a judgment scene between God the Father and God the Son on the way.

In the "hospital," Niggle learns to be more fully human and so more fully an artist. Purgatory is a long process of purging, healing, and, finally, a remedial course in what sub-creation really requires. When Niggle first arrives in purgatory (at a train depot something akin to Dante's ante-purgatory), he faints on the railway platform and is carted off to "the hospital." Niggle is faint, because he has entered a higher realm—he suffers from spiritual altitude sickness and must become stronger before he can go higher. We find out later that Niggle, coming with virtually nothing, has been admitted to the Pauper's Wing. He is put in bed, the doctors and nurses are stern, and he is given bitter medicine. The "bitter medicine" is probably Niggle's confrontation with his own life, what he has done, but, even more, what he has failed to do. As the Catholic mass begins with a confession of sins, Niggle's recovery begins at least with an awareness of them. During the "first century or so," Niggle feels no pleasure in anything and spends most of his time in regrets. Eventually, though, he works through it.

Herbert McCabe explains that purgatory is the place where sinners break out of the prison-like selves they have constructed; the less repentant the sinner, the stronger the bars. This dying to the self, so that a greater self, conformed to Christ, can be born, starts with baptism and is completed in purgatory:

> One effect of sin is that it becomes harder for us to die. Sin, besides turning us from God, binds us closer to ourselves, so that the abandonment of self becomes more difficult. This tendency to self-centeredness is something that may remain even when our sin is forgiven. It is eradicated only by deliberate self-denial. Self-denial, then, is not the same as self-control, nor is it the vice of excessive self-repression; self-control is the attitude of the good man toward his desires with a view to living well, while self-denial is the attitude of a man towards his desires with a view to transcending the good life.[46]

---

46 Herbert McCabe, *The New Creation* (London: Continuum, 2010), 77–8. See also William Golding's novel, *Pincher Martin*, which shows how clinging to one's consciousness is *the* purgatorial trap, like being stranded on a rock in the middle of the Atlantic Ocean.

Self-control is necessary to live a happy, contented life, but self-denial is required for self-sacrifice—for heroism. Tolkien sees this initial stage in Niggle's purgatorial life as the time during which he develops the self-control necessary to exercise free will. Training in self-denial will come later. In his earthly life, Niggle's will had been so diffuse and distracted that he barely had enough to be human. The purgatorial process takes a long time for Niggle, because he still must make the right choice freely—the choice to discipline himself, to cooperate with the treatment. Finally, when he drops his regrets and idle wishes, he just wants to be useful. In the process, Niggle becomes "master of his time." Paradoxically, his mastery is achieved through obedience. He achieves a state that post-modern man, with cell-phone and email hook-up, might well envy:

> [I]t could not be denied that he began to have a feeling of—well, satisfaction: bread rather than jam. He could take up a task the moment one bell rang, and lay it aside promptly the moment the next one went, all tidy and ready to be continued at the right time. He got through quite a lot in a day, now; he finished small things off neatly. He had no 'time of his own' (except in his bed-cell), and yet he was becoming master of his time; he began to know just what he could do with it. There was no sense of rush. He was quieter inside now, and at resting-time he could really rest.[47]

Purgatory has become a monastery for Niggle, and he learns to do everything whole-heartedly—to become a master of time by giving it rather than possessing it. Niggle can no longer be caught in time, as in a trap. His problem has not just been distraction and lack of will, but lack of faith. He needed to know that he could completely let go of his picture, go on with complete attention to another task, and then come back to paint. This offering of time, as a sacrifice, restores his faith in the one who gives time. Niggle begins to see time as gifted to him. Having learned faith, so that he no longer attempts to hoard, his mind is no longer split, and "he could really rest."

Tolkien understands man's fallen nature as insane, divided

---

47 "Leaf by Niggle," in *Tree and Leaf,* 104.

against itself and its Creator. In the uncured Niggle, there are streaks of Tolkien's dragon, Smaug, and of Gollum as well. Purgatory's function is to set that right. As Creation itself is portrayed in Genesis as a process that occurs within time—six days—so Niggle's treatment does not come instantly. He must learn to dissociate the idea of pleasure from work and just do the work. Self-discipline becomes the foundation for experiencing joy.

At this point, Niggle's treatment changes, and he is worked punishingly hard. This is when Niggle goes from learning self-control to the much more difficult and important task of learning what McCabe refers to as "divinely inspired self-denial." The good life is not rejected, but transcended, so that self-sacrificing love becomes possible. Niggle cooperates in his "death" in the service of a new life. McCabe suggests that purgatory is the place where souls accomplish this, if they have not been able to do it on earth:

> It is very tentatively that I finally put forward a view of purgatory. It seems to me that we should see purgatory somewhat on the analogy of mortification rather than on the analogy of punishment (though the theory of punishment is itself so debatable that it is in any case unclear what would count as a punitive theory of purgatory). I suggest that purgatory consists in the personal appropriation of death. This immediately explains three of the main things we know about purgatory. First, that the soul in purgatory is assured of heaven; for grace has done its work, rather as in the case of the baptized infant. Second, that the more a man has sinned the more difficult purgatory is. Third, that the more a man has done penance the easier it is.[48]

Thus, Niggle's labor *seems* to be a punishment, but there is no punishment in purgatory; he is undergoing transformation. It is part of God's mercy that the judgment of Niggle occurs after he has changed. While he is resting in bed, in the dark, he hears two voices. The First Voice represents God the Father and the second, God the Son, who becomes Niggle's judge and advocate. Niggle's heart didn't function properly, the First Voice says, and his head wasn't screwed on tight enough. Yes, says the second, but in his

---

48 McCabe, 78.

own way, Niggle had some talent—"a leaf by Niggle has a charm of its own"—and he took great pains with leaves because he loved them "for their own sake." And even if he neglected many "calls," he also answered "a good many." Finally, Niggle's last bicycle ride on behalf of Mrs. Parish "was a genuine sacrifice." "I rather lay stress on that," the Second Voice says.

Although the First Voice argues that the Second puts it "too strongly," he gives the Second Voice the final decision: "You have the last word. It is your task, of course, to put the best interpretation on the facts. Sometimes they will bear it." That Tolkien succeeds in creating a comically sardonic conversation between two members of the Trinity is no little part of this story's charm: The Second Voice pushes mercy as far as it will logically go and farther, recommending gentle treatment. The First Voice asks Niggle if he has anything to say, and Niggle immediately asks about Parish. He hopes that he is well and maintains that he was a very good neighbor. And with that, even the First Voice has to agree with the Second, that it is time for Niggle to move on.

Niggle is released on a holiday into the country—a country which turns out to be his own painting made real. This is full Enchantment, by Tolkien's definition in "On Fairy-Stories": "Enchantment produces a Secondary World into which both designer and spectator can enter, to the satisfaction of their senses while they are inside; but in its purity it is artistic in desire and purpose."[49] Niggle is so shocked when he sees "his Tree" that he falls off his bicycle. The tree and the country around it are more fully developed than Niggle had consciously imagined for his painting, but he recognizes that it is his, and still in need of finishing. One of Niggle's surprises is that now he can clearly see Parish's influence on his work:

> He went on looking at the Tree. All the leaves he had ever laboured at were there, as he had imagined them rather than as he had made them; and there were others that had only budded in his mind, and many that might have budded, if only he had had time. Nothing was written on them, they were just exquisite leaves, yet they were dated as clear as a calendar.

49 Tolkien, "On Fairy-Stories," 53.

Some of the most beautiful—and the most characteristic, the most perfect examples of Niggle's style—were seen to have been produced in collaboration with Mr. Parish: there was no other way of putting it.[50]

Art, Niggle learns, is not just the endeavor of the individual genius, laboring Romantically by himself, but a communal project. It comes out of human relationship, community, even the community of a disdainful neighbor, in ways that are mysterious. This is the first clue for Niggle and the reader that sub-creation is impossible without love; that, as participation in the Logos, sub-creation is an expression of love and our own intended nature.

As Niggle walks about his country and thinks about completing it, he realizes that he needs Parish: "There are lots of things about earth, plants, and trees that he knows and I don't. This place cannot be left just as my private park. I need help and advice: I ought to have got it sooner." Niggle has two important insights: that the art is not really just his, to own, but part of a larger creative process to be shared. It is after all a "sub" creation, embedded in and dependent on God's creation. Second, this dependency implies that others can and probably must contribute. Help and advice are fundamental to creation, which cannot happen without them. (With regard to getting advice, Tolkien will be true to Niggle's insight that he needs help and advice; he will read *The Lord of the Rings* to the Inklings, at times getting very harsh criticism;[51] saving Middle-earth will not be the project of Frodo alone but of an ever growing Fellowship.) "Leaf by Niggle" reframes the Romantic love of nature and its portrayal of the artist as a lone genius working in solitude by removing the artist from narcissistic absorption in his or her own project and placing him within the community of Catholicism. Niggle cannot complete his painting, in part because he seeks this isolation and resents intrusions upon

---

50 "Leaf by Niggle," 110.

51 Humphrey Carpenter delightfully imagines an Inklings session, "Thursday Evenings," in *The Inklings*, 127–152; on the importance of a writing community to Tolkien, see Diana Pavlac Glyer, *The Company They Keep: C. S. Lewis and J. R. R. Tolkien as Writers in Community* (Kent, Ohio: Kent State University Press, 2007).

it; yet, the intrusions fed the life that could have cultivated Niggle's vocation as a painter. Creation depends on love.

Niggle's prayer for Parish's help, which Niggle doesn't even recognize as a prayer, is instantly granted. Parish, who has also died, is let out of the hospital / prison stage of purgatory sooner because of Niggle, and here Tolkien is surely reaffirming the Church as one body, whether its members are "dead" or alive, members who can and ought to intercede for each other. As they work on the garden together, Niggle becomes more like Parish, building and weeding and planting, and Parish becomes more like Niggle, gazing, contemplating, wondering. Each completes the other, as they complete the painting come to life.

Finally, Niggle goes off with a shepherd into the mountains of his picture, though these mountains, he realizes, are much more than his imaginings. He says good-bye to Parish, who decides to wait for his wife, whose hospital treatment is taking a long time indeed. The land they have worked on together, as artists and gardeners becomes "Niggle's Parish," useful, the Second Voice says, "As a holiday and a refreshment . . . splendid for convalescence . . . and for many . . . the best introduction to the Mountains." In other words, it provides recovery, consolation, and escape.

"Leaf by Niggle" ends with a very short satire, in which two people who knew Niggle talk about him after his death. The very fallen Councilor Tompkins, a minor bureaucrat, dismisses Niggle as being "a useless person," a sentimental artist who couldn't design a poster to save his life, who should have been pushed into the "Great Rubbish Heap" long ago. A school teacher who knew Niggle replies that he really painted leaves quite well. The teacher has found a scrap of Niggle's canvas with leaves. "I can't get it out of my mind," he says.

"Out of what?" Tompkins replies, incredulous, for, once God has been evacuated from the world, minds, equally immaterial, must go too. "The mind" is an anti-materialist heresy.

"Leaf by Niggle" is a joyous affirmation by Tolkien that we and our work may survive cultural representatives like Tompkins and persist and be useful beyond this life. In 1941, in a letter to his son Michael, who was a cadet at Sandhurst, Tolkien wrote, "There is a place called 'heaven' where the good, here unfinished, is completed; and where the stories unwritten and the hopes unfulfilled, are continued."[52] If man is redeemed, his art may be as well, and if man is to remain man, he will continue to have work—to be a sub-creator in the on-going Creation project of God. Niggle, whose name implies smallness, is rather like the hobbit Bilbo Baggins, the bourgeois burglar. Neither is remarkable or has any ambition for wealth or importance.[53] Niggle, while not a full-bodied inhabitant of the magical Realm of Faërie, perhaps comes as close as a modern Babbit or Walter Mitty can get. He is a very ordinary man, but, through God's grace, becomes glorious: a human being fully alive.

52 *Letters*, 55.

53 Hobbits have more than a phonemic resemblance to Sinclair Lewis's George F. Babbit, a caricature of the American bourgeoisie; hobbits are humble, unambitious, and their communal vice is smugness and insularity. Tolkien, we know, had read *Babbit* and, in an interview, suggested the name as a possible unconscious source for "hobbit." J.R.R. Tolkien, interview by Charlotte and Dennis Plimmer, "The Man Who Understands Hobbits," *Daily Telegraph Magazine*, March 22, 1968.

3

THE LOGOS OF ST. JOHN AND TOLKIEN'S CREATION OF ARDA

> "The world is a product of the Word, of the Logos, as St. John expresses it. . . . 'Logos' means 'reason,' 'sense,' 'word.' It is not reason pure and simple, but creative Reason, which speaks and communicates itself. It is Reason that both is and creates sense. The creation account tells us, then, that the world is a product of creative Reason."
>
> POPE BENEDICT XVI[1]

FOLLOWING GENESIS, which has two creation stories, Tolkien offers two of his own in *The Silmarillion*, framing them as Elven texts: the *Ainulindalë*, which in Elven (Quenya[2]) means "The Music of the Ainur," and the *Valaquenta*, which means "The History of the Powers." The Ainur are the Holy Ones (or Powers), first created by "Eru, the One, who in Arda [the Earth] is called Ilúvatar." Tolkien starts with monotheism. Ilúvatar first creates something like a Greek pantheon of lesser but powerful spiritual beings. Essentially, they are the guardian angels and sub-creators of the world in which we live. The *Valaquenta* describes these "powers" and their functions. Eru, the good creator, who will bring even greater good out of evil, and who promises to enter his

---

1 Pope Benedict XVI, *The Faith* (Huntington, IN: *Our Sunday Visitor*, 2013), 26–7.

2 Quenya is "high-elven," the original Elvish language.

81

world, is, it seems, the God of the Bible as understood by a clear-sighted race, the Elves, before Biblical revelation.

In the *Ainulindalë*, the Ainur, under the direction of Ilúvatar, sing the universe (Eä) into being. Ilúvatar is first a composer and choir director. Also, He is the ultimate Creator, since all of the angels have their being through Him. Yet He is a Creator who gives his creatures free will, allowing them, as "sub-creators," to add their own energy and ideas to the physical world. At the moment of completion of the celestial music, Ilúvatar transposes the music into light, displays the light to the angels, and says, "Let it be!" The music, turned into light, becomes the potential physical realization of the world, and the angels who desire to continue with the creative process are given leave to bring the world of their music into being.

Although Tolkien uses many sources from Northern European mythology and Anglo-Saxon literature to construct his own mythology, he acknowledged, as we have seen, that *The Lord of the Rings* is "a fundamentally religious and Catholic work." If Christianity illuminates it "like light from an invisible lamp," the Gospel of John throws much of that light. Aside from what can be inferred from *The Lord of the Rings* itself, there are two independent sources that alert us to Tolkien's interest in John. One is a short letter, in which Tolkien acknowledged John as his patron saint: "I was born on the Octave of St. John the Evangelist, I take him as my patron. . . ."[3] The other is an essay that includes some painful memories of C. S. Lewis.

Sometime in 1964, after he had published *The Lord of the Rings*, and after the death of Lewis on November 22, 1963, Tolkien wrote the "Ulsterior Motive," Ulster being Lewis's birthplace. It was a review of Lewis's book, *Letters to Malcolm*, which Tolkien found "distressing" and "in parts horrifying."[4] Although bits of this unpublished essay are often considered by critics whose interest is the friendship of Lewis and Tolkien, I offer the following anecdote from the essay, edited by Humphrey Carpenter, because it provides insight into the relationship of Tolkien and St. John:

3 *Letters*, 397.
4 Ibid., 352.

"We were coming down the steps from Magdalen hall," Tolkien recalled, "long ago in the days of our unclouded association, before there was anything, as it seemed, that must be withheld or passed over in silence. I said that I had a special devotion to St. John. Lewis stiffened, his head went back, and he said in the brusque harsh tones which I was later to hear him use again when dismissing something he disapproved of: 'I can't imagine any two persons more dissimilar.' We stumped along the cloisters, and I followed feeling like a shabby Catholic caught by the eye of an 'Evangelical clergyman of good family' taking holy water at the door of a church. A door had slammed. Never now should I be able to say in his presence:

Bot Crytes mersy and Mary and Jon

Thise arn the grounde of alle my blysse.

—*The Pearl,* 383–4; a poem that Lewis disliked—and suppose that I was sharing anything of my vision of a great rood-screen through which one could see the Holy of Holies."[5]

The "Evangelical clergyman of good family" was Lewis's satirical label for his father, who was a lawyer. Tolkien's "great rood-screen" refers to Mary, the saints, and the iconic elements of Catholic tradition, through which Christ is not obscured or displaced, but seen more clearly. The "rood screen" of Catholicism includes having one's favorite saints and taking a saint's name at confirmation—for Tolkien, John the Evangelist. The Holy of Holies behind the screen is Christ, of course, but it suggests the Christ of John's gospel. That Christ's mercy, Mary, and John are *all* Tolkien's bliss underscores the importance of the Johannine works to Tolkien.[6]

---

5 Humphrey Carpenter, *The Inklings: C. S. Lewis, J. R. R. Tolkien, Charles Williams and Their Friends* (London: HarperCollins, 1997), 51–2.

6 I doubt that Tolkien would have been unaware of controversy concerning the authorship of the traditional Johannine corpus: John, the letters of John, and Revelations. I assume that "a special devotion to John," however, includes the idea that John is at least the founder of a "school" that produced this material and taken to be the "beloved disciple" of the gospel. Otherwise, a special devotion to John has little content.

Tolkien, the Logos, and the Sacramental Universe

Genesis 1:1–5 establishes a framework within which John 1:1–5 dwells. Here is the *Douay-Rheims* translation of the opening verses of Genesis:

> In the beginning God created heaven, and earth. And the earth was void and empty, and darkness was upon the face of the deep; and the spirit of God moved over the waters. And God said: Be light made. And light was made. And God saw the light that it was good; and he divided the light from the darkness. And he called the light Day, and the darkness Night; and there was evening and morning one day.

The first creation account, which goes through Genesis 2:3, establishes that the world's creation was peaceful, the world was brought into being through speech over time, and that creation was good. It is Catholic theology that the world, however damaged by sin, is still primarily good. The Genesis account also establishes a mild light/dark dualism.

John's creation story retains all of this, by implication, but brings in revolutionary ideas about Christ's part in creation. John 1:1–5 reads as follows:

> In the beginning was the Word [*logos*], and the Word was with God, and the Word was God.
> The same was in the beginning with God.
> All things were made by him: and without him was made nothing that was made.
> In him was life, and the life was the light of men.
> And the light shineth in darkness, and the darkness did not comprehend it.

John assigns the creative activity to Christ, "the Word," who is not only the designer and enactor of Creation, but the supreme human manifestation of God's creative power in the world. This is consistent with Hebrews 1:3, "In these days [God] hath spoken to us by his Son, whom he hath appointed heir of all things, *by whom also he made the world*" (my emphasis), and with Christ's speech in Revelations 21:5, "Behold, I make all things new." As in

Genesis, John introduces the duality of light and darkness, which he emphasizes as a strong, continuing motif throughout his gospel. In many translations, the last line of verse 5 is, "the darkness did not overcome it," and this is more appropriate to the battle between light and darkness that we see both in John and throughout Tolkien's work,[7] even in his scholarly essays.

The Greek *logos*, translated as "Word" in all English versions of John 1:1,[8] refers to God's entire creative action through Christ, both the plan of Creation and God's continuing execution of that plan throughout time. The Logos has two long genealogies, one in Greek philosophy and the other in the Old Testament.

According to the Liddell-Scott *Intermediate Greek-English Lexicon* of 1889, the word *logos* includes the following meanings: "a ground," "a plea," "an opinion," "an expectation," "an account," and most importantly, "reason." Before John used the word, it already had this broad array of meaning and also a complex set of meanings in Greek philosophy. Sophists used the term to mean "discourse," and Aristotle "reasoned discourse."

Heraclitus of Ephesus was the first known Greek philosopher to use the word logos as a philosophical term. For him, it is the eternal divine law, moral as well as natural.[9] For the Stoics, the logos meant the principle of active reason that permeated and animated the universe and engaged in creation. They associated it with God, and in this context the word became influential in Jewish philosophy. Philo of Alexandria, a Jewish Platonist, saw the logos as an intermediary between God and man, the intermediary closest to God in a Platonic system that had a succession of intermediaries. Because it was the highest intermediary, Philo called it "the first born of God,"[10] and he associated it with the

7 See Verlyn Flieger, *Splintered Light*: "The contrast and interplay of light and dark are essential elements in his [Tolkien's] fiction," 4. Flieger concentrates on Northern European mythological sources for this idea with essentially no reference of John's gospel.

8 I make this statement of the basis of the 19 parallel translations listed on *Biblos*. http://Bible.cc/john/1-1.htm, accessed on February 11, 2013.

9 Diels-Kranz 22B1 and 22B2.

10 Frederick Copleston, *Greece and Rome*. Vol. 1 of *A History of Philosophy* (NY: Doubleday, 1997), 458–462.

Angel of the Lord in the Old Testament. Philo wrote, "the Logos of the living God is the bond of everything, holding all things together and binding all the parts, and prevents them from being dissolved and separated." He identified the Logos as the instrument through which God created the universe.[11] Justin Martyr, one of the earliest Christian theologians, associated the Logos not only with Christ, but with the Angel of the Lord and Wisdom: "God begot before all creatures a Beginning, [who was] a certain rational power [proceeding] from Himself, who is called by the Holy Spirit, now the Glory of the Lord, now the Son, again Wisdom, again an Angel, then God, and then Lord and Logos."[12]

The Stoic idea of Logos as creative reason strikingly resembles Proverbs' depiction of Lady Wisdom, portrayed as the master craftsman of the universe:

> The Lord possessed me in the beginning of his ways, before he made any thing from the beginning.
>
> I was set up from eternity, and of old before the earth was made.
>
> The depths were not as yet, and I was already conceived, neither had the fountains of waters as yet sprung out:
>
> The mountains with their huge bulk had not as yet been established: before the hills I was brought forth.
>
> He had not yet made the earth, nor the rivers, nor the poles of the world.
>
> When he prepared the heavens, I was present: when with a certain law and compass he enclosed the depths:
>
> When he established the sky above, and poised the fountains of waters:
>
> When he compassed the sea with its bounds, and set a law to the waters that they should not pass their limits: when he balanced the foundations of the earth;
>
> I was with him forming all things: and was delighted every day, playing before him at all times;

---

11 Philo, *De Profugis*, cited in Gerald Friedlander, *Hellenism and Christianity* (London: P. Vallentine, 1912), 114–115.

12 Justin Martyr, *Dialogue with Trypho*, Chapter 61. New Advent. http://www.newadvent.org/fathers/01285.htm (accessed 10 October 2012).

Playing in the world: and my delights were to be with the children of men.[13]

Wisdom is described in a similar way in the books of Sirach (Ecclesiasticus) and the Wisdom of Solomon, all of which see Wisdom existing before time and having a fundamental role in creation.[14] The Old Testament adds the additional dimension of attaching the concepts of "breath" and "life" to the concept of "word." There are obvious reasons for associating the inspiration and expiration of breath with life, since, when respiration stops, life stops. In Genesis, breath comes to be associated with life, when God breathes into the dust to create Adam: "And the Lord God formed man of the slime of the earth: and breathed into his face the breath of life, and man became a living soul" (Genesis 2:7); and in John's gospel, when Jesus similarly breathes on his disciples, imbuing them with new life: "When he had said this, he breathed on them; and he said to them: Receive ye the Holy Ghost" (John 20:22). Additionally, when one speaks, one expels breath, so the spoken word becomes associated with the breath of life and life itself. God speaks the universe into existence by saying, "Let it be," and the Word, as both breath and meaning, is the essence of life and, hence, creation. Breath becomes wind,

13 Proverbs 8:22–31; The *Jerusalem Bible*'s translation is quite beautiful and adds to the understanding of these verses:

Yahweh created me when his purpose first unfolded, / Before the oldest of his works. / From everlasting I was firmly set, / from the beginning, before earth came into being / The deep was not when I was born, / there were no springs to gush with water. / Before the mountains were settled, / before the hills, I came to birth; / before he made the earth, the countryside, / or the first grains of the world's dust. / When he fixed the heavens firm, I was there, / when he drew a ring on the surface of the deep, / when he thickened the clouds above, / when he fixed fast the springs of the deep, / when he assigned the sea its boundaries / —and the waters will not invade the shore— / when he laid down the foundations of the earth, / I was at his side, a master craftsman / delighting him day after day / ever at play in his presence, / at play everywhere in his world, / delighting to be with the sons of men.

14 See the following Old Testament passages: Wisdom 7:22 to 8:1; Sirach 24:1–9.

and the wind the Holy Spirit, bringing new life, as Tolkien and C.S. Lewis perceived it on Addison's Walk.

Included for John are all of the Old Testament associations that give "Word" immediate spiritual significance as creative power. Taking both Hellenistic and Judaic strands, the word *logos* compresses an astonishing array of harmonious ideas, all focused on creation. It is all at once the power to create and the meaningful blueprint by which creation is structured. Moreover, the world is "good" (on the basis of Genesis 1), not just a morally neutral realm of matter and forces, working in a scientifically comprehensible manner, but a realm brought into existence and ordered by love.

Tolkien's belief, under the influence of Owen Barfield, was that language in its ancient condition reflected this physical and spiritual unity. The word *logos* is an example of the ancient semantic unity described by Barfield in *Poetic Diction* (1928). His argument implied that language itself had become desacralized, as secular meaning split from religious; in which *wind*, for example, meant only moving air and *spirit* only immaterial being, whereas the Latin word *spiritus* originally held both meanings.[15]

Barfield's point was that, when the world becomes disenchanted—dispirited—language follows suit. Barfield's philosophic enemies were those who did most to divorce fact from value in language: Kant and the logical positivists. Tolkien examines the moral consequences of logical positivism in Saruman, the wizard with a mind of gears and wheels, who can make words stand on their heads. But Tolkien, in his development of the languages of Middle-earth, traces a deeper process, "the fall" of language itself, as the children of Ilúvatar become progressively alienated from him after their falls.[16]

In the sacramental understanding of the cosmos, there can be

---

15 Owen Barfield, *Poetic Diction: A Study in Meaning* (Middletown, CT: Wesleyan University Press, 1973), 79–81; and the whole chapter, "Meaning and Myth." Flieger, *Splintered Light*, gives a succinct description of Barfield's theory and its impact on Tolkien, 33–44.

16 Verlyn Flieger, in *Splintered Light*, presents the best explication of this aspect of Tolkien's work.

no division between a secular world and a holy, spirit-filled world, between the natural and supernatural—reality is *all* a spiritual production. Alexander Schmemann expresses the same idea:

> Each ounce of matter belongs to God and is to find in God its fulfillment. Each instant of time is God's time and is to fulfill itself as God's eternity. Nothing is "neutral." For the Holy Spirit, as a ray of light, as a smile of joy, has "touched" all things, all time—revealing all of them as precious stones of a precious temple.[17]

This sacramental vision is thoroughly incorporated into the theology of Thomas Aquinas and is the lynchpin of Dante's *Divine Comedy*. In the last two lines of the great poem, Dante recognizes that the love which orders the universe and the love which impels human beings are the same and have the same source: "My will and my desire were turned by love, / The love that moves the sun and the other stars."[18] David L. Schindler provides a less poetic, but nevertheless beautiful, statement of the idea: "Love is the basic act and order of things. . . . Love is that which first brings each thing into existence, and that in and through and for which each thing continues in existence."[19]

Part of what follows from Logos-centric creation is that all creatures, i.e., created things, participate in and point toward a loving creator as their source. Schindler sets forth the significance of this in a Thomistic form that was fully available to Tolkien:

> The most basic fact or truth of all things is at once their analogically conceived goodness or value as gift, a giftedness that is intrinsic to each thing by virtue of its being generated by the generosity of God. The goodness of things in the cosmos is not rooted most basically in human freedom or intelligence, and thus in human spirit, nor is it first granted by human freedom and intelligence. On the contrary, it is rooted in the creative freedom and intelligence of the creator in which *all things of the*

17 Alexander Schmemann, *For the Life of the World*, 76.

18 Dante Alighieri, *Paradise*, vol. 3 of *The Divine Comedy*, translated by Mark Musa (NY: Penguin, 1986), 394.

19 David L. Schindler, *Ordering Love: Liberal Societies and the Memory of God* (Grand Rapids: Eerdmans, 2011), 1.

cosmos truly participate, and which they just so far "image," each in
its own analogical creaturely way.[20] (original emphasis)

Since love is the "basic act and order" by which the universe is
made, the universe will "image" God, making it fundamentally
sacramental, sacraments being the way in which human beings
participate in God's creative love. "God is love," John says (1 John
4:8); the Logos is love ordering the universe; God's love is available through the specific sacraments of the church and the general
sacramentality of a world ordered by love. This understanding of
St. John's Logos, as developed through 2,000 years of Christian
culture, was part of Tolkien's intellectual DNA.[21]

Che Logos and music

We can think of the Logos as the composer of a grand symphonic
score that orders creation, the score itself, and the playing of that
score: the formulation of a plan, the plan, and the plan in action.
As the idea of the Logos developed in early Christianity, it
became associated with Greek speculation about music and
angelic song. This begins with Pythagoras, appears for the
Hebrews in the angelic choirs of Isaiah and for mankind in the
Gospel of Luke, when the angels announce Christ's nativity. In
"On Music," St. Augustine locates mathematical and musical harmony in Christ as the Logos, and this idea appears continuously
in European thought until the Enlightenment.[22] Knowing this

20 Schindler, 5.

21 Tolkien would have inhaled these connections during his boyhood at
the Birmingham Oratory. More explicitly, they are available in Aquinas *Summa
Theologica*, which Tolkien studied, and in Dante, whom he and Lewis read
together. These ideas were also in Charles Williams' works on Dante. See *Letters*, 377.

22 Isidore of Seville (560–636) wrote: "Nothing exists without music; for
the universe itself is said to have been framed by a kind of harmony of sounds,
and the heaven itself revolves under the tones of that harmony," *Etymologia-
rum sive originum libri*, quoted in E.M.W. Tillyard, *The Elizabethan World Picture* (1943; rpt. NY, 1961); in the second century, Clement of Alexandria
identified the Logos with music: "It also composed the universe into melodious order, and tuned the discord of the elements to harmonious arrangement,

history, as well as Tolkien's myth, C. S. Lewis has Aslan sing Narnia into being.[23]

Pope Benedict XVI, in *The Spirit of the Liturgy*, connects Logos to beauty and art in a manner which virtually explicates the *Ainulindalë*. This is no accident, for Benedict is summarizing the tradition that Tolkien understands and draws on throughout his work:

> [There] was a spontaneous turn at this point [the time of Augustine], from stellar deities to the choirs of angels that surround God and illumine the universe. Perceiving the "music of the cosmos" thus becomes listening to the song of the angels, and the reference to Isaiah chapter 6 ["Holy, holy, holy is the Lord of hosts; the whole earth is full of his glory."] naturally suggests itself.
>
> But a further step was taken with the help of the Trinitarian faith, faith in the Father, the Logos [the Son], and the Pneuma [Holy Spirit]. The mathematics of the universe does not exist by itself, nor, as people now came to see, can it be explained by stellar deities. It has a deeper foundation: the mind of the Creator. It comes from the Logos, in whom, so to speak, the archetypes of the world's order are contained. The Logos, through the Spirit, fashions the material world according to these archetypes. In virtue of his work in creation, the Logos is, therefore, called "art of God".... The Logos himself is the great artist, in whom all works of art—the beauty of the universe—have their origin.
>
> To sing with the universe means, then, to follow the track of the Logos and to come close to him. All true human art is an

so that the whole world might become harmony.... A beautiful breathing instrument of music the Lord made man, after His own image. And He Himself also, surely, who is the supramundane Wisdom, the celestial Word, is the all-harmonious, melodious, holy instrument of God," *Exhortation to the Heathen* (OrthodoxEbooks, 2012), 325–326, http://books.google.com/books?id=t YHjz6J3OrYC&dq=clement+of+alexandria+exhortation+to+the+heathen &source=gbs_navlinks_s (accessed March 10, 2014); John Davies explicates this idea in his 1594 poem, "Orchestra," and John Dryden uses it in his 1687 poem, "A Song for St. Cecelia's Day."

23 This occurs in *The Magician's Nephew.*

assimilation to the artist, to Christ, to the mind of the Creator. The idea of the music of the cosmos, of singing with angels, leads back again to the relation of art to logos, but now it is broadened and deepened in the context of the cosmos. Yes, it is the cosmic context that gives art in the liturgy both its measure and its scope. A merely subjective "creativity" is no match for the vast compass of the cosmos and for the message of beauty. When a man conforms to the measure of the universe, his freedom is not diminished but expanded to a new horizon.[24]

The Music of the Ainur is mythopoetic theology in an imagined world millennia before Christian revelation. But one can see a shadow of the Trinity in it. The Trinity is a society based on love; indeed, the Holy Spirit is the Love that flows between the Father and Son. The Trinity is inherently *kenotic*—self-giving—in that for all eternity it has engaged in a mutual communion of love. Creation flows out of Trinitarian love to a world made for the purpose of participating in that love. Ilúvatar's outpouring of love to the Ainur, through the gift of creative participation, can only be returned by their free outpouring as well. In Christian terms, the Ainur are invited into Trinitarian love. The creation of Eä takes place as an exchange of love, but also, to use Benedict's language, "as an assimilation to the artist, to Christ, to the mind of the Creator." In Tolkien's myth, the Ainur have freedom, but it is subordinate to Ilúvatar's overall plan, and, although one of them refuses any limitations, this is ultimately impossible, because all have their origin and are held in being by Ilúvatar. Finally, the nature of Ilúvatar and his ultimate plan remain mysterious even to the Ainur.

---

24 Joseph Cardinal Ratzinger, *The Spirit of the Liturgy* (San Francisco: Ignatius Press, 2000), 153–4. For an excellent quick summary of the tradition Tolkien draws upon for the music of creation, see Bradford Lee Eden, "'The Music of the Spheres': Relationships between Tolkien's *The Silmarillion* and Medieval Cosmological and Religious Theory," in *Tolkien the Medievalist*, ed. Jane Chance (London: Routledge, 2008), 183.

Chε Logos in the αinulinδalë

Tolkien begins with the Ainur singing by themselves. They discover, in a necessary solitude, the song that is particularly their own, which will come to be enriched in communication with others. Continuing a theme of "Leaf by Niggle," Tolkien shows that God's gift of sub-creation is only perfected in community with others. The Ainur sing for some time, as if Eru were tuning up his angelic choir. But then Eru gets down to the real business by proposing a theme that eventually will be actualized as Creation:

> And it came to pass that Ilúvatar called together all the Ainur and declared to them a mighty theme, unfolding to them things greater and more wonderful than he had yet revealed; and the glory of its beginning and the splendour of its end amazed the Ainur, so that they bowed before Ilúvatar and were silent.
>
> Then Ilúvatar said to them: "Of the theme that I have declared to you, I will now that ye make in harmony together a Great Music. And since I have kindled you with the Flame Imperishable, ye shall show forth your powers in adorning this theme, each with his own thoughts and devices, if he will. But I will sit and hearken, and be glad that through you great beauty has been wakened into song." (15)

Ilúvatar invites his angels into creative song. He is not obligated to do this, but one of his characteristics is overflowing, gratuitous joy, which he wants to share. This is *kenosis*, the gratuitous pouring out of oneself in creation. Everything that goes wrong in Middle-earth will result from a denial of kenosis—a greedy, dragon-like appropriation and hoarding of what one can create or acquire.

There are many remarkable ideas in this passage, which open gateways into the understanding of everything Tolkien wrote. He continues to theologize his idea of sub-creation as a gift from God, impossible without the additional gift of free will. Without free will, participatory joy in creation would be impossible. So Ilúvatar kindles within his creatures "the Flame Imperishable," which confers life and free will. Is the Flame Imperishable, with its suggestion of Pentecostal Fire, an analog of the Holy Spirit? In Note 11 of his "Athrabeth Finrod ah Andreth,"[25] Tolkien offers this extended, albeit tentative definition:

> In the *Ainulindalë* . . . reference is made to the 'Flame Imperishable'. This appears to mean the Creative activity of Eru (in some sense distinct from or within Him), by which things could be given a 'real' and independent (though derivative and created) existence. The Flame Imperishable is sent out from Eru, to dwell in the heart of the world, and the world then Is, on the same plane as the Ainur, and they can enter into it. . . . It refers rather to the mystery of 'authorship', by which the author, while remaining 'outside' and independent of his work, also 'indwells' in it, on its derivative plane, below that of his own being, as the source and guarantee of its being.

The phrase "In some sense distinct from *or within* Him" invites us into the mystery of the Trinity. On the basis of Psalm 103 (v. 30),[26] Catholics see the role of the Holy Spirit in the act of creation, as giving life to creation. The Holy Spirit makes the inanimate become animate, and, in Tolkien's creation myth, is the kindler of free will. In this passage, Tolkien also connects the Flame Imperishable to Eru's immanence in creation, adding another of God's characteristics.

As we shall see, Gandalf is the representative of the Flame Imperishable in Middle-earth. He will be the unidentified bearer of Narya the Great, the Ring of Fire, given to him by the Elf, Círdan: 'Take now this Ring," he said; 'for thy labours and thy cares will be heavy, but in all it will support thee and defend thee from weariness. For this is the Ring of Fire, and herewith, maybe, thou shalt *rekindle hearts* to the valor of old in a world that grows chill" (my emphasis; *The Silmarillion*, 303). Gandalf's main function in Middle-earth will be to rouse people—to throw Bilbo out of his Hobbit hole and send him on the road for an adventure, to give heart to those who have given in to despair. Gandalf is the catalyst of spiritual response.

Finally, the Ainur "assimilate" their singing to the great theme

---

25 *Morgoth's Ring* (NY: Houghton Mifflin, 1993), 345.
26 Douay-Reims numbering.

of Ilúvatar, doing exactly what Pope Benedict says all "true artists" do, finding their freedom within the boundaries of the all-encompassing divine scheme of creation. Without free will, the Ainur could add nothing to creation that Ilúvatar had not given them. He does not want them to be spiritual player pianos, but composers in their own right. Still, Ilúvatar doesn't give them complete freedom, for he has proposed "the Great Theme" that will furnish the framework for their improvisations and, of course, he has created the Ainur themselves. They are invited "to conform to the measure of the universe," to use Pope Benedict's delightful pun, and to create within that broad measure. Their freedom as creatures will reach its full potential only through this framework.

The account of free will offered by Milton and most apologists is that, without it, no genuine relationship with God would be possible. Tolkien includes this by implication, but adds an important and highly original idea—that for a creator to have a full, joyful relationship with his creatures, they also must have the genuine power to create. Free will, therefore, is a necessary gift to creatures who are to participate as creators. But, in Tolkien's myth, freedom without constraint is not only bad, but delusional; the *Ainulindalë* illustrates the Catholic understanding that true freedom and full actualization of the self blossom out of obedience to God.

The Ainur produce beautiful music, "endless interchanging melodies woven in harmony that passed beyond hearing into the depths and into the heights." Tolkien echoes Keats's phrase: "Heard melodies are Sweet, but those unheard are Sweeter." This music that passes beyond hearing represents a truth and beauty so deep and profound that it goes into the imperceptible corners of the world, and it comprehends the deepest levels of natural and moral law. It is consistent with Heraclitus's original understanding of the pervasiveness of the *Logos*.

Despite the beautiful harmony, Tolkien mythologizes that the Ainur do not fully understand Ilúvatar's intent, even when they sing their own parts, and they will not know it until the end of days, when they make an even greater music. The music is teleological—it will achieve a fulfillment at some point, with a new, undisclosed movement, but knowledge of this is closed to all but Ilúvatar. Like the God of Christianity, Eru is the only omniscient being in Tolkien's secondary world, and history is the providential story he writes, known only to him. Like the Logos, the Music is beguiling, beautiful, and, finally, mysterious. Even the Ainur do not know the entire song. Mystery is a component of holiness, and thus, at bottom, Christianity is built on mystery expressed as paradox.[27]

At this point, Tolkien gives us his version of Lucifer's fall—a story he will repeat in variation after variation throughout *The Silmarillion* and *The Lord of the Rings*. Tolkien's predecessor is Milton, Lucifer being replaced by the fallen Ainur, Melkor, but Tolkien adds to Milton's thought by focusing on the dangers of sub-creation. Melkor, the most powerful of the angels, becomes envious of Iluvátar's capacity to create—and especially to bestow free will, the one creative power which is denied him: "To Melkor among the Ainur had been given the greatest gifts of power and knowledge, and he had a share in all the gifts of his brethren." Melkor, who wants to produce beings of his own, has "gone often alone into the void places seeking that Imperishable Flame" (16), with which he could give life to his creations. (He cannot find it because it is "within" Ilúvatar or, in more Christian terms, in Trinitarian relationship within Him. Melkor's quest is ironic, based on his ignorance of Ilúvatar's nature.) The desire to create

---

27 Ross Douthat, in *Bad Religion* (NY: Free Press, 2012) Kindle Electronic Edition, Prologue, Location 310–26, gives this delightful list of the paradoxes at the heart of Christianity: "[O]rthodox Christians insist that Jesus Christ was divine and human all at once, that the Absolute is somehow Three as well as One, that God is omnipotent and omniscient and yet nonetheless leaves us free to choose between good and evil. They propose that the world is corrupted by original sin and yet somehow also essentially good, with the stamp of its Creator visible on every star and sinew. They assert that the God of the Old Testament, jealous and punitive, is somehow identical to the New Testament's God of love and mercy. They claim that this same God sets impossible moral standards and yet forgives every sin. They insist that faith alone will save us, yet faith without works is dead." G.K. Chesterton loves the paradoxes and irresolvable mysteries of Christianity. See "Paradoxes of Christianity" in *Orthodoxy*, 87–108.

with the full power of God grows hot within Melkor and preys on him, as he sings in the heavenly chorus:

> Some of these thoughts he now wove into his music, and straightway, discord arose about him, and many that sang nigh him grew despondent, and their thought was disturbed and their music faltered; but some began to attune their music to his rather than to the thought which they had at first. Then the discord of Melkor spread ever wider, and the melodies which had been heard before foundered in a sea of turbulent sound. But Ilúvatar sat and hearkened until it seemed that about this throne there was a raging storm, as of dark waters that made war upon one another in an endless wrath that would not be assuaged. (16)

Melkor wants a universe of his own, his own worshippers, and, failing this, to destroy.[28] In the choir, he gives full voice to his anger, singing "out of measure" and thereby introducing evil and discord into the world. His music reflects his mind, full of envy and malice, out of control. He is powerful enough to set a dominant tone that takes possession of those around him, and they begin to sing more in sync with him than with Ilúvatar's theme. Some of the Ainur grow despondent. Melkor has reduced them, taken away their joy in creation, induced depression, and here we have the ultimate origin of the Nazgûl, whose presence alone, in *The Lord of the Rings,* causes despair. Moreover, the force of Melkor's will controls the Ainur nearest him, a foreshadowing of Saruman's voice and the power of the Ring.

Oddly, Melkor's attempt to sabotage the chorus does not bother Ilúvatar, who merely smiles, lifts his hand, and begins a new theme, "like and yet unlike to the former theme, and it gathered power and had new beauty." He is working with Melkor's dissonance, playing off it, incorporating it into the larger composition. Ilúvatar's smile is enigmatic. Does He smile because He

---

28 As *The Silmarillion* progresses, we find Melkor wants the impossible: free-willed creatures who are *guaranteed* to love and worship him. Tolkien helps us to understand the irrationality and evil of such a conception. George Orwell shares the same aim in 1984, in the horrifying scene when Winston Smith finally does love Big Brother.

knows Melkor cannot win, or because He is pleased that Melkor has used his free will to break new ground, to add something original and unexpected to the composition? Ilúvatar may have something of a father's pride in Melkor, who is a headstrong and wayward son, but one perhaps who shows potential and who has taken the work in an interesting direction. Further, everything that Melkor does only serves to make the music more beautiful—which is Ilúvatar's intent.

Rather than seeing opportunities to incorporate dissonance into a unified composition, Melkor competes even more dreadfully with the rest of the Ainur, who are weaving music around the second theme: "the discord of Melkor rose in uproar and contended with it, and again there was a war of sound more violent than before, until many of the Ainur were dismayed and sang no longer and Melkor had the mastery." Now, Ilúvatar rises for the second time, but his countenance is stern. Melkor is dominating the other angels, removing their freedom to create. In the first movement, Melkor had done this by entraining the angels with his dissonance, but, in the second instance, he silences many of them. Melkor's sub-creation is destroying the community of sub-creators, exactly what the One Ring of Sauron is meant to do.

Núvatar's third theme grows in response to Melkor:

> [I]t seemed at first soft and sweet, a mere rippling of gentle sounds in delicate melodies; but it could not be quenched, and it took to itself power and profundity. And it seemed at last that there were two musics progressing at one time before the seat of Ilúvatar, and they were utterly at variance. The one was deep and wide and beautiful, but slow and blended with an immeasurable sorrow, from which its beauty chiefly came. The other had now achieved a unity of its own; but it was loud and vain, and endlessly repeated; and it had little harmony, but rather a clamorous unison as of many trumpets braying upon a few notes. And it essayed to drown the other music by the violence of its voice. (*The Silmarillion*, 16–17)

What is the content of this beautiful, deep, unquenchable theme played out against the narcissistic and nihilistic pandemonium of Melkor? I would suggest it is salvation history, moving inexorably through a damaged world toward sacrifice and redemption, a story that Tolkien plays out again and again in *The Lord of the Rings*. It is the most beautiful of all the themes, *because* it is at once sorrowful and joyful. It is the music of eucatastrophe.

Ilúvatar arises for the third time, and his face is "terrible to behold." He raises both his hands, and, in one chord "deeper than the abyss," brings the music to a halt. Then he gives the Ainur a vision of the entire musical composition. "Behold your music," he says to them, and they see their music translated into a new World, "globed amid the Void." The "Valaquenta," Tolkien's second creation myth, refers to the music made visible with Johannine poetry: "they beheld it as a light in the darkness" (25). What the Ainur see is a multi-dimensional design, their music turned into a sculpture of light. As they watch their music unfold, it seems to them alive and growing. Ilúvatar tells them, "This is your minstrelsy; and each of you shall find contained herein, amid the design that I set before you, all those things which it may seem that he himself devised or added" (17). It includes Melkor's dissonance also, which Ilúvatar assures him will only add to the glory of the whole:

> "Thou Melkor, shalt see that no theme may be played that hath not its uttermost source in me, nor can any alter the music in my despite. For he that attempteth this shall prove but mine instrument in the devising of things more wonderful, which he himself hath not imagined." (17)

Certainly, we are meant to see the similarities between Melkor and Satan. Here Tolkien puts his poetic stamp on the *felix culpa*, the fortunate fall that leads not to final disaster, but to eucatastrophe, the unexpected happy ending, love abounding through Christ's death and resurrection. This is the Logos beneath the *telos*—the narrative—of the world. Ilúvatar's final word is "Eä! Let these things be!" (20). Having given being to the design, Ilúvatar sends the Ainur who desire it into the world to "achieve" the vision, and the "powers" become the builders of the world.

✠

This is Tolkien's mythopoetic variation on John 1:1–5, the Music that was in the beginning. It is a retelling of and commentary upon key creation and wisdom texts. It offers a short mythic explanation of the origin of free will and its relation to the fixed frame of God's order. It identifies the origin of evil as an expression of the free will that God allows. Significantly, Tolkien associates the first sin with the act of creation. Melkor's frustrated desire to create with the power of God makes him an envious destroyer—or attempted destroyer—of God's creation. Ilúvatar's gift of sub-creation, because it entails a powerful grant of freedom, has an equally powerful potential to be abused, and it is the tendency of sub-creation to go wrong, because the sub-creator can grow envious of the works of others and fall idolatrously in love with his own. This misdirected love becomes the archetypal pattern of sin in Middle-earth. In opposition, Tolkien sets an equally archetypal pattern of sacrifice and redemption. Tolkien's mythic theodicy makes a promise, at least, that all evil will produce even greater glory and goodness. But how this is possible is not obvious to the Ainur, and perhaps not to us either.

The unfolding of the history of Arda is contained in the crescendos and decrescendos of the Music. The conflict between harmony and dissonance, and its movements, are analogs of the story Tolkien will go on to tell in *The Silmarillion* and *The Lord of the Rings*. The Ainur know their individual songs and they have some knowledge of the musical lines sung by each member of the chorus. They learn more through time. But only Ilúvatar knows the entire composition and fully understands the three themes he propounded. The Logos does not just yield a mechanical system of material cause and effect or provide a detailed map of history, even to the Ainur. It delivers surprises which cannot be accounted for by mere calculation: "for to none but himself has Ilúvatar revealed all that he has in store, and in every age there come forth things that are new and have no foretelling, *for they do not proceed from the past*" (my emphasis; *The Silmarillion*, 18). Tolkien's myth asserts God's continued surprising and creative involvement in the world and that the pattern of history in the music is eucatastrophic: there will unexpected happy endings.

Tolkien was aware that his creation myth differed from the Jewish and Christian versions in one important aspect—evil is built into the world from the beginning rather than brought in, by Satan, from the outside. Tolkien explains this in a draft of an unsent letter to Rhona Beare, who had written with a number of questions about *The Lord of the Rings*:

> I suppose a difference between this Myth and what may be perhaps called Christian mythology is this. In the latter, the Fall of Man is subsequent to and a consequence (though not a necessary consequence) of the 'Fall of the Angels': a rebellion of created free-will at a higher level than Man; but it is not clearly held (and in many versions is not held at all) that this affected the 'World' in its nature: evil was brought in from outside, by Satan. In this Myth the rebellion of created free-will precedes creation of the World (Eä); and Eä has in it, subcreatively introduced, evil, rebellions, discordant elements of its own nature already when the *Let it Be* was spoken. The Fall or corruption, therefore, of all things in it and all inhabitants of it, was a possibility if not inevitable. Trees may 'go bad' as in the Old Forest; Elves may turn into Orcs, and if this required the special perversive malice of Morgoth, still the World could at least err; as the Great Valar did in their dealings with the Elves; or as the lesser of their kind (as the Istari or wizards) could in various ways become self-seeking.[29]

The difference this makes for Tolkien's creation is that the built-in darkness of the world gives it more the flavor of Northern myth, and yet this darkness is just as much a part of the Bible, though it begins in Eden.

Melkor is never able to attain the "Flame Imperishable," because it cannot be appropriated. It is the love of God and can only be gratefully accepted. The contradiction at Melkor's heart is that his own creatures would not worship him, unless coerced by lies and threats. Melkor, as a creator, wants to confer free will, but, at the same time, cannot abide it. What he must settle for are free-willed slaves—slaves whose wills have been bent to his. Melkor can never create anything, love being required for any true creation. All he can do is mar the world by subtracting the good from it, "creating" waste through destruction. Melkor becomes the archetypal nihilist and is later named Morgoth, "the

---

29 *Letters*, 286–7.

Black Foe of the World." He and his servants are never associated with illuminative fire. Rather, his fire is always dark and consumes without illuminating. At the Bridge of Khazad-Dûm, when Gandalf makes his stand against the Balrog, he declares, "I am a servant of the Secret Fire, wielder of the flame of Anor. . . . The dark fire will not avail you, flame of Udûn. Go back to the Shadow!" (330). Gandalf pits the weapons of true Light, the Flame Imperishable, against fire from which Morgoth has subtracted light.[30] Gandalf simply has more "being" than the Balrog, more light and love, and he prevails.

The One Ring, forged by Morgoth's disciple Sauron, is a black hole: when Gandalf throws it into Frodo's fire, it doesn't get hot—light goes in, but doesn't come out. Rather than illuminating the world, like Gandalf's ring, Narya, it obscures, making its wearer invisible and throwing the world into shadow, subtracting being from the wearer and his world. The opposite of the Ring is Galadriel's Phial, which contains the original light of the two trees of Valinor. In the widespread iconography of the Sacred Heart of Jesus, Jesus' heart is shown in flame and great illuminative light, the light of life, the light of the Logos. This is the light associated with the monstrance, the container of the consecrated host. Tolkien's liturgical background provided concrete icons of illumination for *The Lord of the Rings*.

Tolkien provides one traditional answer to the problem of evil, and it is the same as John Milton's: love is only possible if it is freely chosen, and free will means love may be rejected and evil chosen; God allows evil as the necessary price of freely willed love, but providentially uses evil, so that even more good can come of it. The Logos is not just the enemy of evil, but the subverter of it, using what was meant to undo creation as the catalyst for a more glorious creation. The *felix culpa,* the fortunate fall that makes God's love abound, was in His mind from the beginning.

Thus, the long history in the West of the Logos as a reality and an idea, developed in Stoic philosophy, utilized by Philo, revealed

---

30 I am indebted to Stratford Caldecott's excellent section on Gandalf's combat with the Balrog. See *The Power of the Ring: The Spiritual Vision Behind the 'Lord of the Rings'* (NY: Crossroad, 2005), 103–4.

in St. John's Gospel, practiced in the Eucharist, and integrated by Coleridge in a coherent theory of perception and artistic creation, comes to Tolkien, who passes it on to us. This is the foundation on which all his fiction is built.

4

The Fall of Fëanor and Practically Everyone Else

"If more of us valued food and cheer and song above hoarded gold, it would be a merrier world." Thorin Oakenshield, *The Hobbit*[1]

The Old Master had come to a bad end. Bard had given him much gold for the help of the Lake-people, but being of the kind that easily catches such disease he fell under the dragon-sickness, and took most of the gold and fled with it, and died of starvation in the Waste, deserted by his companions. The Hobbit[2]

THE EMBLEM of the fallen creature is the straining, grasping hand. Thus Tolkien's characters sometimes lose a hand (Beren) or a finger (Frodo) to be freed. Melkor does not want *as much* power as Ilúvatar; he wants *more,* and he does not perceive the contradiction that, the more power he hoards, the less capable he will be of creation. The essence of evil is anti-creation: subtraction, sterility, destruction, death. The object of Melkor, like Satan, is to undo creation. Tolkien had a deep understanding that creation is based on an economy of giving oneself away. Its emblem is the open, outstretched arms of Christ crucified. Even for God, self-giving, self-limitation, and pain seem to be necessary. For, if God is to create creatures with free will, he must limit

1 J.R.R. Tolkien, *The Hobbit* (NY: Houghton Mifflin, 1995), 263.
2 *The Hobbit,* 276.

his own power in allowing them to exercise theirs and necessarily incur the risk of evil that comes with power sharing—with giving creatures an actual choice. True creation comes through love—the God of the cross is not a god of domination.

Creation is not just a display of power, but a necessary limitation of it, and this is a matter of logic as well as ethics. Any artist knows, as soon as the first brush stroke or line goes on the painting, that some conceptions must be limited or abandoned in favor of others. For a writer, certain characters can only perform certain actions; character and plot exert mutual limits on each other in a well-constructed and coherent story. All possibilities cannot be realized at once.

Tolkien's heroes accept limitation and suffering and give of themselves to the point of complete self-sacrifice. In this, they imitate God as Creator. Since Jesus is the Word made flesh, God incarnate, our understanding of God as Creator comes most completely and concretely from Jesus as Creator: one who does not appropriate for himself but gives himself out in a continual process of sharing, which includes suffering.[3] Jesus is the final divine statement that creation is worth the price of pain and that even God pays it. Through Jesus, God subjects himself to the laws of his own universe, not transcending it, but putting himself at its mercy. The most direct Christian understanding of God's character as Creator is contained in the Christ hymn of Philippians 2, one of the earliest written documents of the church, quoted by Paul:

> [Christ], Who being in the form of God, thought it not robbery to be equal to God:
> But emptied himself, taking the form of a servant, being made in the likeness of men, and in habit found as a man.
> He humbled himself, becoming obedient unto death, even to the death of the cross.[4]

---

3 See Terence E. Fretheim, *The Suffering of God: An Old Testament Perspective* (Philadelphia: Fortress Press, 1984), who applies this to the God of the Old Testament as well.

4 *The Jerusalem Bible* translated the passage as follows: His state was divine / yet he did not cling / to his equality with God / but emptied himself / to assume

Philippians addresses God's *kenosis*[5] through Christ and sets the heroic ideal for Tolkien.

Given the dangers and uncertainties surrounding human life, the refusal to engage in kenotic, self-emptying love is understandable, but it is always wrong. Bilbo at first doesn't want to leave his hobbit hole, and Frodo would rather remain in The Shire, but to do so means living a smaller life—grasping the "self" that Niggle finally understands must be relinquished. Gandalf, the servant of the "Flame Imperishable" and messenger of grace, must push the two Hobbits out the door—only then do they become fully alive.

Asserting oneself against God through sub-creation is the original sin that blights Middle-earth, built into it by Melkor's disruption of the Music of the Ainur and continued in his wars against the Valar, those of the Ainur whose job is to achieve the communal logos, sung in part with Ilúvatar, who keeps the final movement, the final Word, to himself. *The Silmarillion*, like Genesis, is about how the first sin spreads. The opening shows the creative work of the Valar in the world and the attempt by Melkor to disrupt it, yielding successive periods of creation, destruction, and repair. The "Quenta Silmarillion," the myth about the light-filled jewels created by Fëanor, the Silmarils, is a Johannine tale of darkness trying to overcome the light and succeeding, until the remaining light is sacrificed back to its source in completion of the cosmos's kenotic economy.

The tale begins with light. The most glorious creations of the Valar are the two trees of light that illuminate Middle-earth: Telperion, whose light is silver, and Laurelin, whose light is gold.

---

the condition of a slave / and became as men are / and being as all men are / he was humbler yet, / even to accepting death, / death on a cross.

5 See *The Work of Love: Creation as Kenosis,* ed. John Polkinghorne (Grand Rapids: Eerdman's, 2001). George F. R. Ellis's chapter, "Kenosis as a Unifying Theme for Life and Cosmology," gives the following definition of *kenosis* as potentially experienced by humanity: "a joyous, kind, and loving attitude that is willing to give up selfish desires and to make sacrifices on behalf of others for the common good and glory of God, doing this in a generous and creative way, avoiding the pitfall of pride, and guided and inspired by the love of God and the gift of grace," 108.

When the first born of Ilúvatar, the Elves, migrate to Valinor, the home of the Valar, they take great joy in the Trees. A particular group of the Elves, the Noldor, also learn to carve jewels, which celebrate the light of the Trees. At first, the Noldor, despite their love for the beauty of jewels, have no compulsion to appropriate them: "They hoarded them not, but gave them freely, and by their labour enriched all Valinor" (60).

Tolkien's description of the early Noldor is one of complete freedom, creative joy giving itself away. In two sentences, Tolkien gives us an Edenic emblem of light, freedom, and sub-creation in proper relation, governed by generosity and gratitude:

> [The Elves] walked in the waves upon the shore with their hair gleaming in the light beyond the hill. Many jewels the Noldor gave them, opals and diamonds and pale crystals, which they strewed upon the shores and scattered in the pools. (61)

The light beyond the hill, the light of the Trees, is the illumination by which the freedom of the Elves is realized and that fires the beauty of the jewels which the Elves fashion.

In Telperion and Laurelin, Tolkien reaches back to many sources, including, I suspect, the Menorah of the Old Testament, one of the most important icons of the Hebrew temple, a seven branched candle holder meant to depict an almond tree.[6] The menorah is a tree of light and life,[7] which may itself look back to the burning bush of Exodus[8] and forward to the Christmas tree, lighted with candles. These lighted trees are all symbols of the confluence of light and life, as is Christ in John 1:4 "All that came to be had life in him / and that life was the light of men." The cross itself becomes, then, another tree of light and life. Attempts to destroy

---

6 Exodus 25: 31–39.

7 The menorah symbolizes universal enlightenment; the six lamps inclining inward refer in Jewish tradition to the six branches of knowledge, the seventh middle branch to the light of God. See Chanan Morrison, Abraham Isaac Kook, *Gold from the Land of Israel: A New Light on the Weekly Torah Portion— From the Writings of Rabbi Abraham Isaac HaKohen Kook* (NY: Urim Publications, 2006), 239.

8 Robert Lewis Berman, *A House of David in the Land of Jesus* (London: Pelican, 2007), 18.

this light are demonic, and attempts to control it blasphemous, as Tolkien's story goes on to show. (Other sources for Laurelin and Telperion as "world trees" will be addressed in Chapter 9.)

One of the Noldor, Fëanor, has a vastly greater talent and desire for the sub-creation of jewels than any other Elf. In this he resembles Melkor, the most talented and ambitious of the Valar. Ominously, Fëanor has the most fiery spirit of the Elves, one tilted more toward mastery than contemplation. His wife sees this and tries to ameliorate it:

> Nerdanel also was firm of will, but more patient than Fëanor, desiring to understand minds rather than to master them, and at first she restrained him when the fire of his heart grew too hot; but his later deeds grieved her, and they became estranged. Seven sons she bore to Fëanor; her mood she bequeathed in part to some of them, but not to all. (64)

Fëanor's desire to "master" minds is an ominous shadow of Melkor and foreshadowing of Sauron, who will create the One Ring to control the will of others. Fëanor's artistic inspiration to create jewels, which contain some of the blended light of the two trees of Valinor, coexists from the beginning with his darker tendencies.[9] He labors in secret, as Melkor did, and is astonishingly successful, creating the three Silmarils, which shine with the internal light of Telperion and Laurelin. But Fëanor loves his work too much and hoards it:

> Though at great feasts Fëanor would wear them blazing on his brow, at other times they were guarded, close locked in the deep chambers of his hoard in Tirion. For Fëanor began to love the Silmarils with a greedy love, and grudged the sight of them to all save to his father and his seven sons; he seldom remembered now that the light within them was not his own. (69)

Fëanor's Silmarils begin to possess *him*, and his attitude extends to other artifacts as well: he accumulates "*his* hoard." Burning with desire, Fëanor becomes the first "dragon," for the prime characteristic of dragons is that they guard their hoard jealously, sitting on it,

---

9 The battle between light and dark within Fëanor could be analyzed within the Ignatian framework I propose in Chapter 6.

but not using it. He forgets he is a sub-creator—that the light of the jewels and the material of the jewels is the original creation of Ilúvatar. Fëanor gives himself all the credit and assumes exclusive ownership: "he denied the sight of the Silmarils to the Valar and the Eldar [the Elves], and left them locked in Formenos in their chamber of iron," foreshadowing their next resting place in the iron crown of Morgoth (Melkor's later name). This is Fëanor's spiritual state, which seems to provoke the attack of Melkor and the giant, light-devouring spider, Ungoliant, upon the Trees of Light.

Ungoliant is a potent symbol of evil's essential nature, a portrayal of the black hole at Melkor's center. Her nature is to feed but never to be satisfied. A kind of anti-Christ, she ingests light and spins it into darkness:

> In a ravine she lived, and took shape as a spider of monstrous form, weaving her black webs in a cleft of the mountains. There she sucked up all light that she could find, and spun it forth again in dark nets of strangling gloom, until no light more could come to her abode; and she was famished. (73)

In her attack, Ungoliant does not just feed off the light of the Trees; she injects them with venom, so they cannot feed others. This image of the life-sucking monster, motivated by malice as well as hunger, will be carried into *The Lord of the Rings* in the form of the Ring Wraiths—the Nazgûl—whose very presence sucks the spirit from those near them, and, of course, the great spider Shelob, Ungoliant's descendent. Ungoliant figures forth Melkor's appetite, being the extreme reverse of kenotic generosity, taking everything into herself and giving nothing out. Tolkien understood with Augustine that our hunger is for relationship with God; for Tolkien, the appropriate meal to satisfy that hunger was the Eucharist. But God has been utterly rejected by Melkor and Ungoliant, so nothing is left for them but ravenous, unending, insatiable feeding.[10]

As she devours the light of the trees, Ungoliant spins webs of darkness, "a Darkness that *seemed* not a lack but a thing with

---

10 This was a spiritual truth well understood by C.S. Lewis in *The Screwtape Letters,* whose fiends dine on human souls and then on each other.

being of its own . . . for it was indeed made by malice out of light, and it had power to pierce the eye, and to enter heart and mind, and strangle the very will" (76). The Catholic understanding of evil is that it is not a positive thing, but the subtraction of a God-given good. Evil in Tolkien is a spiritual hole, which makes what is left a negation of life—the "darkness visible" of Milton's *Paradise Lost*. Yet, the argument of *The Lord of the Rings* demonstrates the weakness of evil, which does not recognize its own deficits and so is blind to the strength of what it lacks: humility and the capacity for self-sacrificing love.

As Melkor is the first of the powers to fall, Fëanor is the first of the Elves, and both encounter their temptation within the process of sub-creation. But whereas Melkor's sin flows from jealousy of Ilúvatar's control of the Flame Imperishable and the limits on his own ability to sub-create, Fëanor's proceeds from an inappropriate, anti-kenotic love for the Silmarils. He wants to pull his creation back into himself and, in so doing, he brings curses on his house, on Elves and Men, from generation to generation.

When the Trees are destroyed, Fëanor is faced with a decisive choice, for Middle-earth as well as himself: whether to give the Silmarils to the Valar, allowing them to be opened and destroyed, so the remaining light can rekindle the trees of light and life; or to refuse and keep the Silmarils. It is a hard choice. Fëanor knows he will never be able to make the Silmarils again. Giving them up would be a great sacrifice, one which Fëanor, in many ways the greatest of the Elves, could make: "It may be that I can unlock my jewels, but never again shall I make their like; and if I must break them, I shall break my heart, and I shall be slain; first of all the Eldar in Aman" (78). So Fëanor refuses: "This thing I will not do of free will. But if the Valar will constrain me, then shall I know indeed that Melkor is their kindred" (79).

The Valar cannot constrain him, for the same reasons that no one can make Frodo take the Ring to Mt. Doom. In Tolkien's mythology, the ethical quality of a decision has its own objective reality and influences the world no less than an ax biting into a tree. Fëanor makes a great mistake. As Tolkien well understood, the Eucharistic reality of the world is that kenotic sacrifice is the ground from which light and life springs. The Eucharist may seem, superficially, like an act of appropriation, since the communicant takes Christ into himself, but it is the antidote to all appropriation, since it is the very act of self-sacrifice that is incorporated. Fëanor wants to take in light and life and hoard it; but *attempting* to hoard what can only survive by being shared leads to death and destruction. At the very moment Fëanor refuses to give up the Silmarils, Melkor and Ungoliant invade the home of Fëanor's family, kill his father, Finwë, and take the jewels. Though this may seem like coincidence, causality is operating in a moral dimension.

Fëanor renames Melkor, calling him Morgoth, "Black Foe of the World," and swears a terrible oath to get the Silarmils back. He is followed in this by the members of his family and many of the Noldor, including the fiery Galadriel. This leads first to the great sin of "The Kinslaying," when Fëanor's people attack other Elves to get ships to pursue Morgoth across the sea to Beleriand. It leads to a hopeless war, for Morgoth is too powerful for any army of Elves and Men to defeat. Centuries of war follow, in which Men also become embroiled. Two of the Silmarils are lost forever, and, finally, one is returned to the Valar by Eärendil, who is part Elf and part Man, on behalf of both races. The Silmaril and its "sacrifice" for the benefit of all finally leads to the defeat and exile of Morgoth, returning Middle-earth to a long period of peace and prosperity. The age of the Númenoreans follows, whose story is told in the Akallabêth near the end of *The Silmarillion*. This story is about the fall of Men, but it is not Man's initial fall.

Tolkien's myth about The Fall of Man is strongly consistent with the Bible. It is introduced in *The Silmarillion* and developed in a later dialogue, *Athrabeth Finrod ah Andreth*.[11] In *The Silmarillion*, one of the first men, Bëor, tells the Elves, as his tribe journeys west, "A darkness lies behind us and we have turned our backs upon it, and we do not desire to return thither even in thought. Westward our hearts have been turned, and we believe that there we shall find Light" (141). Tolkien echoes the words of 1 Peter 2:9,

11 J.R.R. Tolkien, "Athrabeth Finrod ah Andreth," in *Morgoth's Ring*, vol. 10 of *The History of Middle Earth*, ed. Christopher Tolkien (NY: Houghton Mifflin, 1993), 301–366.

"You are a chosen race . . . a holy nation, God's own people, that you may declare the wonderful deeds of him who *called you out of darkness into his marvelous light.*" Tolkien wants us to draw the conclusion that Bëor's tribe is running from The Fall and its consequences, however we imagine that aboriginal disaster, and toward the Light. Tolkien gives Bëor's people an understanding verging on the Christian, and his capitalization of "Light" brings us back to the Logos of John. Unlike the Elves, who first woke to see the stars, men woke to see the "Sun"—a slight allusion to the Son of God as the model of mankind, based on the medieval pun.

In 1959 or 1960, Tolkien was writing the *Athrabeth Finrod ah Andreth,* in which Galadriel's brother, Finrod, discusses the murky history of man's past with the wise woman, Andreth, and in it we hear rumors of the original Fall. At first, Andreth is too ashamed to tell Finrod the history, but, after much urging, she reveals one of the legends—that Men, who were meant to be immortal, were seduced by Morgoth into worshipping him as God and, as a result, they became subject to death. Andreth says that, as Men became aware, they heard the voice of their Creator within themselves:

> Some say the Disaster happened at the beginning of the history of our people, before any had yet died. The Voice had spoken to us, and we had listened. The Voice said, 'Ye are my children. I have sent you to dwell here. In time ye will inherit all this Earth, but first ye must be children and learn. Call on me and I shall hear; for I am watching over you.'
>
> We understood the Voice in our hearts, though we had no words yet. Then the desire for words awoke in us, and we began to make them. But we were few, and the world was wide and strange. Though we greatly desired to understand, learning was difficult, and the making of words was slow.
>
> In that time we called often and the Voice answered. But it seldom answered our questions, saying only: 'First seek to find the answer for yourselves. For ye will have joy in the finding, and so grow from childhood and become wise. Do not seek to leave childhood before your time.'[12]

12 *Morgoth's Ring*, 345–46.

But then, "one" who is visible and beautiful appears before Men, calling himself the Giver of Gifts, and offers them an accelerated path to knowledge and power, which they accept, and, eventually, they worship him, reject the Voice, and acknowledge the Giver as God. This is Morgoth. Men, in their desire for knowledge and power, worship the one who promises to give it the fastest. (Saruman, a Maia, or lower-order angel, will recapitulate just this fall in seeking the Ring. One of the "Wise," he fails in the most fundamental virtue, prudence.)[13] Then things get very bad, for the Giver gives power to the strongest and cruelest, and all kinds of atrocities follow. Tolkien gives us a version of Nimrod's world before the Flood. The Voice speaks only once more: "Ye have adjured Me, but ye remain Mine. I gave you life. Now it shall be shortened, and each of you in a little while shall come to Me, to learn who is your Lord: the one ye worship, or I who made him."[14]

Although Men fell, Andreth says, there is also a legend that the Voice made a promise: "They say that the One will himself enter into Arda, and heal Men and all the marring from beginning to end. This they say also, or they feign, is a rumor that has come down through years uncounted, even from the days of our undoing."[15] Andreth doubts the legend, because she finds it hard to conceive how the Author of creation can enter his own work: "This saying of hope passes my understanding. How could Eru enter into the thing that He had made, and than which He is beyond measure greater? Can the singer enter into his tale or the designer into his picture?" In response, Finrod recognizes both God's immanence in Creation and his transcendence of it: "He is already in it, as well as outside. . . . But indeed the 'in-dwelling' and the 'out-living' are not in the same mode."[16] Finrod's point is that Eru already does what Andreth thinks he cannot do. Andreth replies, "But they speak of Eru himself *entering into*

---

13 Prudence is the foundation of the others cardinal virtues, as it puts one in touch with reality, the first step toward moral behavior. See Joseph Pieper, *The Christian Idea of Man* (South Bend, IN: St. Augustine's Press, 2011), 13–17.

14 *Morgoth's Ring*, 347.

15 Ibid., 321.

16 Ibid., 322.

Arda . . . would it not shatter Arda?" In a sense, yes. With this pre-monition of the Incarnation, but bafflement with the mechanics, Tolkien joins his myth to the Christian true myth and completes his indebtedness to the prologue of John's gospel: "And the Word was made flesh, and dwelt among us (and we saw his glory, the glory as it were of the only begotten of the Father), full of grace and truth" (John 1:14).

Tolkien believed in one reality, and, in his mythology, he imag-ined how it might be perceived by Elves and Men in a world which precedes our recorded history. Here we see Tolkien, a few years after publication of *The Lord of the Rings*, trying to imagine a revelation preceding the Old Testament, but consistent with and pointing at Christianity. Andreth's lingering guilt on behalf of her race and her inability to take in how God could enter his own creation is perhaps not very different from our own, 2,000 years after the event.

✠

Once they find the Elves, the early Men learn much and reach their highest development in the civilization of Númenor. But, unlike the Elves, who are destined to live as long as the Earth,[17] Men die early, and their fate after death remains mysterious. That they will not accept this leads to their second fall in Tolkien's combination and revision of the biblical myths of the Flood and Babel and the classical myth of Atlantis. The end of Númenor involves, once again, humanity's tendency to take shortcuts. This time, Men try to appropriate the immortal life they have lost without having to go through the gate of death.

The Men of Númenor are stupider and more evil than Fëanor, who fails, because he cannot sacrifice something that he identi-fies as his very being. The Númenoreans try to crash a metaphys-ical barrier, erected by God, by sheer force: an amphibious landing and attack on Valinor, where they demand the secret of

17 Elves who die in battle or by accident are reincarnated in Valinor, from whence they may return to Middle-earth. The life-span of Elves is identical to that of Middle-earth, though Finrod, in his discussion with Andreth, specu-lates that Ilúvatar may finally extend eternal life to Elves as well as Men.

eternal life. Their attack is really directed against God—Eru Ilú-vatar—who has made the boundaries, and it is he who responds, curving the previously flat Earth into a sphere, so that the sea-lane to Valinor is cut off to Men forever, although the Elves are able to sail it, off the earth and into a different plane of reality.

The mistake of the Númenoreans is to see death as altogether evil rather than a gate—they forget they are destined to a higher level of existence beyond death, and they begin to fear death as darkness.[18] As Tolkien explains in his draft letter to Rhona Beare, they utterly misconstrue the remedy of Ilúvatar for a curse:

> A divine 'punishment' is also a divine 'gift', if accepted, since its object is ultimate blessing, and the supreme inventiveness of the Creator will make 'punishments' (that is changes of design) produce a good not otherwise to be attained: a 'mortal' Man has probably (an Elf would say) a higher if unrevealed destiny than a longeval one [such as the Elves]. To attempt by device or 'magic' to recover longevity is thus a supreme folly and wickedness of 'mortals'. Longevity . . . is the chief bait of Sauron.[19]

The Númenorean fear of death is fanned by Sauron, Morgoth's lieutenant, a lesser spirit, but a powerful one.[20] Though knowing Sauron's relation to Morgoth, the Númenoreans finally fall victim to him, making him their chief counselor, replicating the sin of their oldest ancestors, who were seduced by "The Giver of Gifts." Under Sauron's influence, they build tombs of Egyptian immensity to keep their ancestors "alive," and they offer human sacrifice, in the hope of appropriating their victims' life and adding it to their own. Like Ungoliant feeding on the light of the Trees, they attempt to feed off the spirit of others.

But death is the necessary human sacrifice that the mode of

18 Tolkien is perhaps influenced by the *ars moriendi* of medieval tradition. For an interesting critique of the *ars moriendi,* see Allen Verhey, *The Christian Art of Dying: Learning from Jesus* (Grand Rapids: Eerdmans, 2011).

19 *Letters,* 286.

20 Sauron is another fallen angel, a demon. Sauron, like Gandalf and Saruman, is one of the Maiar, lesser angelic beings sent into Middle-earth to help the Valar bring the world into being.

being human (at least a fallen human) calls for. It is what gives humans the potential to live more intensely and have a greater destiny even than the Elves, whose millennia of existence wearies them of the world. Time, for the Elves of Middle-earth, eventually becomes "a place" in which they have nowhere to go. They might well envy human beings Ilúvatar's gift of death. In grasping at life, the Númenoreans produce a culture of death. Tolkien takes us back to the paradox at the heart of creation: "Whosoever will save his life, shall lose it" (Luke 9:24).

In the curving of the earth, the Númenorean fleet and Númenor itself are destroyed in an immense tidal wave which crashes into the continents of Middle-earth, causing vast damage and geographical change. The earth is remade. Surviving Númenoreans who rejected the evil of their leaders found the new lands of Gondor and Arnor. Like their ancestors, they achieve a long period of peace and prosperity. They even help the Elves defeat the forces of Sauron, and this again results in a long peace.

At this point in Tolkien's mythology, the "One Ring" enters. In many ways, the desire for the Ring reenacts the desire for the Silmarils. An object that contains what human beings, Elves, and even fallen angels want becomes the object of an intense, competitive quest and the generator of great wars. The main difference is that, while the Silmarils are beautiful and not inherently evil, the Ring actually is evil, containing part of the demonic spirit of Sauron and always trying to get back to him. In the plots of *The Silmarillion* and *The Lord of the Rings*, these objects of desire perform the same function: they provide the nexus for characters to scramble around and die for. They are what Alfred Hitchcock called "the McGuffin"—whatever people in the story are trying to get, from secret weapon plans to those valuable "letters of transit" in *Casablanca*.

That the McGuffin shows up again and again in our stories says something about man's character. The "Music of the Ainur," like all great music, repeats themes in different ways, but what Melkor added was boring, disruptive, mindless repetition: an acid rock cacophony of drumming and screaming. McGuffin stories are representations of naked human desire and how it haunts us. The boring repetitiveness of evil is captured by Tolkien in his plot rep-

116

etitions: the endless pursuit of an object, the cycle of hunger, grasping, feeding that is Gollum's mental world; men taking Morgoth as counselor and god, and then taking his lieutenant Sauron as counselor and god. Tolkien's insight about sin, observed throughout history, is its insane repetitiveness. It is a profound reversal that, in Tolkien's greatest story, Frodo goes on a quest to get rid of something—in this sense he is a true pilgrim, for the first process of pilgrimage is simplification and emptying out.

Tolkien tells the initial story of the One Ring and the rings it controls in the last chapter of *The Silmarillion*, "Of the Rings of Power and the Third Age." When Morgoth is finally defeated, Sauron is given a chance to repent and receive judgment. But

> Sauron was ashamed, and he was unwilling to return in humiliation and to receive from the Valar a sentence, it might be, of long servitude in proof of his good faith; for under Morgoth his power had been great. Therefore . . . [he] departed and hid himself in Middle-earth; and he fell back into evil, for the bonds that Morgoth had laid upon him were very strong. (285)

After a long absence, Sauron returns and once again ingratiates himself with the Noldor, because he has technical skills to teach. "Therefore they hearkened to Sauron, and they learned of him many things, for his knowledge was great" (287). The One Ring is created during an era of ring-making. Sauron creates the One Ring to control all the others, causing Men and Dwarves to fall, but not the Elves, who finally realize what Sauron is doing.

⁜

There are many similarities between Tolkien's mythology and Milton's *Paradise Lost,* and, in both, demons are too proud, frightened, and attached to themselves to repent. In *The Lord of the Rings,* Saruman is the exemplar of this perpetual angelic fall. He replicates the most recent version of the Fall, that of modernity: the desire to create a Baconian world in which the secrets of nature are "tortured" out of her and employed for utilitarian purposes in a society of endless "progress" run by technocratic elites, like Saruman.

The fall of Saruman starts with the delusion that reality can be split into material and spiritual components.[21] This mistake cannot be separated from the motivation for power that precedes and feeds it. Saruman wants power he alone controls, and only by splitting the material from the spiritual can it be acquired.[22] (This dissociation of spirit and matter has its physical analog in Sauron's splitting of himself, when he puts part of his spirit into the Ring. Possibly he has made other such investments, for, when the Ring is destroyed, it is not just Sauron but the entire Sauronic realm that is annihilated.)[23] Instead of seeing the world as a sacramental marriage of spirit and matter, Saruman sees it as merely material, and that viewpoint serves his own ambition. As Treebeard says, "He is plotting to become a Power. He has a mind of metal and wheels; and he does not care for growing things, except as far as they serve him" (473).

Saruman falls to the danger inherent in tool-making. Rather than using tools within the constraints of a world ordered by love, the disordered tool-maker uses them to impose his own deficient sense of order. The difference can be seen in comparing Saruman as maker with Galadriel. Saruman proceeds with a hatred of nature, feeding Fangorn forest to the fires of his industrial complex. Fangorn irritates Saruman; it is messy, inefficient, non-utilitarian. Worse, it has a life of its own, apart from Saruman. Men are irritating for the same reasons, so Saruman crosses Orcs with Men to create Uruk-hai, which are usable. In contrast, Galadriel puts her love of the world into all that she makes.[24] The cloaks made of her cloth blend seamlessly into nature, for she

---

21 Charles Taylor in *A Secular Age* (Cambridge: Harvard University Press, 2007), 14, sees the "hiving off of an independent, free-standing level, that of 'nature', which may or may not be in interaction with something further or beyond" as a "crucial bit of modern theorizing." The hiving off of Nature from Super-nature is the first mistake, and the denial of Super-nature the second.

22 David L. Schindler, *Ordering Love: Liberal Societies and the Memory of God,* (Grand Rapids: Eerdmans, 2011), ix: "Modernity's technological logic, or ordering intelligence, can be said to consist in 'theoretical manipulability' (Hans Jonas)."

23 J.K. Rowling uses the same idea with Voldemort's horcruxes in the Harry Potter series.

24 *The Lord of the Rings*, 370.

loves the world; the wearers are lost to view in their surroundings, and it is Galadriel's love which does this. Saruman's creations, built out of the destruction of the country that surrounds Isengard, assert themselves in defiance of their surroundings.

Saruman dissociates the material from the spiritual, and then banishes the spiritual as if it never existed. This view, as C. S. Lewis notes, also abolishes the idea of Man, because it refuses to believe in spirit or mind. It looks to endless progress, but has no transcendent vision against which progress can be measured.[25] Thus "progress" becomes a concept with no content, subject to redefinition, impulse by technocratic impulse:

> There is something which unites magic and applied science while separating both from the 'wisdom' of earlier ages. For the wise men of old the cardinal problem had been how to conform the soul to reality, and the solution had been knowledge, self-discipline, and virtue. For magic and applied science alike the problem is now to subdue reality to the wishes of men: the solution is a technique; and both, in the practice of this technique, are ready to do things hitherto regarded as disgusting and impious. . . .[26]

In Gandalf, Tolkien gives us an example of the "wise man of old," and, in Saruman, the scientific magus of modernity. Saruman doesn't just lose the balance between matter and spirit; he materializes all of reality, which is an ironic fall, since he has been sent into Middle-earth from a more heavenly realm. He suffers a spiritual amnesia, induced by dreams of power, forgetting his origins. Saruman's fall corresponds almost exactly with Alexander Schmemann's understanding of original sin:

> The 'original' sin is not that man 'disobeyed' God; the sin is that he ceased to be hungry for Him and for Him alone, ceased to see his whole life as depending on the whole world as sacrament of communion with God. . . . The fall is not that he preferred the world to God, distorted the balance between spiritual and material, but that he made the world material,

25 See C. S. Lewis, *The Abolition of Man* (San Francisco: Harper Collins, 2001).

26 Ibid., 77.

whereas he was to have transformed it into 'life in God,' filled with meaning and spirit.[27]

Saruman's first impulse with regard to Gandalf is to convert him with the same dream of power and enlist him as a servant:

> 'And listen, Gandalf, my old friend and helper!' he said, coming near and speaking now in a softer voice. 'I said *we*, for *we* it may be, if you will join me. A new Power is rising. . . . We may join with that Power. It would be wise, Gandalf. There is hope that way. Its victory is at hand; and there will be rich reward for those that aided it. As the Power grows, its proved friends will also grow; and the Wise, such as you and I, may with patience come at last to direct its courses, to control it. We can bide our time, we can keep our thoughts in our hearts, deploring maybe evils done by the way, but approving the high and ultimate purpose: Knowledge, Rule, Order; all the things that we have so far striven in vain to accomplish. . . . There need not be, there would not be, any real change in our designs, *only in our means.*' (my emphasis; 259)

Saruman's convinces himself of two lies: that the end justifies the means[28] and that Sauron will share power. The last, as Gandalf tells him, is an astonishing self-deception and the first an abandonment of logic. Saruman would bring about order through destruction. *"On ne saurait faire une omelette sans casser des oeufs,"* said Robespierre before he began the Terror of the French Revolution: "You can't make an omelette without breaking eggs," the lie being that an omelette was sure to follow the breaking. But good does not come out of the indulgence of evil, because lesser realities cannot produce greater ones. This law cannot be broken, though Elves and Men try, again and again, throughout the history of Middle-earth.

Saruman is enticed to evil through his study of Sauron, which

---

27 Schmemann, 18.

28 For an analysis of why justification of ends by means is a moral error, see Robert Spitzer, *Ten Universal Principles: A Brief Philosophy of Life Issues* (San Francisco: Ignatius Press, 2009), 40–4. Summarizing Aquinas, Spitzer writes: "One cannot use an evil means to achieve a good end; the evil of the means will undermine the goodness of the end."

he originally undertakes to combat him. Gandalf goes to Saruman with hope, because, if anyone knows enough to defeat Sauron, it is he. Gandalf tells the Council of Elrond:

> 'Saruman has long studied the arts of the Enemy himself, and thus we have often been able to forestall him. It was by the devices of Saruman that we drove him from Dol Guldur. It might be that he had found some weapons that would drive back the Nine.' (257)

Elrond's terse response is: "It is perilous to study too deeply the ways of the Enemy, for good or for ill" (265). Studying the enemy is dangerous, because one becomes attracted to what the Enemy wants—to assert oneself as a god, but not a god who allows his subjects free will. Like Faustus, he begins to believe that he has found ways, through magic or science, to wield god-like powers, to be the sole creator of himself, his reality, and, finally, everyone else's.

In *The Lord of the Rings,* all sins begin and end with this same idolatry of the self and the next step of imposing one's vision on others. Tolkien explains,

> In my story Sauron represents as near an approach to the wholly evil will as is possible. He had gone the way of all tyrants: beginning well, at least on the level that while desiring to order all things according to his own wisdom he still at first considered the (economic) well-being of other inhabitants of the Earth. But he went further than human tyrants in pride and lust for domination, being in origin an immortal (angelic) spirit. In *The Lord of the Rings* the conflict is not basically about 'freedom', though that is naturally involved. It is about God, and His sole right to divine honour. . . . Sauron desired to be a God-King, and was held to be this by his servants; if he had been victorious he would have demanded divine honour from all rational creatures and absolute temporal power over the whole world.[29]

Tolkien's understanding of how people fall into evil is thoroughly biblical and Catholic, but he adds a piece of theology

29 *Letters,* 243–4.

121

which, I believe, he can claim as his own: the Fall is not just a possible outcome of free will, but one of sub-creative free will. The best gifts are subject to the worst corruptions. The essence of God in Genesis is that he creates. Created in God's image, Adam and Eve will want to create too. But Adam and Eve do not want just to sub-create, i.e., to "garden," within the bounds of Creation. They want to *redraw* the boundaries, "to be as gods." As an artist, this gave Tolkien pause, and he worked out his doubts about sub-creation in "Leaf by Niggle," where gardening and art come together. Sub-creation can only be good, if it is worked out in subordination to the pattern of God's creation, ordered by the Logos of love. Sub-creation itself must be sacramental, a way of participating in grace, or it goes wrong.

5

FRODO'S
BAPTISMAL CAREER

"Amen, amen I say to thee, unless a man be born again of water and the Holy Ghost he cannot enter into the kingdom of God. That which is born of the flesh, is flesh; and that which is born of the Spirit, is spirit." JOHN 3:5–6

"The glory of God is a human being fully alive." ST. IRENEAUS

SACRAMENTS ALWAYS POINT in two directions: to Creation, of which they are an extension, and to God, who gives them their more than natural power. In the sacraments, the border between natural and supernatural is at its most tenuous. The Roman Catholic Church does not believe there is a bold, broad borderline between the natural and supernatural. Bread and wine become indistinguishable from Christ's body and blood; water dissolves not only dirt, but sin; oil becomes the seal of a new life. And this progression is easy, for it is the property of wine to raise the spirit, bread to nourish, water to cleanse, and oil to leave a mark that persists. The sacraments represent not so much a supernatural element joined to a natural one as nature made whole, doing what it was meant to do. (The same can be said for Jesus's healing miracles.) A sacramental vision of the world regards nature as it was meant to be, communicating God's glory and power. Tolkien's characters, even his down-to-earth Hobbits, are closer to this sacramental vision than we are; his Elves are the closest. (Part of what it means to be an Elf is to live within this sacramental vision most, if not all, of the time. An "Elf-friend" is a

Human, Hobbit, or Dwarf who shares this Elvish capacity to an unusual degree and is thus capable of friendship with Elves.)

J. Robert Barth, S. J., in his study of Coleridge's idea of the symbol, offers a definition of "sacrament" that illuminates Tolkien's understanding of the world as sacrament writ large, a representation and participation in the Logos as a whole. For Coleridge, a sacrament was a kind of symbol which both represents and participates in the reality that it represents. This sacramental and symbolic order is present throughout *The Lord of the Rings* as a feature of reality—as its essence, really. When the hobbits cross the river, Nimrodel, after their escape from Moria, and sense its healing power and hear its music, they are experiencing not just cold water but a spiritual event that unifies them with a harmonious cosmos. The mushrooms of Farmer Maggott figure forth human kindness, joy, and solidarity, which in turn connects the Hobbits to those qualities in the divine reality. When Sam sees one star, twinkling over Mordor, it is enough to represent and communicate the higher, transcendental goodness of God. Barth defines this broad sense of sacrament in light of its unifying power as symbol:

> A sacrament is a sensible sign—a spoken word of forgiveness, a ritual gesture, a material object (a piece of bread, a cup of wine)—pointing to something beyond itself. . . . A sacrament is an efficacious sign; it actually makes present what it represents—the grace of God, which is a share in the life of God. [Quoting Coleridge:] It "partakes of the Reality which it renders intelligible" . . . A sacrament—Baptism, Confirmation, Marriage, the Eucharist—involves the union of a subject and an object, the faithful recipient and the material sign in which the grace of God is mediated to the Christian. . . . [Quoting Edouard Schillebeeckx:] Sacraments are ultimately "the properly human mode of encounter with God" . . . an encounter through sensible reality with God.[1]

The battle for Middle-earth is ultimately the battle for a sacramental universe, one in which the physical world is preserved in such a state that it can function as a sacrament, a natural symbol

---

1 J. Robert Barth, *The Symbolic Imagination: Coleridge & the Romantic Tradition*, 2nd ed. (NY: Fordham University Press, 2001), 39–40.

that unifies man with God. Mordor is the attempt to obliterate that possibility.

For Tolkien, the sacraments of the Church were the narrative tropes by which life was structured, and they provided building blocks of *The Lord of the Rings*. Washing has baptismal significance, and eating Eucharistic. There is a range in the sacramental order. At one end is the sacramentality of daily life within a created order; at the other end are the sacraments proper, administered by the Church, which provide a medium for God's grace to flow in unusually powerful ways. In *The Lord of the Rings*, this full range of sacramentality is represented, from bath and supper songs, which are the Hobbits' favorites, to near drownings, entombments, and Frodo and Sam's Eucharistic journey up Mount Doom. Various sacramental motifs occur and recur as continuing features of narrative reality. The journey of Frodo is built on a sacramental arc, an arc which is part of the music of the Ainur, figuring forth the Logos-centric nature of the world. This arc starts in baptism, proceeds through confirmation and confession, and ends in Eucharistic sacrifice. It is the typical arc by which a Christian matures and an analog of the way in which callow youths mature into heroes in the heroic quest genre.

My aim in this chapter is to examine the baptismal narratives that do so much to organize *The Fellowship of the Ring*, the first book of *The Lord of the Rings*. There are three of them: 1) the Hobbits' encounter with Old Man Willow, who tries to both bury and drown them, and their rescue by Tom Bombadil; 2) the entombment of the Hobbits by the Barrow-wight and their rescue, once again, by Tom Bombadil; and 3) Frodo's near destruction from being wounded by a Nazgûl blade and his rescue by the flame-tipped waters of the Bruinen. Even from this brief list, one of the most important elements of baptism becomes clear, that it is a rescue, achieved not by our own efforts, but when, like infants, we are at our weakest and most vulnerable.

⊹

Baptism is a spiritual death and resurrection into life with Christ, dramatically accomplished through symbolic drowning by total immersion in water. During the early years of the church, people were sometimes baptized in tubs containing extremely cold water, so they would experience a physical shock to mark the spiritual transition. Taken naked from the water, they were anointed with oil, wrapped in white cloth, given a candle lit from the paschal candle (most baptisms taking place during Easter vigil), and presented to the congregation as new human beings. They were like babes coming out of the amniotic fluid of Mother Church.

The primary sacrament of initiation into the Church, Baptism is a spiritual workhorse, accomplishing many things at once. It is not only a spiritual death and resurrection, but a cleansing. Baptism washes away the stain of original sin—our human proclivity to keep doing the wrong things—and all sins incurred up to that point. It includes an exorcism, in which the devil and his ways are renounced. It incorporates the person baptized into the body of Christ and infuses him or her with the Holy Spirit. The candles held by the baptized are symbols of the light of Christ that now fills them, and they have Pentecostal significance as well, since to be part of the Church is to be incorporated in the mission of the church, which is to spread the gospel and to baptize. The oil, used to cover the entire body of those baptized in the early church, but now applied with the sign of the cross to the forehead "seals the Christian with the indelible spiritual mark (*character*) of his belonging to Christ. No sin can erase this mark, even if sin prevents Baptism from bearing the fruits of salvation."[2] All of these elements, except the application of oil, are included in one or more of three baptismal episodes in the first book of *The Lord of the Rings*.

The clearest and fullest statement about baptism in the New Testament occurs in Romans 6:3–11:

> You have been taught that when we were baptized in Christ Jesus we were baptized in his death; in other words, when we were baptized we were sent into the tomb with him and joined him in death, so that as Christ was raised from the dead by the Father's glory, we too might live a new life.

2 *Catechism of the Catholic Church*, 2nd ed. (Washington, DC: United States Catholic Conference, 1994), no. 1272, 324, original emphasis.

> If in union with Christ we have imitated his death, we shall also imitate him in his resurrection. We must realize that our former selves have been crucified with him to destroy this sinful body and to free us from the slavery of sin. When a man dies, of course, he has finished with sin.
>
> But we believe that having died with Christ we shall return to life with him: Christ as we know, having been raised from the dead will never die again. Death has no power over him any more. When he died, he died, once for all, to sin, so his life now is life with God; and in that way, you too must consider yourselves to be dead to sin but alive for God in Christ Jesus.

The "death" of baptism is being sent into the tomb and resurrected into a new, stronger life. This happens in all three baptismal episodes for the Hobbits, and, in the pursuance of their quest, each develops greater fortitude, confidence, and maturity.[3] For Tolkien's baptismal scenes, the pervasive New Testament imagery linking baptism to death, rebirth, washing, and the infusion of spiritual light is very important, and he relies on this imagery throughout.

The Hobbits and Old Man Willow

Baptism seals those baptized into Christ once and for all and cannot be performed twice. But, like every other Catholic, each time Tolkien entered the church and left it, except during Lent, he would have dipped his fingers in holy water and crossed himself in remembrance of his baptismal vows. At every baptism, the congregation renews its baptismal vows, so baptism remains a fresh reality. Frodo goes through three "baptismal adventures" in the first book of *The Lord of the Rings*, but I am not arguing that he has been baptized three times or that he is being baptized at all. Tolkien uses "baptismal episodes," because baptism is the Catholic archetypal instance of transition from immaturity to maturity,

---

3 In John, the locus classicus for the necessity of baptism occurs in the context of Jesus's dialogue with Nicodemus (John 3:5): "I tell you most solemnly, unless a man is born through water and the Spirit, he cannot enter the kingdom of God."

from individuality to incorporation into a close knit group, from old life to new, which we work on for our entire lives. In the broad sense, baptism is something Catholics relive, and Tolkien uses the baptismal sequence of Frodo to show his deepening initiation and maturation.

Tolkien sets up his baptismal sequence by plunking his Hobbits "safely" in the Shire with his parodic Encyclopedia Britannica-style prologue, "Concerning Hobbits." The Hobbits, built low to the ground, are a humble "unobtrusive" people, who "love peace and quiet and good tilled earth," who had come to "think that peace and plenty were the rule in Middle-earth and the right of all sensible folk." If baptism for the Christian is rebirth into new life with Christ, for the four questing Hobbits, who enjoy six meals a day, if they can get them, pipe weed, good beer, and a comfortable bed, it is death to self-satisfaction and smug security and rebirth into a vast, seemingly chaotic world of danger, self-sacrifice, and almost certain failure.

Baptism is like crossing a border through the medium of water, and rivers in *The Lord of the Rings* are one of the most significant markers of geographical and spiritual transition.[4] Successive river crossings put the Hobbits farther from their old life and into the new one. The first is the crossing of the Brandywine River to Buckland; Tolkien emphasizes the baptismal significance for Sam Gamgee:

> Sam was the only member of the party who had not been over the river before. He had a strange feeling as the slow gurgling stream slipped by: his old life lay behind in the mists, dark adventure lay in front. He scratched his head, and for a moment had a passing wish that Mr. Frodo could have gone on living quietly at Bag End. (99)

The Hobbits are pursued by the demonic Ring Wraiths, the nine Black Riders. On the ferry in the dark, the Hobbits barely make out one Black Rider, sniffing along the shore they have just left.

---

4 The crossing of rivers and bridges are significant transitional points in Celtic and Norse myth as well. See Marjorie Burns, "Bridges, Gates, and Doors," in *Perilous Realms*, 44–74.

Sam is blocked from his old life, once he crosses the river to where a new begins, whether he will or no.

The next day, the Hobbits continue toward Rivendell, into the Old Forest. In Middle-earth, the older forests, like Fangorn, have stored centuries of grudges, and the forest the Hobbits enter to evade the Ringwraiths is under the vengeful control of Old Man Willow. The forest determines the path of the Hobbits, blocking off openings in one direction and allowing passage in another, steering the Hobbits in the direction it wants them to go, preventing back-tracking, giving them only one way, deeper inward, like an enormous Venus fly-trap. They emerge in the "queerest" part of the Old Forest, the Withywindle River valley, at the center of evil influence: the ancient, malevolent willow.

Here, all four become unaccountably drowsy, as they walk along the river: "Sleepiness seemed to be creeping out of the ground and up their legs, and falling softly out of the air upon their heads and eyes" (116). Merry and Pippin are overcome first and rest against the willow; Frodo tries to get them up, but soon he too finds the torpor overwhelming and falls asleep with his feet in the river. Sam is the only one to remain conscious. When he sees Frodo being held under water by a tree root, Sam pulls him, coughing and sputtering, from the river, and they find Merry and Pippin have been enveloped—buried alive—in the trunk of the tree, which has opened and closed. Pippin is gone, and Merry's legs stick outside.

After trying to free Merry and Pippin by threatening the tree with fire—which nearly gets the two trapped Hobbits crushed— "Frodo, without any clear idea of why he did so, or what he hoped for, ran along the path crying *help! help! help!*" (original emphasis, 118). The elements of baptism up to this point are clear. The Hobbits, except for Sam Gamgee, are put to sleep by a spell, an evil spell, easy to associate with sin, arising from Old Man Willow's hatred of creatures who can move freely. Tolkien says of the Hobbits, excepting Sam, that "They *gave themselves up* to the spell" (my emphasis; 116). Their wills and resistance to evil are weak at the beginning of the journey, and they must be strengthened for what is to come. Frodo is immersed in the Withywindle and almost undergoes death by drowning. The only thing Frodo can do is cry for help, and it is important to see that he has no "clear idea" why he is doing it. He just does it. Something very similar will happen to Frodo in his next two baptismal adventures, as if his own asking for help is itself brought about by grace, which, in the Catholic understanding, it is. Frodo's cry is a spontaneous prayer. Baptism is a rescue operation, but the rescue begins even before baptism, in the grace-induced desiring of it.

The next important moment follows immediately in the arrival of the rescuer, Tom Bombadil, who is singing "nonsense" carelessly and happily. Tom, along with Treebeard, is one of the strangest of Tolkien's creations. Starting his career independently of *The Lord of the Rings*, as a character singing nonsense rhymes and having adventures that Tolkien wrote for his children, Tom is enigmatically incorporated into *The Lord of the Rings* as its major outlier, immune to the powers of the Ring, not especially concerned with the problems of Middle-earth, someone whose function is to save the day and chuckle good-naturedly. Three Hobbits undergo near death and a symbolic resurrection, as they are saved—Frodo from the river by Sam, and Merry and Pippin from entombment in the tree by Tom.

Tom has a blue coat, a long brown beard, is about halfway between Hobbit and human in height, and wears great yellow boots; "his eyes were blue and bright, and his face was red as a ripe apple, creased into a hundred wrinkles of laughter." He comes singing a song of praise and thanksgiving whose main subjects are his wife, Goldberry, and nature. In his hands he bears a gift for her, a large leaf on which are piled white water-lilies.

As Goldberry will say, Tom is Master, because Tom has never been "caught"; within his limited realm, he has the musical antidote to Melkor's dissonance. Tom is so fully tuned to the music of Ilúvatar, it would seem, that he doesn't worry about outcomes. He is sure that goodness will triumph, and evil has no purchase in him. In Tom, Tolkien has imagined an unfallen being. This makes him the ideal first rescuer of the Hobbits, since the Catholic belief is that baptism erases all traces of original sin,[5]

---

5 *Catechism of the Catholic Church*, no. 1263: "By Baptism *all sins* are forgiven, original sin and all personal sins, as well as all punishment for sin. In those who

and who better to do that or illustrate what that ultimately might mean than one who is free from it? Tom becomes a priest, completing the sacrament.

Song turns out to be one of Tom's habitual modes of speech, the best way to communicate joy and praise, which Tom does without ceasing. Tom himself is like an unblemished refrain in the Music of the Ainur, part of the choral Word, and his singing a joining in that heavenly choir that harmonizes the world. The power of the Logos is strong in Tom, as he uses language to manage nature. He rescues Merry and Pippin with one song and puts Old Man Willow to sleep with another.

The element of water is present in many ways throughout this baptismal episode. Not only is Frodo nearly drowned, but it rains hard for most of the time the Hobbits are with Tom, and they wake up to hear Goldberry singing a "rain song." Goldberry, their hostess, is the daughter of the River, and we first see her "enthroned" by the water lilies that Tom has brought to her. It is Goldberry's "washing day," her time to do the autumnal laundry. This extends the baptismal significance of the episode with Old Man Willow to the Hobbits' entire stay with Tom and Goldberry: their visit with Tom is a step toward sanctification.

fRodo's dReams

In the Hobbits' visit with Tom, Tolkien provides a theological frame for what will happen to Frodo as the book proceeds; he

have been reborn nothing remains that would impede their entry into the Kingdom of God, neither Adam's sin, nor personal sin, nor the consequences of sin, the gravest of which is separation from God," 322; no. 405: "Although it is proper to each individual, original sin does not have the character of a personal fault in any of Adam's descendants. It is a deprivation of original holiness and justice, but human nature has not been totally corrupted; it is wounded in the natural powers proper to it; subject to ignorance, suffering, and the dominion of death; and inclined to sin—an inclination to evil that is called 'concupiscence.' Baptism, by imparting the life of Christ's grace, erases original sin and turns a man back toward God, but the consequences for nature, weakened and inclined to evil, persist in man and summon him to spiritual battle," 201.

inducts Frodo into a prophetic experience just beyond the reach of Frodo's comprehension. First, the Hobbits are introduced to a deep domestic bliss, not unlike their life in the Shire, but more profound. As baptism brings the baptized into a new, grace-filled life with Christ, Frodo and his companions taste a heavenly bliss with Tom and Goldberry. At the sight of Goldberry, Frodo feels his heart moved "with a joy that he did not understand." The delight he feels in her presence is "less keen and lofty" than he feels in the presence of Elves, yet "deeper and nearer to mortal heart; marvelous and yet not strange." In this description, there is much of the Virgin Mary, and, for Hobbits, whose nature is to love hearth and home, a deep and comfortable love is the best. "Fear nothing," she says, and although the phrase "fear not" is biblically familiar, what resonates with her use is Luke 2:10, where the angels address the shepherds: "Fear not: for, behold, I bring you good tidings of great joy." The Hobbits wash for dinner, and, as they are eating and conversing, become suddenly aware that they are "singing, merrily, as if it was easier and more natural than talking" (125). They have entered a grace-filled realm, where song is the natural language. They are in measure with the Music of the Ainur.

The Hobbits spend two nights in Tom Bombadil's house, and on each Frodo has a prophetic dream. But, before these, Frodo has had another, in his house in Crickhollow, the night before entering the Old Forrest. These three dreams at the beginning of Frodo's journey make a set, situating Frodo within prophetic time. The first dream possibly looks to the far past, the second to the near past, and the third to the future.

At the beginning of Frodo's first dream, the Black Riders are crawling and snuffling after him. This memory of the preceding days' trauma gives way to a more profound vision:

> Then he heard a noise in the distance. At first he thought it was a great wind coming over the leaves of the forest. Then he knew that it was not leaves, but the sound of the Sea far-off; a sound he had never heard in waking life, though it had often troubled his dreams. Suddenly he was out in the open. There were no trees after all. He was on a dark heath, and there was a strange salt smell in the air. Looking up he saw before him a

tall white tower, standing alone on a high ridge. A great desire
came over him to climb the tower and see the Sea. He started
to struggle up the ridge towards the tower: but suddenly a
light came in the sky, and there was a noise of thunder. (108)

Frodo has entered a numinous realm where the psychological is
penetrated by a higher reality. In this dream of great foreboding,
what Frodo may sense, amid the thunder and light, is the inun-
dating wave that destroyed Númenor. Tolkien had a repeating
dream of a great wave,[6] as did his son Michael, and he may have
considered it to be a "memory" of an actual event; it was the
inspiration for his Atlantis story about Númenor. Faramir relates
the same recurring dream to Éowyn, as they wait for word of
Aragorn.

Frodo's great desire to climb the tower and see the Sea is full of
hope and longing, but an unknown threat replaces these emotions with rising fear. Frodo has not gotten the full dream—it is
cut off in the thunder—and, like Frodo, the reader is left wondering. We have not seen the tidal wave, but the "strange salt smell
in the air," the great far off noise, and the frightening weather are
suggestive. Without *The Silmarillion*, published nearly twenty
years after *The Fellowship of the Ring*, and Tolkien's letters, the
idea of the tidal wave would be out of reach, and perhaps this is
just an anxiety dream about gathering trouble.[7] But the tidal
wave dream would make sense here, since Sauron laid the foundation for the destruction of Númenor. It would also suggest the
fuller context of Frodo's quest. He understands at least that a
horrendous force is growing in the darkness, and that is enough.

The second dream takes place on September 26, the first night
with Tom and Goldberry, and is a straightforward vision of Gandalf's plight on September 18 at Orthanc, where Gandalf is
trapped on the Tower and rescued by the mighty eagle, Gwaihir.
More like a news bulletin than a nightmare, this dream tells us

6 For Tolkien's writing about his "Atlantis" dream, see *Letters*, numbers 163,
180, 257, and 276.

7 Tolkien's earlier drafts continued the nightmare with the arrival of the
Black Riders, but Tolkien's decision to cut that part is a deliberate move
toward ambiguity, which emphasizes the uncertainty of Frodo's quest.

something about both Frodo and the house of Bombadil, which is a place where people dream dreams and have visions, for the other Hobbits are having dreams as well. In Tom's house, the mind works differently—distances of time and space become less real, and the Logos more available. Frodo, the Elf-friend, has a mind more open to these dimensions of reality than most Hobbits. His capacity for vision is magnified. The threatening tower of the first dream resolves into the tower that Gandalf escapes from, as if by divine grace: "But they that hope in the Lord shall renew their strength, they shall take wings as eagles" (Isaiah 40:31).

Just before he rises to leave Bombadil's house after his second night there, Frodo has his third dream:

> [E]ither in dreams or out of them, he could not tell which, Frodo heard a sweet singing running in his mind: a song that seemed to come like a pale light behind a grey rain-curtain, and growing stronger to turn the veil all to glass and silver, until at last it was rolled back, and a far green country opened before him under a swift sunrise. (135)

This dream completes the first, as the hidden foreboding gives way to joy, the giant wave (perhaps) to a gentle curtain of rain. The anxiety dream of thunder, lightning, and a thwarted quest to see the Sea opens to a vision of heaven, or one of the stops on the way—in Tolkien's mythology, the Undying Lands, where Frodo will finally go with Gandalf, Bilbo, and Galadriel, when this vision will become reality. Tolkien may have 2 Corinthians 5:17 in mind, as Frodo sees this new, unstained world: "Therefore if anyone is in Christ, he is a new creation: old things have passed away; behold, all things have become new."

Frodo has been given a big hunk of the larger tale he is in, and it is a great gift, because, even though he doesn't understand it, that he has been shown his own story is a eucatastrophe. There is hope. Verlyn Flieger argues persuasively that these dreams are a kind of time travel.[8] Although Flieger does not mention Catholic

---

8 Verlyn Flieger, *A Question of Time* (Kent, OH; Kent State University Press, 1997), especially chapters 3 and 8. Flieger finds convincing literary and parapsychological sources for Tolkien's ideas of time and time travel in contemporary

sources for the idea, they would have been readily available to Tolkien. Orthodox Catholic theology holds that God is outside of time, meaning all time is present to Him at once. Tolkien is speculating that sometimes people are granted access to this eternal perspective, as are Frodo and Faramir, another prolific dreamer. Frodo's dreams hint that he is within a providential narrative that ends in joy.

Bombadil and The Ring

Before we leave the house of Tom Bombadil, two more baptismal aspects of the Hobbits' stay have to be considered. The first is Tom's complete immunity to the Ring—extending to his inability even to take it seriously. The later would be a mistake for anyone else in Middle-earth; even Gandalf, a lower-order angel, cannot afford to touch it for fear of its seductive power. For Bombadil, however, laughing at the Ring is based on a deeper understanding of reality. With no anxiety, Bombadil just asks Frodo for the Ring: "'Show me the precious Ring!' he said suddenly in the midst of the story: and Frodo, to his own astonishment, drew out the chain from his pocket, and unfastening the ring handed it at once to Tom" (132).

No one can part with the Ring without difficulty, but Tom's immunity to the Ring temporarily extends to Frodo, who astonishes himself by easily giving it up. (In the terminology of Charles Taylor, Frodo's self is *porous* to Tom, open to his influence.[9]) There must be something in a person—the proclivity toward sin—to which the Ring, like a magnet, attaches itself. Tom doesn't have this tendency, and, when Frodo is with Tom, this resistance becomes available to Frodo, as if he has been baptismally washed clean of any attraction to sin. Sin has no foothold in Tom; he is a

writing; obvious and relevant biblical and theological sources go unmentioned. One cannot avoid the impression that Flieger has a secular academic filter in place.

9 Charles Taylor, *A Secular Age*, especially Chapter 1, "The Bulwarks of Belief." Taylor's distinction between the modern "buffered" self and the medieval "porous" self is implicit in *The Lord of the Rings*, in which Frodo's porous self is susceptible to invasion by both good and evil "spirits."

communicator of grace to all the Hobbits. Sin goes deeper into even the best Hobbits than they can consciously understand; it is part of the condition of living in a fallen world, apart from any particular act that is wrong. To be in the realm of Bombadil is to be partly taken out of that condition:

> It [the Ring] seemed to grow larger as it lay for a moment on his big brown-skinned hand. Then suddenly he put it to his eye and laughed. For a second the Hobbits had a vision, both comical and alarming, of his bright blue eye gleaming through a circle of gold. Then Tom put the Ring round the end of his little finger and held is up to the candlelight. For a moment the Hobbits noticed nothing strange about this. Then they gasped. There was no sign of Tom disappearing! Tom laughed again, and then he spun the Ring in the air—and it vanished with a flash. Frodo gave a cry—and Tom leaned forward and handed it back to him with a smile. (132–33)

Not only does the Ring not affect Tom, he controls it. He can make it larger; he can make it disappear rather than submitting to it and disappearing himself. The piece of black technology that has put the survival of Middle-earth at risk is for him a bauble. But Tom's most telling action is one that Frodo cannot yet appreciate: when Tom's "bright blue eye" gleams through the Ring, he is burlesquing the "Eye of Sauron," the fiery eye in which Sauron has embodied himself and which is searching for the Ring. Frodo hasn't seen the Eye yet, but he will on Amon Hen at the end of the second book, and it will nearly take possession of him. Yet, for Tom, that Eye is the object of a joke.

Blue is the color of heaven and the sea, the color of the tassels on Hebrew prayer shawls, which has great relevance to Tom's joke. "When you use these tassels, the sight of the cord will remind you of all the commandments of the Lord and you will do them, *without prostituting yourself going after the desire of your hearts and your eyes*" (Numbers 15:39). The point of the Ring is to make the wearer do exactly the opposite—to go after the desire of his heart and eyes, prostituting himself to Sauron, ultimately becoming a wraith. In making his own eye a laughing parody of Sauron's, Tom acknowledges that the Logos is ultimately in control and, knowing this, he is freed to be a cheerful warrior.

Tom's most notable trait, with his perpetual song, is laughter. My speculation is that Tolkien meant Tom to be an incarnation of the Divine Joy in the creation of a particular geographical area of Middle-earth: the Withywindle River Valley. Tolkien has, perhaps, imagined God's joy in the creation of just the English Midlands and made it Bombadil. As the incarnate Joy of this small part of creation, Tom seems to have come into being with it. Elrond says that the earliest Elves knew him as Iarwain Ben-adar, "oldest and fatherless" (265). He is "eldest," older even than the Elves. Now, as Gandalf says, Bombadil has withdrawn into a little land, within bounds that he has set, though no one else can see them. As Divine Joy, even circumscribed in a small geographical area, there is no place for evil to enter Tom. He is a creature of constant laughter and merriment. Since the Ring is parasitic on desire, it has no place to grab onto Tom, no ground on which he can be "caught." Tom is all gratitude.

Laughter can express sheer joy and exuberance, exhilaration, and gratitude at our participation in the order of the Logos. A closely related laughter arises when we are released from a perception that is incongruous with reality. Evil wants itself to be taken very, very seriously, and The Ring wants to be taken seriously as a dangerous instrument of power, but the idea of putting the world within the confines of a ring and thereby controlling it is just ridiculous to Tom, who sees it against the vast backdrop of joyful Creation and finds its pretensions ridiculous. Laughter works in a similar way, when Gandalf dissolves in mirth, as Saruman, stranded in Orthanc by the Ents, tries to bluff his way out by selling himself as wise:

> Then Gandalf laughed. The fantasy vanished like a puff of smoke.
>
> 'Saruman, Saruman!' said Gandalf still laughing. 'Saruman . . . you should have been the king's jester and earned your bread, and stripes too, by mimicking his counselors. Ah me!' he paused, getting the better of his mirth 'Understand one another? I fear I am beyond your comprehension. But you, Saruman, I understand now too well.' (582)

Saruman's understanding of the world is so tightly wound about his own ego, he has lost the capacity to see the world, to be one of the Wise. When the paltry, having given itself cosmic pretensions, is suddenly seen for what it is, cleansing laughter often comes to those who have been taken in. But Saruman is curved in on himself, and his reaction is a sneer. On the stairs of Cirith Ungol, Frodo and Sam are able to step outside themselves, to see themselves as part of a bigger story, in which they might even look just a little ridiculous, and it makes Frodo laugh: "a long clear laugh from his heart. Such a sound had not been heard in those places since Sauron came to Middle-earth" (712). Weapon and armor both, laughter defies evil, transcends it, shrinks it to its gargoyle proportions. Joy in creation, when it produces silent wonder, can do the same, as it does for Sam when he sees a star in the sky from the midst of Mordor:

> Peeping among the cloud-wrack above a dark tor high up in the mountains, Sam saw a white star twinkle for a while. The beauty of it smote his heart. . . . For like a shaft, clear and cold, the thought pierced him that in the end the Shadow was only a small and passing thing: there was light and high beauty forever beyond its reach. . . . Now, for a moment, his own fate, and even his master's, ceased to trouble him. (922)

If Tom is Divine Creative Joy, even in only a very small part of the universe, then it is significant that Tom withdraws into one of its most damaged portions, the Old Forest, which needs healing as much as any land we encounter outside Mordor. Tom's presence is a token of God's faithfulness to fallen creation, to even the tragically ruined portions of the world.

Frodo is rather irked that Tom takes the Ring so lightly. He puts it on his finger, ostensibly to find out whether the Ring is still the one he gave Tom, but, really, because possessiveness has gotten into him. Frodo disappears, confirming the Ring hasn't been switched, but he doesn't disappear to Tom, who tells him to stop playing games and sit down. In response to Tom's demonstration of goodness, Frodo has actually sinned: "Frodo was delighted (in a way): it was his own Ring all right." Delighted "in a way"—part of Frodo wants the ring back and the power that goes with it. "It was *his own* Ring all right." It is already digging into him. "[T]he grace of Baptism delivers no one from all the weakness of nature. On the contrary, we must still combat the movements of concupiscence that never cease leading us into evil."[10]

Frodo is engaged in "spiritual warfare" throughout the book, a struggle that he fights mainly within himself against the power of the Ring. He cannot escape the fight, but has to encounter it. The Catholic baptismal rite includes exorcism as part of the preparation of the baptized for spiritual warfare,[11] and this is proclaimed in the gospels of Matthew, Mark, and Luke, where, immediately after his baptism by John, Jesus goes into the wilderness to encounter Satan and his temptations. Frodo's baptismal sequence is his preparation for entry into the wilderness of Mordor and facing his own temptations.

In the Tomb of the Barrow-wight

The first baptismal episode ends, and the second begins, as the Hobbits leave Tom Bombadil and Frodo realizes they haven't said good-bye to Goldberry, which causes him great distress. From the bottom of a green hollow he turns around to see her: "There on the hill-brow she stood beckoning to them: her hair was flying loose, and as it caught the sun it shone and shimmered. A light like the glint of water on dewy grass flashed from under her feet as she danced" (135). The Hobbits hasten up the hill to speak with her, and she gestures with a wave of her arm to look around. They survey all directions of the compass, and they are filled with hope and energy. Then she sends them out:

> Goldberry spoke to them and recalled their eyes and thoughts. "Speed now, fair guests!" she said. "And hold to your purpose! North with the wind in the left eye and a blessing on your footsteps! Make haste while the Sun shines!" And to Frodo she said: "Farewell, Elf-friend, it was a merry meeting."

10 *The Catechism of the Catholic Church*, no. 978, 255.

11 "Almighty and ever-living God, you sent your only Son into the world to cast out the power of Satan, spirit of evil, to rescue man from the kingdom of darkness, and bring him into the splendor of your kingdom of light. We pray for this child: set him (her) free from original sin, make him (her) a temple of your glory, and send your Holy Spirit to dwell with him (her). We ask this through Christ our Lord."

> But Frodo found no words to answer. He bowed low, and
> mounted his pony. (136)

When they get to the bottom, Frodo sees Goldberry at the top:

> Like a sunlit flower against the sky: She was standing and still
> watching them, and her hands were stretched out towards
> them. As they looked she gave a clear call, and lifting up her
> hand she turned and vanished behind the hill. (136)

Tolkien has crafted this ligature between baptismal episodes
almost completely from biblical tropes and the end of the Catholic mass. "Mass" comes from the Latin word *missa* meaning "to
send." The point of the mass is to restore the congregation, so it
can hold to its baptismal purpose of spreading the gospel, which
it is sent out to do with energy: "I tell you, open your eyes and
look at the fields. They are ripe for harvest," Jesus tells the disciples in John 4:35. Goldberry has given the Hobbits a benediction,
an invocation of divine blessing, and she has sent them out on
their mission. "To make haste while the sun shines" is a slight
twist of Proverbs 10:5, "Make hay while the sun shines." Haste is
what the Hobbits are to make in their battle against evil. The
Hobbits are speechless in Goldberry's presence. All they can do is
bow solemnly—very much in the spirit of genuflecting before
one leaves the church.

The sun reoccurs through this scene with Goldberry. She is the
flower, always bent towards the sun; her hair catches the sun and
shimmers, and the dewy grass "flashes" under her feet as she
dances. Daughter of the Withywindle, minor nature deity or
angel, she is the archetype of communion with the sun, and Tolkien, of course, was quite familiar with the perpetual medieval pun
on Sun and Son. For Tolkien this is not an allegorical connection
but a sacramental one: the sun just does remind us of the Son in a
sacramental universe. It is not only an atomic furnace, but, like
the light of John 1, a proclamation of God's glory. As a reflector of
the sun, Goldberry is a type of Mary, who reflects her Son.

✚

Jonah is one of the Old Testament books whose applicability to
baptism has long been recognized. Tolkien was asked to translate

it by the general editor of *The Jerusalem Bible* (1966), Fr. Anthony
Jones, who was impressed by *The Lord of the Rings*.[12] Perhaps Fr.
Jones recognized that the baptismal echoes in Tolkien's work res-
onated with those in Jonah. In his attempt to escape Yaweh's
command to go to Nineveh, Jonah is thwarted, when a great
storm threatens the ship he has taken and the sailors cast him
into the sea, where he is swallowed by a giant fish. Jonah's prayer
to Yaweh, from the belly of the fish, prefigures several baptismal
motifs—drowning, burial, and the "resurrection" of Jonah, when,
in response to his prayer, Yaweh causes the fish to vomit him up
on the shore:

> From the belly of Sheol I cried.
> and you have heard my voice.
> you cast me into the abyss, into the heart of the sea,
> and the flood surrounded me.
> All your waves, your billows,
> washed over me. . . .
> The waters surrounded me right to my throat,
> The abyss was all around me. . . .
> I went down into the countries underneath the earth,
> to the peoples of the past.
> But you lifted my life from the pit,
> Yahweh, my God.
> While my soul was fainting with me,
> I remembered Yahweh
> And my prayer came before you
> into your holy Temple.
> Those who serve worthless idols
> forfeit the grace that was theirs. (Jonah 2:3–10)[13]

The general proposition that "those who serve worthless idols
/ forfeit the grace that was theirs" might be taken as the central
theme of *The Lord of the Rings*; however, much in Jonah's prayer
also connects specifically to Frodo's second baptismal episode, in

12 Tolkien also worked on Proverbs. See *The Tolkien Library*, http://www.
tolkienlibrary.com/press/888-Book_of_Jonah_Translated_by_Tolkien.php
(accessed 11/26/2012)

13 Tolkien's translation of Jonah, *The Jerusalem Bible*, ed. Alexander Jones
(NY: Doubleday, 1966), 1494–5.

which there is a metaphorical drowning in a rising "sea" of fog; the Hobbits are "swallowed" in a tomb, surrounded by ancient treasure, and Frodo, like Jonah, must call for aid.

Tom Bombadil has warned the Hobbits to stay away from the Barrow Downs, the burial sites of ancient kings. The Hobbits try to do this, but, as in their encounter with Old Man Willow, natural obstacles force them off their desired path. They become disoriented, the day is hot and muggy, and, once again, they feel a more than natural desire to sleep.

At mid-day on their journey, they come to a hill "whose top was wide and flattened, like a shallow saucer with a green mounded rim." They cross the hill and see more hills, just like the one they are on, with standing stones. That sight is "discomforting." Somehow, though they don't seem to realize it, the Hobbits have gotten into the beginning of the barrows. They turn back, going down "into the hollow circle," on which there is one stone standing. "It was cool, as if the sun had no power to warm it; but at the time this seemed pleasant" (137). The stone, like the Ring, doesn't give off heat. It only absorbs. They all go to sleep with their backs on the stone.

The Hobbits' continued lack of resistance to sleep can be associated with acedia, a spiritual symptom, a flight from the divine good to sloth. (We will encounter it again in Théoden's deep depression.) *The Oxford Concise Dictionary of the Christian Church* defines it as "a state of restlessness and inability either to work or to pray."[14] In the grip of acedia, despair and ennui are so strong that one does not even care that one does not care. Acedia makes the fulfillment of baptismal vows impossible, and so it becomes sloth, one of the seven deadly sins; it is, in a sense, a nullification of the Holy Spirit, who gives energy and joy, and, in both of their sleepy adventures, the Hobbits consent to the dragging force of torpor and become culpable.[15]

---

14 "Accidie," *The Concise Oxford Dictionary of the Christian Church*, ed. E. A. Livingstone, Oxford University Press, 2006. Oxford Reference Online. Oxford University Press. 1 November 2011.

15 A literary precursor is the Redcrosse Knight in Canto 7 of Spenser's the *Faerie Queene*, who falls asleep, signifying the same spiritual problem.

When the Hobbits wake up, they find themselves in a Jonah-like situation, being engulfed by a rising sea:

> They found that they were upon an island in the fog. Even as they looked out in dismay towards the setting sun, it sank before their eyes into a white sea, and a cold grey shadow sprang up in the East behind. The fog rolled up to the walls and rose above them, and as it mounted it bent over their heads until it became a roof: they were shut in a hall of mist whose central pillar was the standing stone. (138)

The imagery of both drowning and entombment are here, as the sea-like fog turns into a barrow. At this point, the Hobbits mobilize their wills and try to escape. They mount their ponies and set off from the hill, but, in the fog, they lose track of each other. Frodo finally confronts the Barrow-wight on his own, "a tall dark figure like a shadow against the stars." The wight seizes Frodo in a strong, cold grip, and, when he wakes, he is in a tomb, surrounded by the treasures of a long dead king from a lost realm. Frodo and the Hobbits have entered that world described by Jonah: "a country beneath the earth," whose origin and treasure derive from "peoples of the past." The Hobbits are in a Northern Sheol, the land of the dead.

Frodo finds himself on his back, on a slab of stone, and, lying beside him, on their backs, Sam, Pippin, and Merry, gold circlets on their heads, gold chains about their waists and rings on their fingers, laid out like the dead kings of old. As they had lain with their backs on the standing stone, they now lie on an altar stone. They are in a kind of dragon's hoard. Swords are at their sides, but across their necks "one long naked sword." Frodo hears a song, "a cold murmur, rising and falling." The voice seems "immeasurably dreary," a "formless stream of sad but horrible sounds," impossible to understand, but "grim, hard, cold words, heartless and miserable." Like the black speech of Mordor or Melkor's original dissonance, this song represents the anti-logos, the attempt to unmake creation through language; it is a song of universal death, and Frodo is "chilled to the marrow." The Word throughout the Bible brings forth life;[16] this anti-Word brings

---

16 There are a great many references to the word as an active, life-giving

forth death. Frodo is being engaged in combat at the spiritual level, but also at the physical: a long arm enters the chamber, groping with its fingers at the hilt of the sword. The disembodied arm, like the disembodied Eye of Sauron, is an image of how evil subtracts from the being of a creature. The cold fear felt by the Hobbits, which threatens to paralyze Frodo's will, is the psychic manifestation of evil subtraction.

The episode shows the spiritual maturation of Frodo. He is not simply saved, as he was before, by Sam and then Tom. He finds the courage to fight successfully, despite his terror. He is tempted to escape, to put on the Ring and leave his companions, but his courage and love are stronger than his fear. Tolkien's description of Frodo is a tribute to the English yeomen, with whom Tolkien served in the trenches of the Great War:

> There is a seed of courage hidden (often deeply, it is true) in the heart of the fattest and most timid Hobbit, waiting for some final and desperate danger to make it grow. Frodo was neither very fat nor very timid; indeed, though he did not know it, Bilbo (and Gandalf) had thought him the best Hobbit in the Shire. He thought he had come to the end of his adventure, and a terrible end, but the thought hardened him. He found himself stiffening, as if for a final spring; he no longer felt limp like a helpless prey. (140)

Frodo grabs a sword and hacks the hand off the crawling arm. There is a shriek, and the sword shatters up to the hilt. Suddenly Frodo remembers Tom Bombadil, and even thinking of him makes Frodo stronger. He remembers the song he is to sing, if he gets into trouble within Tom's realm:

> *Ho! Tom Bombadil, Tom Bombadillo!*
> *By water, wood and hill, by the reed and willow,*
> *By fire, sun, and moon, harken now and hear us!*
> *Come, Tom Bombadil, for our need is near us!* (142)

---

principle in the Bible. Some of the more important examples are, as we have seen, creation through language in Genesis and John 1. See also Isaiah 55:11 and Psalm 33.

Frodo's cry is not just a prayer, though it is that. The songs of Tom, and this song to him, have much in common with several Psalms in praise of creation, such as 8, 19, 104, 139, and 148. They pit the glory of creation against the un-creation of death.

Tom not only wakes the Hobbits from their "death," but it's an awakening that recalls Jesus exit from the tomb, stone rolled aside; Tom sings: *"Dark door is standing wide; dead hand is broken. / Night under Night is flown, and the Gate is open!"* (original emphasis; 143). In addition, Tolkien gives Tom the words of a baptismal exorcism. The Catholic exorcism at baptism consists mainly of one sentence: "Almighty and ever-living God, you sent your only Son into the world to cast out the power of Satan, spirit of evil, to rescue man from the kingdom of darkness, and bring him into the splendor of your kingdom of light." Tom's exorcism, in the spirit of John's Gospel, casts light against darkness, rescuing Frodo and company from the wight's kingdom of darkness, bringing them into the bright sunshine of day:

> Get out, you old Wight! Vanish in the sunlight!
> Shrivel like the cold mist, like the winds go wailing,
> Out into the barren lands far beyond the mountains!
> Come never here again! Leave your barrow empty!
> Lost and forgotten be, darker than the darkness,
> Where gates stand for ever shut, till the world is mended. (142)

Whatever the wight's eternal fate, he is banished "till the world is mended," as Tom goes on to plunder the barrow itself, the danger having been removed. (The eschatological reference, "till the world is mended," alludes to the promise of a remade Creation that goes throughout the New Testament; Tom, it seems, has inside information.) He carries the three sleeping Hobbits out of the tomb, extracting them from the realm of death. Then the baptismal theme goes to full completion. The Hobbits, clad in old rags by the wight (as if clad in sin), are bidden by Tom to "Be glad my merry friends, and let the warm sunlight heat now heart and limb! Cast off these cold rags! Run naked on the grass!" (144). The Hobbits become like those baptized in the early church; reborn in water and emerging naked, they shed their previous selves to find their real selves. Tom's final baptismal word to the

Hobbits is, "You've found yourselves again, out of the deep water. Clothes are but little loss, if you escape from drowning" (144).

As baptism is a great reception of the gift of the Holy Spirit, this episode ends with Tom giving out gifts from the barrow—things the Hobbits can use in the coming days, such as daggers, which are big enough for the Hobbits to use as swords. (Merry will make good use of his in The Battle of Pelennor Fields.) The most enigmatic find in the barrow is a blue brooch, "set with blue stones, many-shaded like flax-flowers or the wings of blue butterflies." Tom looks at it a long time and says, rather wistfully, "fair was she who long ago wore this on her shoulder. Goldberry shall wear it now, and we will not forget her!" (145). Although it seems impossible to pin this brooch to a specific lady from The Silmarillion, Melian or Luthien are good candidates, because of their great beauty, and because Tom would venerate both of them. But even if we cannot identify the lady, perhaps the most important thing is that Tom remembers her and that the brooch will be worn by Goldberry in memory of someone who is gone. As baptism brings the Christian into a church whose members are dead, living, and yet to be born, so the exorcism of the barrow reminds the Hobbits that they are part of a community that extends into an ancient past, still alive in memory, and which looks to the mending of the world.

This concludes the first "movement" of Tolkien's story, which takes Frodo and his companions from Hobbiton to Bree and is mainly concerned with overcoming a split in their minds: the need to leave the Shire and the desire to stay. Out of this very natural conflict emerges the vulnerability that both Old Man Willow and the Barrow-wight exploit.

By any reasonable standard, the Hobbits show an astonishing indifference to possessions and comfort. Frodo drops everything to do his duty, and Sam, Merry, and Pippin follow him out of love, casting their longing for home aside. The Hobbits' indifference to possessions and other attachments that get in the way of their mission flows directly into Tolkien's work from New Testament sources about what is required of Jesus's disciples[17] and is

17 Matthew 8:22; Luke 9:62; Mark 10:17-30.

stressed in Ignatius's Spiritual Exercises in "The First Principle and Foundation":

> Man is created to praise, reverence, and serve God our Lord, and by this means to save his soul.
>
> The others things on the face of the earth are created for man to help him in attaining the end for which he is created.
>
> Hence, man is to make use of them in as far as they help him in the attainment of his end, and he must rid himself of them in as far as they prove a hindrance to him.
>
> Therefore, *we must make ourselves indifferent to all created things, as far as we are allowed free choice and are not under any prohibition.* Consequently, as far as we are concerned, we should not prefer health to sickness, riches to poverty, honor to dishonor, a long life to a short life. The same holds for all other things.
>
> Our one desire and choice should be what is more conducive to the end for which we are created.[18]

We admire Frodo for his ready capacity to sacrifice for the Shire. We admire Sam, Merry, and Pippin for their love of Frodo. And their sacrifice does not pertain so much to possessions as to the merriment, joy, and comfort they find in an ordinary life with friends. Frodo thinks how nice a retired life at Crickhollow would be; the Hobbits enjoy the coziness of Farmer Maggot's dining room and the merry house of Tom Bombadil, all of which remind them of home. But it makes them want to hold back. Old Man Willow turns this reluctance into a late afternoon stupor; the Barrow Wight uses it against them, after they lazily linger near the barrows after lunch. In both cases, some or all of the Hobbits find themselves propped against a support that drains them of energy—Old Man Willow and the giant standing stone—as they drift off to sleep.

The second obstacle to the Hobbits is not one of their doing— it is the age-old structural sin built into Middle-earth since the fall of Melkor and made worse since then. The Old Forest, which has

---

18 St. Ignatius of Loyola, *The Spiritual Exercise of St. Ignatius,* trans. Louis J. Puhl, S. J. (Chicago: Loyola Press, 1951), 12; See also Ignatius's exercise on "The Three Classes of Men," 64–65.

endured for epochs the depredations of creatures that can move, has an immense store of malice that it aims at those who travel through it. It is rotten at the heart, a victim of sin and damage, and it wants revenge. The Barrow Wight episode connects the Hobbits to the distant historical past, when the Witch King of Angmar, now the King of the Nazgûl, was human and battled Elves and Men. When Merry emerges from the tomb, he arises with the memory of one of the fallen in those battles: "'The men of Carn Dûm came on us at night, and we were worsted. Ah! the spear in my heart!'" (143). The Shire *seems* to have escaped the past. On the road, the Hobbits find that they can escape neither their personal past nor the historical or even geological past. They are part of a deeply rooted story, as Sam will come to understand more and more, as the book progresses. At the beginning of their quest, they are roughly introduced to this reality, and they want to shrink from it. But, in their first confrontations with the past, they are given specific graces that will help them meet what is ahead, some in the form of treasures from the barrow, such as the long knife that Merry will use to avenge the death of the man whose memory of death he has mysteriously inherited.

Frodo Fords the Bruinen

In the final baptismal episode, Frodo and the Hobbits directly confront what has been chasing them since the beginning of the novel, the Black Riders, the most potent servants of Sauron, the nine kings whose beings have been eaten away by Sauron's rings. During the Nazgûl attack on Weathertop, Frodo once again finds himself calling for help and, once again, doesn't know where the words come from. They are just on his lips. As when he ran, calling "help, help, help," after Old Man Willow swallowed Merry and Pippin, Frodo is helped to pray by something outside himself, and what helps him to pray also responds to the prayer. Tolkien is writing with the Holy Spirit in mind, and the commonplace is Romans 8:26: "Likewise the Spirit also helpeth our infirmity. For we know not what we should pray for as we ought; but the Spirit himself asketh for us with unspeakable groanings."

Frodo hears himself crying aloud "O Elbereth! Gilthoniel!" It is the second time in the novel that Elbereth is mentioned, the first occurring in the song of the Elves led by Gildor Inglorion (79). "Elbereth" is the Sindarin name for Varda, the consort of Manwë and queen of the powers of Middle-earth; Gilthoniel means "star-kindler," and it is Varda's task of sub-creation to actualize that part of the Music which brings the stars into being. On the night in which they entertain Frodo, Pippin, and Sam, Gildor Inglorion and the Elves sing this praise to Elbereth:

Snow-white! Snow-white! O Lady clear!
  O Queen beyond the Western Seas!
O Light to us that wander here
  Amid the world of woven trees!

Gilthoniel! O Elbereth!
  Clear are thy eyes and bright thy breath!
Snow-white! Snow-white! We sing to thee
  In a far land beyond the sea.

O stars that in the Sunless Year
  With shining hand by her were sown,
In windy fields now bright and clear
  We see your silver blossom blown!

Many commentators have noted the Marian aspects of Elbereth (as they have with Galadriel), including an unnamed "critic" to whom Tolkien refers in a letter,[19] and there are good reasons to make the connection.[20] Tolkien himself acknowledges that this song is a "hymn" and that "these [invocations to Elbereth] and

19 *Letters*, 288, "[O]ne critic [probably Robert Murray, S.J.], asserted that the invocations of Elbereth, and the character of Galadriel as directly described (or through the words of Gimli and Sam) were clearly related to Catholic devotion to Mary." Tolkien is seldom reticent to correct a misreading; he does not correct this, but cites it. See also Matthew Dickerson, *Following Gandalf: Epic Battles and Moral Victory in "The Lord of the Rings"* (Grand Rapids: Brazos Press, 2003), 191–3.

20 Stratford Caldecott is especially perceptive on Marian influence in *The Lord of the Rings,* and my comments are indebted to him. See his book, *The Ring of Power: The Spiritual Vision Behind the Lord of the Rings* (NY: The Crossroad Publishing Co., 2005).

other references to religion in The Lord of the Rings are frequently overlooked."[21] The song which Tolkien's Elves address to Elbereth is striking similar to a popular Marian hymn, "Hail Queen of Heaven, the Ocean Star," written by an English priest, Fr. John Lingard (1771–1851):

> Hail, Queen of heaven, the ocean star,
> Guide of the wanderer here below,
> Thrown on life's surge, we claim thy care,
> Save us from peril and from woe.
>
> Mother of Christ, Star of the sea
> Pray for the wanderer, pray for me.

I am not arguing that Elbereth is an allegorical stand-in for Mary. But, like Mary, the Queen of Heaven, she is associated with stars. She is pure and white, which echoes the Catholic belief in Mary's sinlessness. Both Elbereth and Mary are invoked as lights of guidance, and, as Elbereth is a lady of the western sea, so Mary is called the star of the sea, who guides struggling mariners and wanderers. The Elvish song promises that Elbereth, whom some of the Elves have known in Valinor, will not be forgotten; the hymn to Mary contains the rosary prayer that she not forget us: "Holy Mary, mother of God, pray for us." At the very least, these parallel songs show the deep human desire for a mother's guidance and protection. They also proclaim the power of beauty and love to dispel evil. As Richard Purtill notes, Frodo and others *just do* call on Elbereth at the times a Christian would pray,[22] and specifically at the times a Catholic Christian would pray to Mary for her intercession.

That Mary was deeply important to Tolkien is evident in several of his letters. To Fr. Murray, he writes, "I think I know exactly what you mean by the order of Grace; and of course by

21 *The Road Goes Ever On: A Song Cycle*, poems by J.R.R. Tolkien set to music by Donald Swann (London: George Allen & Unwin, 1968), 65, quoted in Tom Shippey, *The Road to Middle-Earth: How J.R.R. Tolkien Created a New Mythology* (NY: Houghton Mifflin, 2003), 203.

22 Richard Purtill, *J.R.R. Tolkien, Myth, Morality, and Religion* (San Francisco: Ignatius Press, 1984), 127.

your references to Our Lady, upon which all my own small perception of beauty both in majesty and simplicity is founded."[23] Tolkien describes the importance of her Assumption in the draft to Rhona Beare: "The Assumption of Mary, the only unfallen person, may be regarded as in some ways a simple regaining of unfallen grace and liberty: she asked to be received, and was, having no further function on Earth."[24] Grace to fight evil and regain his liberty is exactly what Frodo needs from Elbereth.

Frodo's plea is heard. As the Nazgûl King attacks him on Weathertop, Frodo regains the will to resist. He strikes at the Nazgûl's foot, but misses. Still, his assertion of will is important. It saves his life, even though the Nazgûl wounds him in the shoulder. As Aragorn says later, "More deadly to him was the name of Elbereth" (198).

At this point, another sacrament, that of anointing the sick, also comes into play, as Aragorn tries to heal Frodo by application of a poultice made of the plant *athelas*, or "kingsfoil." Even the fragrance of the steam, when Aragorn boils the leaves, is refreshing, and the Hobbits feel their minds "calmed and cleared." The Catholic Catechism states the purpose of anointing is to commend those who are ill "to the suffering and glorified Lord, that he may raise them up and save them. And indeed [the Church] exhorts them to contribute to the good of the People of God by freely uniting themselves to the Passion and death of Christ."[25] The "calming and clearing" effect of the *athelas*, not only on Frodo, but on everyone else, is a spiritual good, for it dispels what Frodo's injury can lead to mentally, "anguish, self-absorption, sometimes even despair and revolt against God."[26]

With a broken piece of the Nazgûl blade still inside him, Frodo begins a three-front personal war: he must both bear the Ring and deal with his wound in two dimensions, physical and spiritual. He must hang on until he gets to Rivendell, where Elrond may be able to help him. Frodo keeps a grip on life from October

23 *Letters*, 172.
24 Ibid., 286.
25 *The Catechism of the Catholic Church*, no. 1499, 375.
26 Ibid., no. 1501, 375.

6 to October 20[27], when he crosses the Bruinen, and then for an additional three days in Rivendell, before Elrond can extract the piece of broken blade, seventeen days altogether (222). Frodo's spiritual struggle begins with a dream, "in which he walked on the grass in his garden in the Shire, but it seemed faint and dim, less clear than the tall black shadows that stood looking over the hedge" (202).

As Frodo fights the process in which he begins to fade, the Black Riders loom over the boundary of his garden. But Frodo does get help along the way. The group meets the Elf, Glorfindel, who has been riding to find them; to Frodo, he appears "a white light . . . shining through the form and raiment of the rider, as if through a thin veil" (209), and there is brief Eucharistic scene in which Glorfindel gives the Hobbits a little liquor from a silver flask, from which "strength and vigour seemed to flow into all their limbs" (211). Together with some stale bread and fruit, it "seemed to satisfy their hunger better than many a good breakfast in the Shire had done." The main struggle comes when Frodo has to ride, on his own, across the River Bruinen on Glorfindel's horse. Again, Frodo comes into direct contact with wills that seek to overbear his. As Frodo is pursued by the Black Riders to the Ford of the Bruinen, a "strange reluctance" seizes him and he brings his horse to a walk. But having been through such experiences twice before, Frodo is quicker to realize what is happening: "Suddenly he knew in his heart that they were silently commanding him to wait. Then at once fear and hatred awoke in him" (213). With an order from Glorfindel, his horse takes off across the Bruinen, the crossing of which begins the baptismal episode. Frodo gets up the bank on the other side and faces the Black Riders from across the river. Once again, he invokes Elbereth: "'By Elbereth and Lúthien the Fair,' said Frodo with a last effort, lifting up his sword, 'you shall have neither the Ring nor me!'" (214).

The Black Riders cross the river for Frodo, who is virtually paralyzed. But Gandalf and Elrond, unknown to Frodo, are now par-

---

27 See Appendix B, *The Lord of The Rings*, 1092, and also Karen Wynn Fonstad, *The Atlas of Middle Earth* (NY: Houghton Mifflin, 1991), 157.

ticipating in his rescue, and they unleash the waters of the Bruinen:

> At that moment there came a roaring and a rushing: a noise of loud waters rolling many stones. Dimly Frodo saw the river below him rise, and down along its course there came a plumed cavalry of waves. White flames seemed to Frodo to flicker on their crest, and he half fancied that he saw amid the water white riders upon white horses with frothing manes. The three Riders that were still in the midst of the Ford were overwhelmed: they disappeared, buried suddenly under angry foam. Those that were behind drew back in dismay. . . .
>
> The black horses were filled with madness, and leaping forward in terror they bore their riders into the rushing flood. Their piercing cries were drowned in the roaring of the river as it carried them away. (214–215)

This scene literally depicts evil being washed away under the power of water: "the washing of regeneration" with a vengeance. The roar of the water makes Frodo, in his half-conscious condition, think that he is "drowning, with . . . friends, enemies, and all" (224). The White Riders of the river "overwhelm" the Black. These water riders—"a touch of my own," Gandalf will later tell Frodo with some pride—did not have to be added. A tidal wave alone would have worked as well. But that Gandalf wants to add them emphasizes the difference between Gandalf, who is in love with beauty, and Saruman, who would think beauty a frivolous consumption of energy that ought to be put to more utilitarian purposes. The universe, Gandalf understands, is not so much meant to serve a purpose beyond itself as to show forth the glory of God. Beauty itself fights evil, adding where evil subtracts.

The flames that flicker on the crests of the horses are like Pentecostal fire.[28] With this image Tolkien directly connects what seem to be opposites, fire and water, which always go together in baptism: water becomes the vehicle for the infusion of spiritual fire, the Holy Spirit, or, in Tolkien's myth, The Flame Imperish-

---

28 The combination of roar and flame in this passage is so startlingly similar to the reading for Pentecost, Acts 2:1–11, that one is forced to speculate Tolkien used this Bible passage as a model.

able. Gandalf, bearer of the Ring of Fire, is its servant. A possible source of Tolkien's inspiration for the flame-crested water cavalry may come from the Easter Vigil, in which the big paschal candle, signifying the light of Christ, is put into the baptismal water to bless it. The light of Christ, communicated to the water, will then be used in the multiple baptisms of Easter Vigil. Tolkien would have seen that rite throughout his life.

Frodo is taken to Rivendell and healed by Elrond, who removes the splinter, an evil that was "deeply buried, and . . . working inwards." It is an image of the removal of sin through baptism. Gandalf's private concerns about Frodo are also baptismal. Frodo had begun to fade and, within a few hours, without the aid of Elrond, would have become a wraith. The Ring and the wound have both had their effect on Frodo:

> To the wizard's eye there was a faint change, just a hint as it were of transparency, about him. . . .
> 'Still that must be expected,' said Gandalf to himself. 'He is not half through yet, and to what he will come in the end not even Elrond can foretell. Not to evil, I think. He may become like a glass filled with a clear light for eyes to see that can.' (223)

The image of "a glass filled with a clear light" echoes New Testament imagery about being "filled with the Holy Spirit." (Acts 2:4) and the body being a Temple of the Holy Spirit (1 Cor. 6:19–20). It also foreshadows Frodo's association with the Phial of Galadriel, which will become an emblem of Frodo himself. Gandalf does not know Frodo's fate—he is only speculating and hoping. Despite the gifts of baptism for the Christian, it too offers no guarantees. The baptized can lose their faith and lose salvation, but they can also be filled with light.

✠

Baptism is the beginning step in the Catholic Church and thus the logical place for Tolkien to begin Frodo's journey. Both Christian baptism and the baptismal episodes at the beginning of *The Lord of the Rings* share the narrative pattern of eucatastrophe that Tolkien identifies as fundamental to fairy stories. Eucatastrophe exemplifies the beatitude that the meek are blessed and shall inherit the earth. Frodo and the Hobbits are built low to the earth, which they love. They know they need to be rescued, they have no compunctions about calling for help, and they *are* helped. Each of the three baptismal episodes pushes the eucatastrophic envelope a little farther. The rescues become more hairbreadth and spectacular, and Frodo is prepared for the more dangerous part of his journey.

A quest is always part *Bildungsroman*. The Hobbits, who appear the size of children, grow to fit the heroic mold. Frodo's adventures already show him increasing in understanding and heroic stature. He is rescued in his last adventure by Hobbits, Elves, a Man, and a Wizard, but, as Gandalf tells him, he would not have survived, had he not put up a stubborn fight: "'Yes, fortune or fate have helped you,' said Gandalf, 'not to mention courage. For your heart was not touched, and only your shoulder was pierced; and that was because you resisted to the last'" (222).

Baptism starts the Christian on a quest. It initiates the new Christian into the body of the Church, so that the mission of the Church might be fulfilled, which is to preach the gospel for the salvation of mankind and, ultimately, to defeat Satan and his minions. Frodo's mission is the salvation of Middle-earth, and his "baptisms" awaken his courage and determination, preparing him for the next step: confirmation as the Ring-bearer in a Fellowship whose mission is to defeat the dark powers of Mordor.

6

"I WONDER WHAT SORT OF TALE WE'VE FALLEN INTO?"

Reading the Sacramental Universe of The Lord of the Rings

"The unity of a human life is the unity of a narrative quest. Quests sometimes fail, are frustrated, abandoned or dissipated into distractions; and human lives may in all these ways also fail. But the only criteria for success or failure in a human life as a whole are the criteria of success or failure in a narrated or to-be-narrated quest. A quest for what?" ALASDAIR MACINTYRE[1]

"Strictly speaking, the whole of history is nothing but the story of God's activity." JEAN PIERRE DE CAUSSADE[2]

THE BASIC FACT of a Logos-centric universe is that it can be read—not easily, and not completely, "for even the wise cannot see all ends," but to some degree, because it is both teleological and sacramental. In Christian thought, the world is God's story, and, in a sense, we inhabit it as characters. We inhabit a world that is trying to tell us our part in a larger story. Thus, in *The Lord of the Rings*, virtually all the characters are continually trying to "read" the course of events, to find themselves in the

---

1 Alasdair MacIntyre, *After Virtue* (Notre Dame, IN: University of Notre Dame, 1981), 219.
2 de Caussade, *Abandonment*, 44.

story, to "confirm" their roles, to make the decisions that are appropriate, given the teleological arc of history. This means that narrative is the principle mode through which truth is understood. Characters look for a narrative understanding which is not only consistent with events as they know them, but which has the impact of truth, the holistic feel of it, in imaginations formed by the transcendental ideas of truth, beauty, and goodness.

Let's consider three representative episodes in which characters consciously search for a narrative pattern in events, so they can make good decisions and understand the part they are to play: the Council of Elrond; Aragorn's crises of decision-making, beginning at the Falls of Rauros and ending in Gandalf's return in "The White Rider"; and Sam's ruminations about story as he and Frodo trek toward Mordor.

narrative within narrative: providential design at the council of elrond

Because reality is a narrative—with beginning, middle, and end—conflict and resolution—within the Music of the Ainur—Truth will be narratival. The Council of Elrond is called, because a great decision has to be made: what to do with the Ring, now that it has been found. "The Wise" make that decision on the basis of a communally constructed narrative that combines the testimony of Elrond, Gandalf, Aragorn, Frodo, and Boromir to form a history of the Ring. The Council as a whole finds this narrative compelling.

There are other modes besides narrative in the search for truth—propositions to be tested and experiments to be performed. Gandalf, for instance, confirms the identity of the Ring by putting it into Frodo's fire. But by the end, it is the overall narrative account that forces conviction and points directly to Frodo as the one person capable of finishing the story. As Elrond says at the beginning, "the Tale of the Ring shall be told from the beginning even to this present. And I will begin that tale, though others shall end it" (242). Elrond and Gandalf recognize they are operating within a larger story, governed by the Music, and their project of discernment, on which the fate of Middle-earth depends, must be worked out within the context of the providential scheme. This is repeatedly made clear by the language of Elrond and Gandalf, who can only set forth a narrative to the Council. Frodo's confirmatory call comes, when he realizes that it is his task to end the tale. His discernment of his role amounts to "finding out" his place in a narrative, and this is a typically Christian framing of the issue of vocation: where do I fit into the grand salvation narrative set forth in the Gospels and communally elaborated by the Church?

That the Council is being held at all is providential. Elrond has summoned no one for the meeting, but, mysteriously, the people who need to be there have come to Rivendell more or less at the same time. Legolas, from the Elves of Northern Mirkwood, had to deliver news of Gollum's escape, so he is there; the Dwarves, Glóin and his son Gimli, have come looking for Bilbo, because they know that Sauron is looking for the Hobbit with the Ring, and because they crave Elrond's advice about the gathering threat of Sauron; Frodo is there as the result of Gildor's advice to go west and his subsequent meeting with Aragorn in Bree; Gandalf comes, having escaped from Orthanc, because he assumes Frodo has gotten the message he left with Barliman Butterbur, telling him to go to Rivendell; Boromir, the most unlikely, arrives on his quest to find the meaning of his brother Faramir's dream. Elrond begins the Council by stating its purpose and noting the strangeness of how they have come together:

> 'The Ring! What shall we do with the Ring, the least of rings, the trifle that Sauron fancies? That is the doom that we must deem.
>
> That is the purpose for which are called hither. *Called, I say, though I have not called you to me*, strangers from distant lands. You have come and are here met, in this very nick of time, *by chance as it may seem*. Yet it is not so. Believe rather that *it is ordered* that we, who sit here, and none others, must now find counsel for the peril of the world.' (my emphasis; 242)

This meeting is all about providential calling and discernment of the Ring's tale.

When Gandalf tells his own story about searching for the identity of the Ring and his betrayal and capture by Saruman, his consciousness of providence is pervasive. Gandalf notes that the Ring was found by Frodo in the same year that the Necromancer of Dol Guldur, who turned out to be Sauron, was driven out of Mirkwood: "a strange chance, if chance it was" (250). Gandalf relates his process of discernment, as he journeys toward Saruman—something was troubling him but he could not make the picture come clear: "I had a foreboding of some danger, still hidden from me but drawing near" (256). On the way he meets Radagast the Brown, another of the Istari, who tells him, "The Nine are abroad again," and one of Gandalf's intuitions is clarified: "I knew then what I had dreaded without knowing it" (257). As Gandalf approaches the gates of Isengard, Saruman's stronghold, he notes, "suddenly I was afraid, though I knew no reason for it" (258). Gandalf gets the reason in his conference with Saruman, who imprisons him on the top of Orthanc. Part of the persuasive power of Gandalf's narrative is the way he shows how his own prophetic worries were clarified.

When Frodo learns that Isildur, Aragorn's ancestor, had cut the Ring from Sauron's finger, he immediately tries to return the Ring to Aragorn as the rightful "owner." Like Gandalf, Frodo wants no part of it:

> 'Then it belongs to you, and not to me at all!' cried Frodo in amazement, springing to his feet, as if he expected the Ring to be demanded at once.
> 'It does not belong to either of us,' said Aragorn; 'but it has been *ordained* that you should hold it for a while.' (emphasis added; 247)

Tolkien consistently moves the reader into the realm of discernment and vocation within the language of calling and chance that is really not chance, but ordination. This is a confirmation in which the pressure on Frodo steadily builds, until he is forced to recognize that he must make a decision, that he has only one right, *ordained* answer, though he is free to give the wrong, unordained answer.

After the tale is told, the Council considers all alternatives for dealing with the Ring. Destroy it? It can only be destroyed in the Cracks of Doom. Give it to Bombadil for safe-keeping, since he is immune to it? Bombadil just wouldn't take the job seriously, and even he is not safe from Sauron. Use the Ring against Sauron, as Boromir suggests? This would just create another Sauron. The only way to get rid of the Ring is to walk into Mordor, take it to the Cracks of Doom in the volcano, Orodúin, and throw it in, unmaking it in the fires where it was created.

Old Bilbo volunteers, and this is important as well as comic. Frodo loves no one more than Bilbo. Although Bilbo is too aged to go, he is serious in his offer and shows Frodo an example of courage, doing what godparents are supposed to do for their godchildren. But, after gently disqualifying Bilbo, the Council waits in silence:

> No one answered. The noon-bell rang. Still no one spoke. Frodo glanced at all the faces, but they were not turned to him. All the Council sat with downcast eyes, as if in deep thought. A great dread fell on him, as if he was awaiting the pronouncement of some doom that he had long foreseen and vainly hoped might after all never be spoken. An overwhelming longing to rest and remain at peace by Bilbo's side in Rivendell filled all his heart. At last with an effort he spoke, and wondered to hear his own words, *as if some other will was using his small voice.*
>
> 'I will take the Ring,' he said, 'though I do not know the way.' (emphasis added; 270)

Tolkien has used the idea of responding to "calls" before. When Niggle is in Purgatory, one of the things the two Voices discuss is the number of calls he received and how many he answered. Here, Frodo is not just given a call, but the grace to accept and fulfill it—that is what the sacrament of Confirmation is all about, and, like a bishop laying his hands on Frodo's head, Elrond confirms Frodo's calling:

> Elrond raised his eyes and looked at him, and Frodo felt his heart pierced by the sudden keenness of the glance. 'If I understand aright all that I have heard,' he said, 'I think that this task is appointed for you, Frodo; and that if you do not find a way, no one will. . . .
>
> 'But it is a heavy burden. So heavy that none could lay it on another. I do not lay it on you. But if you take it freely, I will say that your choice is right.' (270)

Frodo has been confirmed, but not compelled. He couldn't be, for no one compelled could ever succeed in the task. The Ring would devour him. The complex of discernment, calling, and confirmation which Tolkien addresses in The Council of Elrond is typical of that stage of life when Christians are particularly concerned with vocational choices, but, as is the case with baptism, it is a process which continues, even though the sacrament occurs only once. Frodo has been fitted into the story of the Music. He is "appointed." It is "the hour" of the Shire folk.

Bilbo, the old author, understands that life really is a story. He is working on his own Hobbit's tale and wants Frodo to take good notes, because he knows Frodo's tale is just a continuation of his own. It is not only important to live the story, but to tell it! Telling the story affirms and records the events related and also confirms the story-like nature of the world. During the council, after Frodo gives the full account of his adventures from Bag End to Rivendell, Bilbo, his literary mentor, tells him:

> 'Not bad, . . . You would have made a good story of it, if they hadn't kept on interrupting. I tried to make a few notes, but we shall have to go over it all again together some time, if I am to write it up. There are whole chapters of stuff before you ever got here!' (249)

For Bilbo, now on the sidelines, Frodo's near-death experience is food for contemplation in the form of a story that can be crafted out of the greater story on which Bilbo's literary project depends. Frodo is not quite comfortable with being the cannon-fodder for literary pleasure. Before he leaves Rivendell, Bilbo asks him whether he's thought of any ending for the story ahead, and Frodo replies: "Yes, several, and all are dark and unpleasant." Bilbo's response comes out of faith and hope that the meaning of the world doesn't lead to such an ending:

> 'Oh, that won't do!' said Bilbo. 'Books ought to have good endings. How would this do: *and they all settled down and lived together happily ever after?*'
> 'It will do well, if it ever comes to that,' said Frodo.
> 'Ah!' said Sam. 'And where will they live? That's what I often wonder.' (273–74)

Courage amounts to playing one's part in the story, however it unfolds. Sam asks where the characters will live ever after. The question, as incongruently mundane as it may seem, is in the Christian mind, simply the most important of all.

aragorn's decision to pursue merry and pippin: heart and head in concert

As John proclaims, God *is* love (1 John 4:8). This makes love the hermeneutic key to understanding a Logos-centric universe and the primary consideration in decision-making. The word "logic" derives from logos, but a fully Logos-centric wisdom would include much more than rules for constructing syllogisms or a catalog of fallacies to avoid; it would include imagination, intuition, feeling, and above all, love. Tolkien almost never uses the word "reason," but rather the more broadly informed "wisdom."

In "The Breaking of the Fellowship," "The Riders of Rohan," and "The White Rider," Tolkien shows Aragorn's struggle to make wise decisions in difficult circumstances, berating himself for assumed mistakes, only to find out that, "by chance, as it may seem," he has been making the right choices all along. His choices have gone right, because he has not ignored the demands of love.

Aragorn's first choice after the Fellowship is split at the Falls of Rauros is between pursuing the Uruk-hai, who have captured Merry and Pippin, or going into Mordor after Frodo and Sam, to help them finish the quest to destroy the Ring. It would seem to be an easy decision for a responsible military leader: keep your focus on the mission, even if it means sacrificing some troops. Aragorn, however, does not make this choice.

Aragorn starts from a position of self-doubt. The Fellowship is encamped at the Falls of Rauros, and Frodo has taken an hour to go off on his own and decide which way to carry the Ring: across the river to Mordor or in the opposite direction, to Gondor. Aragorn and Sam become worried about the long-overdue Frodo. Boromir returns to camp, speaks a few suspicious sentences, and then says no more. This increases their concern, and Aragorn and Sam go looking for Frodo. On Amon Hen, Aragorn hears the great horn of Boromir, indicating an attack: "Alas! An ill fate is on me this day, and all that I do goes amiss" (413). Aragorn finds Boromir dying, surrounded by dead Orcs. With Frodo missing and Merry and Pippin captured by the Orcs, Boromir confesses that he tried to take the Ring. Aragorn concludes, "It is I that have failed. Vain was Gandalf's trust in me," and a little later, "All that I have done today has gone amiss" (414). We may think that Aragorn is being absurdly hard on himself, but Gandalf has given him responsibility, and the Fellowship is now in shambles. What to do?

Legolas contributes to Aragorn's thinking process by slowing him down: the body of Boromir must be given burial. Love and decency demand as much. On the mountain, digging a grave or building a cairn will take too long, so they decide to give Boromir to the River Anduin, over the falls. But they take their time with this. They put him in a boat, load it with his own weapons and those of the Orcs he killed, and tow him into the river, which takes him over the falls; then they sing a funeral dirge, made up on the spot. Despite the emergency, love is shown to Boromir and to those who will wait for him in vain, in Gondor. His dignity as a human being is preserved, and this is what fighting Sauron is all about. Evil cannot be defeated by evil actions. Tolkien wants us to see this contrast, when, later that day, Aragorn, Gimli and Legolas come upon five dead, unburied Orcs, left out to rot.

The burial of Boromir helps Aragorn make haste slowly. He is able to figure out from tracks and two missing backpacks that Frodo and Sam have indeed taken the path to Mordor. But he is left with important questions. Were the "great Orcs" from Isengard? Does Saruman know of Gandalf's fall? Are the Orcs returning to Isengard?

Aragorn's conversation with Gimli puts the problem of reading the world and making choices up front:

> 'Well, we have no time to ponder riddles,' said Gimli. 'Let us bear Boromir away!'
> 'But after that we must guess the riddles, if we are to choose our course rightly,' answered Aragorn. (416)

Much of Aragorn's ability as a tracker and hunter comes from having an empathetic imagination. He has the capacity to put

163

himself in the place of what he is tracking, and his imagination informs his reason. Frodo, he realizes, has gone into Mordor alone, because he does not "wish to lead any friend to death with him." Although he doesn't reveal it to Gimli or Legolas, Aragorn also understands it was Boromir's attempt to take the Ring that finally moved Frodo to go on his own. Having put reason and imagination to their utmost use, Aragorn still has to make a decision—how to engage his will: "And now may I make a right choice, and change the evil fate of this unhappy day," he says. This is a petition, and what follows, like a prayer:

> He stood silent for a moment. 'I will follow the Orcs,' he said at last. 'I would have guided Frodo to Mordor and gone with him to the end; but if I seek him now in the wilderness I must abandon the captives to torment and death. *My heart speaks clearly at last*: the fate of the Bearer is in my hands no longer. The company has played its part. Yet we that remain cannot forsake our companions while we have strength left.' (my emphasis; 419)

The petition "thy will be done" in the Lord's Prayer is the acceptance of God's action in history, his providential scheme, and, by implication, a desire to act in accordance with it. Aragorn is composing himself as a willing participant in the larger story. He assumes that his heart and his reason will not be in conflict, that, if his heart says "no" to one path, then either that path is wrong or his heart has not been fully informed. Tolkien isn't portraying an emotive, "follow your bliss" approach to making choices, but one in which imagination, reason, and the heart's demands—the demands of love—are fully in concord. Internal discord is an indication that the truth has not yet been reached. Despite the exigencies of the circumstances, Aragorn takes the time to make sure he decides correctly before going ahead. Once he makes up his mind, internal struggle ceases. He is single-minded. "Forth the Three Hunters!" he cries: "On and on he led them, tireless and swift, now that his mind was at last made up" (420).

As night falls on the first day of their pursuit of the Orcs, Aragorn must make another choice: whether to keep going in the dark and chance losing the trail, or to rest and allow the Orcs to get farther ahead. Legolas says that his heart urges him on, but he gives the decision to Aragorn, who replies, "You give the choice to an ill chooser. . . . Since we passed through the Argonath my choices have gone amiss" (426). Aragorn decides to wait until daybreak; once again, reason and the heart have concurred. Losing the trail in the dark is too big a risk.

It is a very Christian perception that what looks like failure on Good Friday is often triumph thereafter. A role that looks inconsequential or vain may not be, and Aragorn goes wrong, though not badly, in failing to see this. When Gimli wishes that they had the Phial that Galadriel had given to Frodo to light their way for a nighttime pursuit, Aragorn replies:

> 'It will be more needed where it is bestowed. . . . With him lies the true Quest. Ours is but a small matter in the great deeds of this time. A vain pursuit from its beginning, maybe, which no choice of mine can mar or mend. Well, I have chosen. So let us use the time as best we may!' (426)

Aragorn is correct that the Phial is with the right person—he would not presume to second-guess Galadriel. And his declaration that they must use the time, according to his decision, in the best way possible, is also true, an echo of Gandalf's declaration to Frodo, "All we have to decide is what to do with the time that is given us" (51). But although he is right, in a sense, that Frodo has "the true Quest," Aragorn's decisions—together with a chain of events he has no part in—are critical to Frodo's success. Events in Rohan and Gondor, though far from Frodo, will help him get the Ring to Mt. Doom, and this is part of Tolkien's genius for plotting. The moral point is thoroughly Christian: in a universe ordered by love, the effects of good deeds cannot be calculated and may have far wider impact than one would guess.

When Aragorn, Legolas, and Gimli are reunited with the resurrected Gandalf, he explains that their pursuit has not been vain, but exactly right. Because of their abduction by Saruman's Orcs (as Saruman double-crossed Sauron and attempted to get the Ring for himself), Merry and Pippin have ended up in Fangorn Forest, where their news will stir the angry Ents into action against Eisengard. Moreover, the pursuit has brought Aragorn to the exact point of the battlefield where he is most needed, Rohan:

'Come, Aragorn, son of Arathorn!' he said. 'Do not regret your choice in the valley of the Emyn Muil, nor call it a vain pursuit. You chose amid doubts the path that seemed right: the choice was just, and it has been rewarded. For so we have met in time, who otherwise might have met too late. But the quest of your companions is over. Your next journey is marked by your given word.' (500)

Aragorn's "given word" is to Éomer, who, contrary to the laws of Rohan, has lent him three horses, on condition that Aragorn return them when he can. Both strategic need and moral duty, Gandalf tells him, point the way to Edoras. Aragorn's council with Éomer in "The Riders of Rohan" picks up many of these themes about reading the world and decision-making. It affirms both the sacramental nature of the world and how a man must act in it.

Éomer is amazed to see a Dwarf, an Elf, and a Man together, and more amazed yet that they claim to have been to Lothlórien and have escaped, and that Aragorn is heir to throne of Gondor. Finally, Éomer believes Aragorn, but is still amazed: "Do we walk in legends or on the green earth in the daylight?" he asks. Aragorn's reply is Chestertonian[3]: "The green earth, say you? That is a mighty matter of legend, though you tread it under the light of day!" (434). What we take for granted, day after day, is a miracle, a "matter of legend," and, as Tolkien says, it is the function of fairy stories to help us recover that insight.

After hearing Aragorn, the amazed Éomer asks how a man can judge what to do in such times. Aragorn replies like his teacher Gandalf: "Good and ill have not changed since yesteryear; nor are they one thing among Elves and Dwarves and another among Men. *It is a man's part to discern them*, as much in the Golden Wood as in his own house" (my emphasis; 438). Good and evil do not change—we have that set standard to go by. Ecclesiastes 12:13 says, "Let us hear the conclusion of the whole matter: Fear God, and keep his commandments: for this is the whole duty of

---

3 Chesterton's work is saturated with the understanding that the world, properly seen, is astonishing throughout. See especially *Orthodoxy* (San Francisco: Ignatius Press, 1995).

man."[4] Given a transcendental standard of morality, one's main task is to make decisions in accord with it, no matter what the consequences. This is what separates a sacramental world from Mordor. In addition, people must *discern* the path God wants them to follow, a term of art in Ignatian practice, in which "motions of the soul" are considered, until clarity of direction is achieved. When Aragorn, after a period of silence, declares that *his heart* has told him what to do, it means that he has a global sense of rightness about his choice, though doubt creeps in again.

What Tolkien outlines for us in these episodes with Aragorn, Sam, Éomer, and Gandalf is an ideal Christian decision-making process, in which choices are based on the harmonious working of the imagination, which provides the data, the reason, which critiques it, and the will, which then acts. Presiding over this at every stage is love, which informs Sam's imagination about Frodo's path and Aragorn's decision to rescue Merry and Pippin. When Aragorn tells Éomer that good and ill do not change, he is saying, in other words, that love must be engaged at all points of decision-making. If it is not, we will miss seeing things and pursue the wrong things.

Aragorn and Sam deeply inhabit the present moment to make the right decisions. Jean-Pierre de Caussade, in *Abandonment to Divine Providence*, says of "the sacrament of the present moment":

> God speaks to every individual through what happens to them moment by moment. . . . The events of each moment are stamped with the will of God . . . we find all that is necessary in the present moment[5] . . . faith sees the Creator acting in all things.[6]

The desire Caussade describes is to discern the voice of God in the present "sacramental" moment and follow it. We are in a story, Tolkien believes, written by Christ, the Logos, and we know the general contours of the story and what it requires. We

---

4 I've quoted the King James version in this case; the Douay-Reims uses much less elegant language: "Let us all hear together the conclusion of the discourse. Fear God, and keep his commandments: for this is all man."

5 de Caussade, *Abandonment*, 20.

6 Ibid., 36.

may struggle to understand our specific part in that story, but we do know that love is the guide. The same holds in Middle-earth.

Sam Gamgee Finds himself in a Bigger Story

Aragorn's heart-felt decision is repeated in Sam, who also does his best to use his head and his heart. In Sam we see how the heart forms the imagination, allowing him to see things that others miss. In "The Breaking of the Fellowship," as he and Aragorn scramble around Amon Hen looking for Frodo, Sam is the first to understand where Frodo has gone; Sam understands Frodo better than anyone, because he loves him more. Sam is able to put himself in Frodo's position and understand what Frodo would do. It becomes instantly clear that Frodo has gone off toward Mordor on his own. Sam's love for Frodo informs his imagination—even his limited appreciation for Boromir comes into play—and when he sees the truth, he doesn't need to make a decision. His plan has always been to stick with Frodo. His will is engaged.

On Cirith Ungol, when Sam believes that Frodo is dead from Shelob's sting, but then overhears the Orcs who take Frodo's body say that he has only been put to sleep, he berates himself, saying "You fool, he isn't dead, and your heart knew it. Don't trust your head, Samwise, it is not the best part of you. The trouble with you is that you never really had any hope" (740). If any character in *The Lord of the Rings* has a big heart, it is Sam, though even his is an imperfect one. But, as Tolkien acknowledged in his letters, Sam does suffer from small mindedness, and he lets his inadequate reason sometimes close his heart, when his heart ought to be opening his mind. Although Sam is too hard on himself here, he has, in general, understood himself correctly.

✠

Hellenic philosophy and Christianity bring together the sense that life is a particular kind of story: a quest for the good. For Plato, the meaning of life is the pursuit of the Good, and all human beings are duty bound to seek it. Aristotle agrees and calls the highest good "happiness." For Christians, happiness and the highest good are union with Christ, and this is conceived as a quest by Augustine, who, in *Confessions*, describes his life as a search for God: "You made us for yourself and our hearts find no peace until they rest in you."[7] God, then, has made human beings questers after Himself. This quest is pursued with the baptized virtues of Greek and Roman classicism: prudence, justice, temperance, and fortitude, and the three Christian virtues of faith, hope, and love, above all, self-sacrificing love. These virtues develop during the quest, and their development is indeed part of the goal of the quest.

The Hobbits start as decent but unremarkable people. Their quest is to protect the good they know, their homes, and their friends, but, as they proceed, they find themselves in a vaster world, and their sense of the good increases proportionately. Their commitments broaden: Merry's to Théoden and Éowyn, Pippin's to Faramir and Gandalf, Frodo's to Gollum, Sam's to the Elves, Gimli's to Galadriel, and Gimli's and Legolas's to each other. They find themselves fighting for an entire world that they barely knew existed. In the process, they develop the virtues and receive the grace to complete their quest. In seeking the good, they learn what the good is. "A quest is always an education both as to the character of that which is sought and in self-knowledge."[8]

Tolkien is very careful to give all his characters a discernible past, a starting point, but he is most careful with his four Hobbits. It may seem eccentric to start a novel with a parodic encyclopedia entry, "Concerning Hobbits," which gives a detailed and comically pedantic summary of Hobbit history, geography, agriculture, genealogy, social customs, and special achievements, such as the invention of the "art" of smoking pipeweed. But Tolkien wants us to understand that no one begins a quest without a moral starting point. The Hobbits inherit their roles from the very soil on which they plant their furry feet, from their family histories (Baggins, Brandybucks, and Tooks being more than

---

7 Saint Augustine, *Confessions*, trans. R.S. Pine-Coffin (London: Penguin, 1961), 21.

8 MacIntyre, *After Virtue*, 219.

usually up for an adventure) and from the culture they are born in: a slow-paced, agrarian life that requires work, but provides plenty of time for leisure. It is a culture marked by a traditional happiness that satisfies the basic bodily pleasures: eating well, smoking pipeweed, and drinking ale; a love of celebration (especially birthdays); an indifference (for the most part) to the accumulation of property; and a tendency to smug satisfaction and insularity. Frodo bears the Ring, because he wants to protect the Shire, and Sam, Merry, and Pippin go with Frodo because they love him. But, as they begin to understand what the Ring is, they all become defenders of the Shire and then the world.

They reach the apogees of their quest in self-sacrificial moments: Merry in the battle of Pelennor Fields, Pippin before the Black Gate, and Sam and Frodo at the Cracks of Doom. When they return to the Shire, they realize they have been part of a story whose bounds were far wider than they'd ever expected.

The most self-reflective passage in *The Lord of the Rings* occurs in "The Stairs of Cirith Ungol," when Sam speculates that he and Frodo have wound up in a story. He has listened to the brave things in old tales and songs, assuming that adventures were trips wonderful folk looked for, to make life more exciting, like Bilbo's story of his adventures with Thorin Oakenshield. But he realizes that, in the "tales that really matter," folk just seemed to land in them, that "their paths were laid that way, as you put it." In other words, they are following an ordained route, one that God had laid before their feet:

> 'I expect they had lots of chances, like us, of turning back, only they didn't. And if they had, we shouldn't know, because they'd have been forgotten. We hear about those as just went on—and not all to a good end, mind you; at least not to what folk inside a story and not outside it call a good end.' (711)

Sam considers the possibility of abandoning the quest. Free will allows that abandonment, but it is perforce also an abandonment of love and shrinks the soul and the world. Sam wonders whether he and Frodo are in a happy adventure, like Mr. Bilbo's, or one of the "tales that really matter," which may end unhappily: *"I wonder what sort of tale we've fallen into"* (712). It is, perhaps, the basic question a human being asks, and, if no satisfactory answer can be found, life drifts into a chaotic, meaningless jumble. When Denethor in despair abandons his quest for the good of Gondor, his only alternative is suicide. No story is left to hold his life together.

Sam's major revelation comes, when he realizes he is in a story that is far bigger than even the War of the Ring. The tale goes back at least as far as Beren's quest for the Silmarils, to win the hand of Luthien:

> 'Beren now, he never thought he was going to get that Silmaril from the Iron Crown in Thangorodrim, and yet he did, and that was a worse place and a blacker danger than ours. But that's a long tale, of course, and goes on past the happiness and into grief and beyond it—and the Silmaril went on and came to Eärendil. And why, sir, I never thought of that before! We've got—you've got some of the light of it in that star-glass the Lady gave you! Why, to think of it, we're in the same tale still! It's going on. Don't the great tales never end?' (712)

Frodo quietly replies that they don't end—only the parts people have to play; "Our part will end later or sooner."

Readers had to wait twenty years for *The Silmarillion* to be published, before they saw the tales Tolkien had imagined before he wrote *The Lord of the Rings,* and then they found out about Beren, Luthien, Eärendil, and much more. But even without this knowledge, readers sensed the vast history behind *The Lord of the Rings,* which Tolkien had started in the hospital in 1917, while recovering from trench fever. This sense of the past and its importance is another facet of the Christian imagination. Everything that has happened since the beginning of the world is part of a story that tells Christians who they are.

Sam's shock, that his story is directly connected to a larger story that has been unfolding as the history of Middle-earth is exactly the opposite of the shock one feels as a tiny consciousness looking out into a universe that makes people disappear. That is the shock of modernity. Sam's shock is to find that he is in a story that *does* make sense; and, though it is vast and sublime, it does not decrease the meaning of his quest, but increases it.

This is Tolkien's fundamental metaphysical position. We live in a universe where it does make sense to understand our lives as stories embedded in the larger story of human history, which in turn is embedded in a meaningful Creation, one that was ordered into existence by love. If this were not true, the actions of all Tolkien's characters would be insane, inconsequential, random. All the reasons that they give for their actions would be delusions, as Denethor finally comes to believe.

Camilla Unwin, the daughter of Tolkien's publisher, Rayner Unwin, wrote to Tolkien once as part of a school project, asking him to answer the question, "What is the purpose of life?" Tolkien answered, in part:

> If you do not believe in a personal God the question: 'What is the meaning of life?' is unaskable and unanswerable. To whom or what would you address the question?
>
> Those who believe in a personal God, Creator, do not think the Universe is in itself worshipful, though devoted study of it may be one of the ways of honouring Him. And while as living creatures we are (in part) within it and part of it, our ideas of God and ways of expressing them will be largely derived from contemplating the world about us. . . .
>
> So it may be that the chief purpose in life . . . is to increase according to our capacity our knowledge of God by all the means we have, and to be moved by it to praise and thanks. To do as we say in the Gloria in Excelsis: . . . We praise you, we call you holy, we worship you, we proclaim your glory, we thank you for the greatness of your splendour.[9]

The acceptance of a loveless universe leads to T.S. Eliot's Wasteland and Tolkien's Mordor, a splendorless world that cannot be understood, in which "meaning" has no meaning. The first importance of Tolkien's sacramental vision is that it declares the universe to be a meaningful place, the second is that we have access to this meaning as a grace conferred by creation itself, the third is that we can act meaningfully in the world. That Tolkien strives to create a beautiful, wondrous world for his Hobbits to

9 *Letters*, 400.

walk through is part of his general declaration that the world is graced. But even in Tolkien's glorious sub-creation, there are specific moments when the sacramental nature of reality is especially powerful, and these bear resemblance to the formal sacraments of the Church, both in what they accomplish and how they do it.

7

Discernment and Calling on the Way to Amon Hen

"For each one of us, there is only one thing necessary: to fulfill our own destiny, according to God's will, to be what God wants us to be."
Thomas Merton[1]

"He does not call those who are worthy, but those whom He pleases."
Thérèse of Lisieux[2]

I<small>N</small> *The Fellowship of the Ring*, the first book of *The Lord of the Rings*, we follow Frodo.[3] Tolkien moves back and forth from omniscient narrative to one more limited to Frodo's perspective, where we perceive the world mainly from his standpoint and get far more of his interiority than any other character's. This enables Tolkien to make Frodo a Christian Everyhobbit—not in

1 *No Man is An Island* (NY: Harcourt, 1983), 131.
2 *Story of a Soul: The Autobiography of St. Thérèse of Lisieux* (Washington, DC: ICS Publications, 1976), 13.
3 On patterns of "following" in narrative, see Rick Altman, *A Theory of Narrative* (NY: Columbia University Press, 2008). Using the Hobbit point of view pushes Tolkien's narrative toward the commonplace and novelistic and away from the epic and thus provides a comfortable viewpoint for modern readers. Tolkien almost always follows the Hobbits, and different ones at different times, which is part of the genius of splitting them to three different parts of the battlefield. In "The Taming of Sméagol," Tolkien switches to Sam as the viewpoint Hobbit, which he must do to keep Frodo as the focal character. Through Sam's eyes, he can most effectively show what the Ring is doing to Frodo.

174

the sense that Frodo is typical, but because his path illustrates the diastolic and systolic of Christian spiritual life and is marked, roughly, by the stages of Christian maturation, which Tolkien describes in baptismal scenes, as we have seen, in his confirmation by Elrond as Ring-bearer, and in Eucharistic scenes of self-sacrifice. Frodo follows a path of maturation that Tolkien sees as the universally right path—the Catholic quest.

Frodo's journey can be divided into three parts. The first takes him from the Shire to Rivendell. This baptismal journey, marked by descent into death, resistance to evil, and rescue by higher powers, prepares him to carry the Ring to Mordor, though, along the way, he still hopes to be rid of the task, believing that, once he gets to Rivendell, somehow someone else will take responsibility for the Ring. The second part of his journey, from Rivendell to Amon Hen, leads to another confirmation with Galadriel and his decision to head toward Mordor alone. He accepts that disposing of the Ring is his special task and he is strengthened to complete it. The last third of his quest is the hardest, the Eucharistic quest of sacrificing himself to annihilate the Ring, to dump an immense piece of cosmic sin into the Cracks of Doom. Self-sacrificial love is the Christian vocation, in whatever manner it is exercised. "Do you really want this vocation?" Jesus asks James and John, when they look for status in the kingdom of heaven. "Are you able to drink the cup that I drink and be baptized with the baptism that I am baptized with?" (Mark 10:38). That is the question Frodo confronts at the end of *The Fellowship of the Ring*.

The second half of *The Fellowship* is sacramentally structured by confirmation, which was introduced as a sacrament about the year 200. It took place at the time of baptism and was seen as an extension of baptism.[4] It is held to have much the same

---

4 The bishop would lay his hands on the baptized, seal them by making the sign of the cross on their foreheads with oil, and pray for the blessing of the Holy Spirit. As the church grew and expanded into remote areas, bishops could not handle every convert personally. Priests began to do the baptisms and bishops confirmations. This has continued, and confirmation is something of an odd sacrament, described by some as "a sacrament in search of a theology." William J. Bausch, *A New Look at the Sacraments* (Mystic, CT: Twenty-Third Publications, 2006), 92.

function as baptism, augmenting baptismal gifts. "The effect of the sacrament of Confirmation is the special outpouring of the Holy Spirit, as once granted to the apostles on the day of Pentecost."[5] It brings about a "deepening of baptismal grace" by uniting the confirmed "more firmly to Christ," increasing the gifts of the Holy Spirit; "rendering [the Christian's] bond with the Church more perfect," "giving special strength to spread and defend the faith by word and action as true witnesses of Christ, to confess the name of Christ boldly, and never be ashamed of the cross."[6]

The grace or "charism" associated with confirmation is that specifically given to pursue one's individual calling as a Christian. Karl Rahner distinguishes the grace of baptism from that of confirmation by their "directions":

> The grace of God has a double direction or movement. It is the grace of dying with Christ, a grace of the cross, of the downfall of the world, of being taken out of the aeon of the law, death, sin, and also of all aims and purposes that belong to this world alone. All that is expressed in baptism as a descent into death with Christ.

Frodo has made that descent three times. His inner life changes. He becomes tougher, more courageous, and more knowledgeable with each encounter. But now he will experience the other movement of grace, outwards, which helps him assume the specific role of Ring-bearer:

> [At] the same time the grace of Christ is the grace of incarnation, a grace of acceptance of the world for its transfiguration, a grace the victory of which will be visible in the world, in its healing, preservation, redemption from the nothingness to which it is subject, and such a grace is also one of mission to the world, work in the world, world-transformation. The particular function of the grace that is given more particularly to the individual as his special task is decided by God's vocation [for the individual] and by the distribution of the charismata of

5 *Catechism of the Catholic Church*, no. 1302, 330.
6 Ibid.

the Spirit, which are nothing but the special directions in which one and the same Spirit unfolds its action.[7]

The gifts of the Holy Spirit are traditionally said to be wisdom, understanding, wonder and awe (fear of the Lord), right judgment, courage, knowledge and reverence.[8] In addition, the Holy Spirit bestows individual "charismata," special talents to be used in the service of God. The gift of healing is an example, manifested in Aragorn, as he becomes king,[9] but "charismata" include Legolas's ability with a bow and Sam's loyalty to Frodo. The gifts of the Holy Spirit catalyze in their receivers twelve traditional fruits: charity, joy, peace, patience, kindness, goodness, generosity, gentleness, faithfulness, modesty, self-control, chastity.[10]

The sacrament of confirmation, then, administered by the bishop, confers the grace to pursue the various vocations that God ordains for confirmed Christians. It affirms the particular gifts—charisms—of the confirmands. All are ordered by self-sacrificing love, in one walk of life or another. This is what happens to Frodo. Following the metaphorical drownings of his "baptisms," Frodo solidifies his vocation as Ring-bearer by the confirmations of those who, like the bishop, have spiritual authority: Gandalf, Elrond, and Galadriel.

Confirmation and decision-making, especially having to do with vocation, go together; much of *The Lord of the Rings* is about decision-making in the midst of spiritual warfare. This is Ignatian territory, and the spiritual exercises of St. Ignatius Loyola may have provided Tolkien a model for thinking about discernment of spirits and for understanding the terrain of the Christian spiritual life. Given that Tolkien's oldest son, John, was a priest who trained at a Jesuit Seminary (Stonyhurst College), that Tolkien

---

7 Karl Rahner, *The Church and the Sacraments* (London: Burns and Oates, 1963), 91.

8 This list goes back to early church fathers, who write about it with great familiarity, including Augustine, John Cassian, and Hilary of Poitiers. See *Catechism*, section 1831, 450.

9 In 1 Cor. 12 Paul provides a long list of special graces, among them healing; see also Rom. 12:6–8.

10 *Catechism*, no. 1832, 451; based upon Gal. 5:22–23.

corresponded with Jesuits, read the poetry of Gerard Manley Hopkins, virtually grew up in the Birmingham Oratory, was fostered there by Fr. *Francis Xavier* Morgan, and even encouraged the conversion of Robert Murray, who became a Jesuit and a close friend of the Tolkien family,[11] it is a reasonable speculation that Tolkien knew about Ignatian meditation techniques and "discernment of spirits."

Discernment has an intimate connection with confirmation and quest, in that it helps the Christian answer the perpetual question, "What now?" The rules developed by St. Ignatius, the founder of the Jesuit Order, are meant to discern between the promptings of good and evil spirits, where "spirit" is meant in the broad sense of an interior prompting, whether the origin is physical, psychological, spiritual, or a combination of these. Ignatius teaches that these incitements to action arise out of two spiritual states, those of "consolation" and "desolation." He analyzes the spiritual life as an oscillation between these states and gives advice on how to recognize them, how to recognize the spirits that proceed from them as good or evil, and what actions to take in response. Frodo experiences a pattern of desolation and consolation that we have already seen established in *The Fellowship of the Ring*. Frodo, Sam, and Pippin are initially pursued by Black Riders, a time of desolation—but then make it to the safety and consolation of Farmer Maggot's house; they are once again pursued by the Riders—but make it to the consolation of baths and dinner provided by Merry and Fatty Bolger at Crickhollow; they are nearly drowned or buried by Old Man Willow—but then are given hospitality by Tom Bombadil and Goldberry; their nearly fatal encounter with the Barrow-wight ends with a naked frolic in the sun and gifts from the treasure hoard; Frodo's wound from the Morgûl blade is tended in the most wonderful place yet, Rivendell. Each episode of desolation is followed by one of consolation, if the Hobbits can hold on. Each period of consolation reenergizes them and affirms the good things their quest seeks to preserve, helping them discern what to do and marshal the will

---

11 See Joseph Pearce, *Tolkien, Man and Myth* (San Francisco: Ignatius, 1998), 101–102.

to do it. This pattern continues until Sam and Frodo leave their companions at Amon Hen for their long and lonely Eucharistic journey to Mt. Doom, where Frodo must go on, even without hope. Without this baptismal and confirmatory path, and without having had experience in discernment, the Eucharistic part of the quest would be impossible for Frodo.[12]

fRoðo the Ring-beaReR

Frodo is appointed the task of bearing the Ring four times: 1) initially by Gandalf, when Frodo is still in the Shire, 2) when he assumes the task voluntarily at the Council of Elrond, as explored in the previous chapter, 3) when he offers Galadriel the Ring and she refuses to take it, and 4) on Amon Hen, when he accepts that he will have to take the Ring into Mordor alone, although Sam goes with him anyway. Each of these is a confirmation of Frodo's calling, and each, except the last, comes after a period of desolation and consolation, during which he accepts once more the vocation thrust on him. In all of them, Frodo contends with opposing "spirits," some of which clearly originate outside himself, but are registered as "voices" or "commands" within his own mind. The most important battleground in the War of the Ring is Frodo's soul. We have seen how evil manifests itself within Frodo as a paralytic attack on his will, either by lulling him to sleep or terrifying him, in his conflicts with Old Man Willow, the Barrow-wight, and the Black Riders at the Ford of the Bruinen, and this spiritual warfare will engage him on Amon Hen, in the caves of Shelob, and on the trek up Mt. Doom. Frodo's good spirits are his native courage and his humility, aided by many within and without the Fellowship.

Frodo begins his career as Ring-bearer without bearing the Ring at all. He gets it in an envelope from Gandalf soon after Bilbo leaves Bag End. "I should not make use of it, if I were you.

---

12 Discernment of spirits is a complicated process, best undertaken with a spiritual director. There are a raft of fine books on the subject by William A. Barry, S.J. and others: Barry's *A Friendship Like No Other* and *Finding God in All Things* provide a good place to begin.

But keep it secret and keep it safe," Gandalf tells him. Frodo has no idea what he has, and even Gandalf's understanding is not yet settled. But in the second meeting, Gandalf is sure that the ring is the One Ring and that it is Frodo's destiny to *bear* it, in all senses of the word.

After many years pass, Gandalf returns again to tell Frodo that the Ring is utterly evil and dangerous to the wearer, who finally will be possessed by its power and begin to fade, if he wears the Ring too long. It is a device for mind-control, contains part of Sauron himself, and, if Sauron gets it back, he will use it to enslave the world.

This long conversation with Gandalf inaugurates Frodo's call. He is in much the same position as an Old Testament prophet, like Moses, who initially sees his calling as both impossible and catastrophic: "Who am I to go to Pharaoh and bring the sons of Israel, out of Egypt? . . . What if they will not believe me or listen to my words?" (Exodus 3:11; 4:1).

When Frodo realizes that he and The Shire are in great danger because of the Ring, his first instinct is to get rid of it. Gandalf, however, tells him that he, like Bilbo, has been handed a vocation, whether he likes it or not. Bilbo was meant to find the Ring and Frodo to have it:

> 'Behind that [Bilbo's finding the Ring] there was something else at work, beyond any design of the Ring-maker. I can put it no plainer than by saying that Bilbo was *meant* to find the Ring, and *not* by its maker. In which case you also were meant to have it. And that may be an encouraging thought.' (original emphasis; 56)

It is *not* an encouraging thought to Frodo, who says "I wish I had never seen the Ring! Why did it come to me? Why was I chosen?" (61).

Gandalf answers that the choice of Frodo must be right, despite the lack of any obvious reason:

> 'Such questions cannot be answered,' said Gandalf. 'You may be sure that it was not for any merit that others do not possess: not for power or wisdom, at any rate. But you have been cho-

sen, and you must therefore use such strength and heart and wits as you have.' (61)

Why Frodo has been chosen becomes clear as the novel progresses. He has the right charisms: great courage and endurance, and great love for the Shire and Gandalf, which finally extends to Men and Elves and all of Middle-earth. He is truly humble—perhaps the least temptable of Hobbits, the one creature in Middle-earth capable of enduring the Ring and taking it all the way to the Cracks of Doom. Gandalf understands that even he himself has too great a desire for power to perform the task. When Frodo begs him to take the Ring, Gandalf's answer is the clearest statement of why it must be Frodo:

> 'With that power I should have power too great and terrible. And over me the ring would gain a power still greater and more deadly . . . . I do not wish to become like the Dark Lord himself. Yet the way of the Ring to my heart is by pity, pity for weakness and the desire of strength to do good. . . . The wish to wield it would be too great for my strength.' (61)

Gandalf's very strengths make him a weak Ring-bearer. He knows that callings are individual and not to be usurped by or passed off to another, even though superficially the uncalled person may seem the better qualified.

Frodo is prepared for the Council of Elrond by his long period of convalescence in Rivendell. In Ignatian terms, it is a time of "consolation," and Elrond's house offers Frodo many of the consolations Tolkien discusses in "Of Fairy Stories," not least of all stories and a reunion with Bilbo, who has retired there:

> That house was, as Bilbo had long ago reported, 'a perfect house, whether you like food or sleep or story-telling or singing, or just sitting and thinking best, or a pleasant mixture of them all.' Merely to be there was a cure for weariness, fear, and sadness. (225)

He enters a world that is closer to eternity than the human: "Time doesn't seem to pass here: it just is" (231). Frodo is put under a healing spell, simply by being with the Elves, who, like Tom Bombadil, love to sing. And even though Frodo doesn't know Elvish, the words of the songs convey meaning. The logos of Elvish is not a barrier but a portal:

> At first the beauty of the melodies and of the interwoven words in elven-tongues, even though he understood them little, held him in a spell, as soon as he began to attend to them. Almost it seemed that the words took shape, and visions of far lands and bright things that he had never yet imagined opened out before him; and the firelit hall became like a golden mist above seas of foam that sighed upon the margins of the world. . . . There he wandered in a dream of music that turned into running water. (239)

The Elvish words are translucent to reality. They are comparatively free of linguistic corruption, and through them Frodo sees the glory of the world and its fundamental sacramentality, going from the logos of elven-song to the Music of the Ainur, captured in the flow of water. In this moment, Frodo gets a taste of divine love. He sees Elrond, Aragorn, and Arwen together in a kind of Trinitarian tableau, the love of which includes him:

> Elrond was in his chair and the fire was on his face like summer-light upon the trees. Near him sat the Lady Arwen. To his surprise Frodo saw that Aragorn stood beside her; his dark cloak was thrown back, and he seemed to be clad in elven-mail, and a star shone on is breast. They spoke together, and then suddenly it seemed to Frodo that Arwen turned toward him, and *the light of her eyes fell on him from afar and pierced his heart.* (emphasis added; 238)

The Trinity, "that sweet society,"[13] which shares love from the beginning, sets it into the frame of the world and orders it accordingly, gives out love as part of its nature. Thus, "God is love,"[14] says St. John, and desires mankind to participate in that love. As the Trinity communicates its love to the world, Elrond, Arwen, and Aragorn, for a moment form a trinity of their own and communicate their love to Frodo. Arwen, who for an instant

---

13 The phrase is that of the famous Puritan preacher and theologian, Jonathan Edwards.

14 1 John 4:8.

becomes an emblem of the Holy Spirit, shares it with him: "the light of her eyes fell on him from afar and pierced his heart." Gimli will have this experience with Galadriel. Both the light and the piercing of the heart are important. In John's first letter, it is light that unifies, just as the light from Arwen's eyes unifies Frodo with the tableau of Elrond, Aragorn, and Arwen: "[I]f we live our lives in the light, as he [God] is in the light, we are in union with one another, and the blood of Jesus, his Son, purifies us from all sin" (1 John 4:7). Frodo is comforted by unifying love, purified by it, and it is love which pierces his heart and so serves as the anti-type to the evil blade with which the Nazgûl king had meant to pierce Frodo's heart. The piercing of hatred and enslavement is replaced by piercing love. This period of consolation and this moment especially prepare Frodo for the Council of Elrond and his confirmation as Ring-bearer.

At the Council, though Frodo feels an "overwhelming long-ing" to remain at peace with Bilbo, it would be a "false consola-tion" to do so. Evenly poised between the wrong choice and the right one, Frodo gets help from another Will, and he hears him-self say the words he cannot quite say on his own: "I will take the Ring . . . though I do not know the way" (270).

Sam Gamgee's discernment and vocational calling are con-firmed before Frodo's, which hints at the role of providence in both their vocations. In the Shire, Sam had decided to follow Frodo no matter what. That is sealed by another authority, Gildor Inglorion, when they meet the Elves on their first night out: "*Don't you leave him! they said to me. Leave him! I said. I never mean to. I am going with him, if he climbs to the Moon*" (87). Sam's role is once again confirmed by Elrond, who acknowledges that Frodo and Sam cannot be separated. Sam's vocation is as impor-tant as Frodo's, so much so that Sam will himself become Ring-bearer for a while and then bearer of the Ring-bearer.

Boromir Takes his Brother's Call

Tolkien sets off Frodo and Sam's confirmatory episodes with an anti-type, Boromir's bad decision to take Faramir's call away from him and answer it in his stead. Here, Tolkien gives us an example of an anti-confirmation. Boromir, son of Denethor, who rules Gondor as Steward, tells the Council that, on the eve of the sudden attack on the bridge at Osgiliath, which he, his brother Faramir, and their troops were holding, his brother had a dream, which came to him often thereafter, and then once to Boromir himself. In the dream he hears a voice crying:

> *Seek for the Sword that was broken:*
> In Imladris it dwells;
> There shall be counsels taken
> Stronger than Morgul-spells.
> There shall be shown a token
> That Doom is near at hand,
> For Isildur's Bane shall waken,
> *And the Halfling forth shall stand.* (246)

Imladris is Rivendell, where Boromir has come. At the beginning of the Council, he stares at Frodo and Bilbo in astonishment—he has never seen Hobbits before, or even known of their existence, but there stand the Halflings. He learns that Aragorn is Isildur's heir and has the broken blade that cut the Ring off Sauron's finger, signifying that Aragorn is the rightful king of Gondor. And Frodo has "Isildur's Bane," the ring that led to Isildur's death.

Explaining why he has come, Boromir says, "[M]y brother, seeing how desperate was our need, was eager to heed the dream and seek for Imladris; but since the way was full of doubt and danger, I took the journey upon myself" (246). It does not seem to occur to Boromir that the quest of the Ring is not his but his brother's. Out of his Beowulfian pride and, perhaps, an undervaluing of his brother's strengths, Boromir usurps his calling. (Boromir has been given the dream only once, and probably so that he can understand Faramir's need to go to Rivendell and encourage *him* to follow the quest of the dream. Boromir's dream is like the dream that explains Mary's pregnancy to Joseph—it is sent on behalf of another.) Boromir's mistake will get him killed and seem to put the quest in jeopardy by splitting off Frodo and Sam from the rest of the Fellowship.

We do not know Faramir yet, even by name, since Boromir only refers to him as "my brother." However, when he appears later, we see why it was his calling to go with Frodo and not Boromir's. A student of Gandalf's, Faramir has the same spiritual qualities as Frodo and would not be tempted to use the Ring. Faramir later tells Frodo that, if the Ring were lying in the road, he wouldn't stoop to pick it up, and we come to realize Faramir has spoken the truth. Faramir's natural humility and carefulness, as opposed to Boromir's pride and rashness, make him stand out from the rest of his family and would have made him an ideal member of the Fellowship.

As with the character pairs, Théoden-Denethor, Gandalf-Saruman, and Frodo-Gollum, Tolkien uses the Faramir and Boromir pair to explore the range of human potential. In the Council of Elrond, Boromir becomes the foil for Frodo, taking a quest that is not his, while Frodo, if he could, would like to give his quest to someone else. Boromir's quest is ultimately disconfirmed, while, from this point on, Frodo's is confirmed by all figures in authority and events to come. Frodo is moved by a will not his own, which is "using his small voice." Boromir makes his voice heard over his brother's—and the sender of the dream. In Frodo's case, we have successful discernment, in Boromir's, failure. Boromir is not the first character we have seen to "blow it" in response to a call. Gandalf had called upon Barliman Butterbur to deliver the crucial message to Frodo to start his journey, but Butterbur, the beleaguered host of the Prancing Pony, simply forgets. As Gandalf ruefully notes, "fat men who sell ale have many calls to answer" (261), and the important one gets lost.

Moria and the Crown of Durin

The Fellowship leaves Rivendell at dusk on December 25, according to Tolkien's chronology.[15] On the basis of John's Gospel, with the birth of Christ, light comes into the world at a time in Jewish history that seems darkest. Israel is oppressed and occupied by the Romans, and the destruction of the Temple and the razing of Jerusalem are only 70 years away, a destruction so thorough that Josephus claims over a million people were killed. Into this seem-

---

15 Appendix B of *The Lord of the Rings*, 1092.

ingly hopeless situation, Christ, "the light that enlightens all men," is born, and out of the wreck comes salvation. When Frodo leaves Rivendell, darkness seems at its greatest. Gondor is besieged and losing a war that promises to end in its total destruction. If Sauron wins, Rivendell and Lothlórien will eventually be destroyed. No one has much hope, and the darkness seems to progress as *The Lord of the Rings* advances, but Tolkien's picking of December 25 as the beginning of the Fellowship's quest is a bit of eucatastrophic irony: the world is better than his heroes believe or can know (which also goes for readers who have not been to *The Lord of the Rings'* appendices, the only place the date is mentioned!). With the decision of the Council and Frodo's willingness to bear the Ring into Mordor and destroy it, light begins to enter the world at its darkest hour. Although resistance to Sauron may seem more hopeless, and the future of the world progressively darker, as Tolkien takes us toward the siege of Minas Tirith and the cave of Shelob, on the day Frodo leaves Rivendell, he and the Fellowship begin their participation in a world where light is coming back.

Tolkien goes out of his way to make the light/dark imagery of St. John a physical reality in *The Lord of the Rings*. The date of December 25, close enough to the winter solstice, signals the turning point at which the days grow longer. Frodo prepares to leave Bag End on September 22, the day of the autumnal equinox, and does so the following day. On March 25, the vernal equinox, as set in the Julian calendar, Gollum bites the finger off Frodo's hand and falls with the Ring into the Cracks of Doom. Tolkien has deliberately framed his story between the equinoxes, using December 25 as the midpoint, with a descent into darkness and from there an ascent into light. Light begins to overcome darkness at the vernal equinox—hence Easter's close location to that point. This is a yearly replication of the pattern of desolation and consolation that Ignatius explicates in his rules and, above all, another way in which the Logos makes itself known in a natural cycle. From the Fellowship's perspective, however, the world is not coming out of the darkness, but entering it.

The first evil the Fellowship must confront is the path over Caradhras, the Red Horn gate, where the Hobbits nearly freeze to death in a snowstorm, and the Fellowship is forced to take the path through the mines of Moria, a descent into death like the Barrow-wight episode, on a grander scale. An entire underground kingdom has become the tomb of Balin and the dwarves who tried to resettle it. Even before the Fellowship enters Moria, it is forced through an anti-baptism, waddling through fetid and stagnant water, rather than the "living" water of a fresh stream. Since Hobbits don't wear shoes, they slog through the polluted water barefoot: "[U]nder the weedy pools were sliding and greasy stones, and footing was treacherous. Frodo shuddered with disgust at the touch of the dark unclean water on his feet" (302).

The Fellowship is confronted with monsters all the way, as they battle "The Watcher," who tries to pull Frodo into the vast, stagnant, lake at the entrance, as well as Orcs, Trolls and finally, the Balrog. As orcs and trolls are Elves and Ents, transformed by the tortures of Morgoth, so Balrogs were once lower-order angels of Gandalf's Maia class. With the Balrog, Gandalf meets another polar opposite. The Balrog is a creature of flame and, paradoxically, darkness; in contrast, the flame that Gandalf wields is one of light. His battle with the Balrog is the most specifically Johannine conflict in *The Fellowship of the Ring*: light going up against dark fire, a servant of the Holy Spirit versus a demon.

Gandalf defends the Bridge of Khazad-dûm, so the rest of the Company can escape, but dies doing it, going into the abyss as the bridge collapses and then fighting the Balrog to the death. Unlike Bombadil's encounter with the Barrow-wight, this fight requires the rescuer to sacrifice his life, so that the others may re-emerge into light and life. The connection between baptism and the Eucharist is explicit in the trip through Moria. Gandalf's Christ-like death is what makes emergence from the tomb possible for the rest of the Fellowship, which proceeds to Lothlórien in grief.

Aragorn says they must do without hope (333), but there are two instances of consolation. Once out of the mines, they pass the small mountain lake, "the Mirrormere, Kheled-zäram." Gimli has been longing to look into it, and he makes a fast detour to get to its shores, along with Frodo and Sam. The property of Mirrormere is to mirror stars, even during broad daylight; the pattern of the stars is a crown, the Crown of Durin, the Dwarf who initially made a kingdom of Moria:

> There like jewels sunk in the deep shone glinting stars, though sunlight was in the sky above. Of their own stooping forms no shadow could be seen.
>
> 'O Kheled-zâram fair and wonderful!' said Gimli. 'There lies the Crown of Durin till he wakes. Farewell!' he bowed, and turned away, and hastened back up the greensward to the road again. (334)

In this scene, we see Tolkien's symbolic imagination in full Coleridgean career: a lake that contains an eternal promise, reflecting two realities, one the surrounding mountains, and the other stars, visible during the day. Are these stars actually in the daylight sky, or are they a reality apart even from that? For Gimli they signify a final crown for Durin, the first of the Dwarves and representative of the race, "when he wakes." It is a promise to the Company, having passed through a kingdom of death, that there is another kingdom. Gimli, Frodo and Sam are given a glimpse of underlying order and glory that should give them hope, an echo of the original Music, a Logos-centric promise of victory, even in death, so profound that it silences the three. It also is a portent that Gandalf has not utterly perished, though they don't read it so. "Be thou faithful unto death: and I will give thee the crown of life" (Revelations 2:10).

Free from Moria, the members of the Company get a chance to wash the muck and pollution from their feet in the River Nimrodel, whose waters carry baptismal grace: "It was cold but its touch was clean, and as he [Frodo] went on and it mounted to his knees, he felt that the strain of travel and all weariness was washed from his limbs" (339).

Tolkien is always demonstrating how sacramental significance emerges from the common practices of life. Here is the "washing of regeneration" in process. Washings just do make us feel better and "lift our spirits." Baptism may occur only once, but baptismal grace again and again, for baptism heightens and intensifies a grace already contained in the Logos-centric foundations of Creation. Though Arda is marred, its sources of joy go all the way down. The Elf Haldir understands this, echoing the proclamation of Ilúvatar in "The Ainulindalë": "though in all lands love is now mingled with grief, it grows perhaps the greater" (349).

In Lothlórien Frodo has another very important confirmatory experience with Galadriel, but this is so tightly connected to the confirmation of the Fellowship as a whole and Galadriel's gift-giving, that I will defer discussing it until the next chapter.

ƒroðo on Amon hen

For Frodo and Boromir, final confirmation—and disconfirmation—comes in the final chapter of *The Fellowship of the Ring*, "The Breaking of the Fellowship." Having made it down the River Anduin to the Falls of Rauros, the Company is split on what to do and where to go. They are prepared to follow Frodo, but he is trying to screw up his courage to go into Mordor alone. Boromir has decided that he has to take the Ring from Frodo and bring it to Gondor. Frodo asks for an hour by himself to decide his course and walks to the top of Amon Hen, the Hill of the Eye, named for the view it commands. Boromir follows him and attempts to get the Ring, first through talk, then through action. Tolkien shows two opposite movements occurring at the same time—Frodo's affirmation of his calling and Boromir's disconfirmation for the quest. When Boromir finds Frodo alone, he becomes his tempter.

Frodo acknowledges his fear to Boromir: "I know what I should do, but I am afraid of doing it, Boromir, afraid." Boromir asks, "Are you sure that you do not suffer needlessly?"

But Frodo is wary of Boromir's advice:

'I think I know already what counsel you would give, Boromir. . . . And it would seem like wisdom but for the warning of my heart . . . [the warning] Against the way that seems easier. Against refusal of the burden that is laid on me. Against—well, if it must be said, against trust in the strength and truth of men.' (397)

Tolkien may have had Matthew 16:21–26 (and Mark 8:33) in mind in composing this scene:

189

Jesus began to shew to his disciples, that he must go to Jerusalem, and suffer many things from the ancients and scribes and
chief priests, and be put to death, and the third day rise again.
And Peter taking him, began to rebuke him, saying: Lord, be it
far from thee, this shall not be unto thee. Who turning, said to
Peter: Go behind me, Satan, thou art a scandal unto me:
because thou savourest not the things that are of God, but the
things that are of men. Then Jesus said to his disciples: If any
man will come after me, let him deny himself, and take up his
cross, and follow me. For he that will save his life, shall lose it:
and he that shall lose his life for my sake, shall find it. For what
doth it profit a man, if he gain the whole world, and suffer the
loss of his own soul? Or what exchange shall a man give for his
soul?

Boromir takes the part of Peter, tempting Frodo not to commit
the necessary sacrifice of going into Mordor, and Frodo takes the
part of Jesus, telling Boromir that he does not trust "the truth of
men." Boromir, like Peter, can only see the typical human solution of fighting fire with fire, in the same way of the Enemy. Like
Jesus to Peter, Frodo tells Boromir his faith in men is misplaced.
His intuitions tell him that refusing the cross and taking "the way
that seems easier" is the opposite of wisdom. Frodo fights within
himself to do the will of God, despite his fears, while Boromir
encourages his desire to avoid the task. When Boromir finally
demands the Ring, Frodo confirms his role: "The Council laid it
upon me to bear it" (399). Then Boromir tries to take the Ring by
force, and Frodo can only escape by putting on the Ring and disappearing.

After struggling with the invisible Hobbit and losing him,
Boromir almost immediately comes to himself. In a sense, he has
been "possessed," and one of the brilliancies of Tolkien is to
show this gradual possession, from the time we meet Boromir at
the Council of Elrond until this point. He is a good person, but
pride is his fatal flaw. He is oriented to seeing enemies on the outside, not within himself, and the Ring has been working on him
as well as Frodo. Later, when Frodo meets Boromir's brother,
Faramir almost guesses what has happened before Frodo and
Sam tell him:

'I can well believe that Boromir, the proud and fearless, often rash, ever anxious for the victory of Minas Tirith (and his own glory therein), might desire [the Ring] and be allured by it. Alas that ever he went on that errand! I should have been chosen by my father and the elders, but he put himself forward, as being the older and the hardier (both true), and he would not be stayed.

'But fear no more! I would not take this thing, if it lay by the highway.' (671)

Faramir proves true to his word, letting Sam and Frodo go to Mordor with the Ring.

The attack by Boromir sends Frodo, invisible, to the top of Amon Hen, where the Ring gives him the power to see what is happening in Middle-earth, from Minas Tirith to Minas Morgul. Frodo sits upon a stone seat and gazes at the forming battle. But the Eye becomes aware of him as well. Here, Tolkien writes the most graphic description of demonic attack in the book:

And suddenly he felt the Eye. There was an eye in the Dark Tower that did not sleep. He knew that it had become aware of his gaze. A fierce eager will was there. It leaped towards him; almost like a finger he felt it, searching for him. Very soon it would nail him down, now just exactly where he was. Amon Lhaw it touched. It glanced upon Tol Brandir—he threw himself from the seat, crouching, covering his head with his grey hood.

He heard himself crying out: *Never, never!* Or was it: *Verily I come I come to you?* He could not tell. Then as a flash from some other point of power there came to his mind another thought: *Take it off! Take it off! Fool, take it off! Take off the Ring!*

The two powers strove in him. For a moment, perfectly balanced between their piercing points, he writhed, tormented. Suddenly he was aware of himself again, Frodo, neither the Voice nor the Eye: free to choose, and with one remaining instant in which to do so. He took the Ring off his finger. (original emphasis; 401)

This is as brilliant a dramatization of "discernment of spirits" as exists in English literature. The "Voice" is Gandalf's, a point Tolkien wants us to miss in our first reading of *The Lord of the*

Rings, but the clues are there: "Fool!" is one of Gandalf's characteristic expressions, and if Frodo has had a tutelary spirit, it is Gandalf. When Ignatius wrote about contending good and evil spirits in the human soul and acting on the good, this was exactly the situation he had in mind. The tempting spirit is met and thwarted by a good spirit, but the tide of the battle must be turned by the free will of the tempted. Frodo is given the temporary grace of Gandalf's intervention, but only for so long as it takes him to mobilize his will to take off the Ring. Frodo has a strong will, and it has been trained in virtue since he left Bag End, trial after trial, or he would be unsuccessful in meeting this challenge. Frodo's baptismal and confirmatory episodes give him the grace and maturity to survive Sauron's assault. He has the final say, but without grace in the form of Gandalf's intervention, he would have been lost.

Gandalf, unknown to Frodo, has been resurrected, "sent back," and so the power he projects through Frodo is truly Christ-like, but, because God grants us free will, it would be wrong for Gandalf to achieve Frodo's victory for him; he can only help. Sauron's attack on Frodo is the final confirmation of Frodo's mission. The great saints, with the greatest tasks, are subject to the blackest attacks, the deepest periods of desolation. The vanguard is always in the thickest part of the fray.

Another baptism and two confirmations occur in this episode. As the Fellowship comes under attack by Uruk-hai, and Frodo makes his way to the river, alone, he pushes off in one of the boats, just as Sam runs to the bank and flings himself into the river after him. Frodo has to return and pull him out. "I drownded," Sam says as Frodo grabs his hand. "It is plain," Frodo concludes, "that we were meant to go together." Sam is baptized and confirmed as Frodo's indispensible companion. They will make the final Eucharistic journey as virtually equal partners. Boromir, who bravely dies defending Merry and Pippin in the Uruk-hai attack, achieves a final confirmation. His role as a great warrior finds him, and he fulfills it.

"Baptisms" and "confirmations" structure much of *The Fellowship of the Ring,* but we do not see so many of them in the rest of *The Lord of the Rings*. They are rituals of initiation, and initiation is over for Frodo and Sam—they understand their goal and are as ready to pursue their quest as they ever will be.

It may seem that I have pushed my argument about baptism and confirmation too far—that every dunking and every vocational confirmation cannot be intended by Tolkien as sacramental. I do believe, however, that is exactly the case, from bath night in Crickhollow to Frodo's anti-baptism in the Dead Marshes. The progression of Christian life lies in closer and closer conformity of the individual soul to Christ, and this is achieved, through grace, by successively dying to the self and rising with a new self, again and again, until the process is complete, even if, as with Niggle, it takes Purgatory to achieve. That Tolkien understood this is evident in many of the letters he wrote to his children, particularly the one to Michael, expressing the need to regularly take "the Blessed Sacrament."[16] Receiving grace through sacramental repetition is the pattern of Catholic life, occurring every time a Roman Catholic enters a church and crosses herself with holy water, remembering her baptism, or goes to communion to participate in the sacrifice and triumph of Christ. It is the pattern of *The Lord of the Rings*.

16 *Letters*, 338.

8

THE FELLOWSHIP CONFIRMED: GALADRIEL AND HER GIFTS

"Gift giving is an intriguing, universal behavior that has yet to be interpreted satisfactorily by social scientists."[1]

"Charity in truth places man before the astonishing experience of gift. Gratuitousness is present in our lives in many different forms, which often go unrecognized because of a purely consumerist and utilitarian view of life. The human being is made for gift, which expresses and makes present his transcendent dimension."
POPE BENEDICT XVI[2]

THE ENCOUNTER of the Fellowship with Galadriel in "The Mirror of Galadriel" and "Farewell to Lórien" is one of the most complex transactions in *The Lord of the Rings*. With Galadriel functioning as priest, it is a reconfirmation not only of Frodo, but the entire Fellowship. It includes a penitential section as a prelude to the confirmations and concludes with gift-giving. Surprisingly, out of all this comes Galadriel's final self- understanding and confirmation of who she is.

There is a clear logic in the progression from confession (requiring an examination and assessment of one's spiritual con-

---

1 John F. Sherry, Jr., "Gift Giving in Anthropological Perspective," *Journal of Consumer Research* 10, no. 2 (Sept. 1983): 157.
2 *Caritas in Veritate*, section 34.

dition and tendencies) to confirming a vocation (inquiring about what one is suited to do and the internal obstacles to doing it) to receiving gifts to aid in the achievement of that vocation. In the Catholic tradition, confirmation is preceded by confession, and, as explained in the preceding chapter, the gifts of the Holy Spirit are increased[3] and individual talents—charisms—recognized.

the figure of galadriel

One of the least convincing criticisms of Tolkien is that he doesn't create complex characters, but merely goodies and baddies. If the modernist idea of a "complex character" is an inner theater of conflicting desires and ambiguities, then there are conflicts aplenty in Tolkien's characters, in the form of self-doubt and temptation—though his good characters are usually able to overcome their temptations, while his bad characters are not. These are made apparent to the reader by the characters' admissions, actions, and their emotional responses to others and the landscapes they travel though. Moreover, Tolkien is interested in human potential, which he explores through character pairs, Gollum representing a dark potential in Frodo and Saruman in Gandalf.

Galadriel is one of Tolkien's most complex characters, a rebel, who defied the Valar to follow Fëanor after the Simarils, who wanted a kingdom of her own to rule, whose athleticism and battle prowess emphasized her masculine character more than her feminine. Her biography is more that of an Amazon or Valkyrie than a spiritual guide.[4] Her shadow double is Shelob. And yet, Tolkien connects her more closely to Mary than anyone in his legendarium except Elbereth (Varda). Her literary ancestors are Melian, the Maia wife of Thingol from *The Silmarillion*, Morgan le Fay, the Celtic goddess Morrígan, and H. Rider Haggard's

---

3 *Catechism of the Catholic Church*, no. 1303, 330.

4 For an analysis of Galadriel as Valkyrie, see Leslie A. Donovan, "The valkyrie reflex in J.R.R. Tolkien's *The Lord of the Rings*: Galadriel, Shelob, Éowyn, and Arwen," in *Tolkien the Medievalist*, ed. Jane Chance (London: Routledge, 2003), 106–132.

Ayesha.[5] For Galadriel, submitting to the will of Erú Ilúvatar takes millennia of tragic experience, and only with her final renunciation of the Ring does her character ultimately conform to Mary's.

Galadriel's roots as a Celtic fertility goddess can be seen in her association with water, which borders so much of Lothlórien: the Nimrodel, the Silverlode, and the Anduin, making Lothlórien a peninsula; and in her Ring Nenya, which is the Ring of Waters. Her gift to Sam not only brings back the vegetation of the Shire, but produces a record number of marriages and children, introducing Galadriel's own blond hair to the Shire. (Galadriel's kinship to fertility goddesses does not put her at odds with Mary, whose only child created the world and was born to renew it entirely.)

When the Fellowship enters Lothlórien, a land on which "no shadow" lies, Frodo senses "a light was upon it for which his language had no name" (350), and Sam says, "this is more Elvish than anything I ever heard tell of. I feel as if I was inside a song, if you take my meaning" (351). Haldir tells them they are feeling the power of the Lady Galadriel, and then they see something unusual. They look across a great expanse, across the River Anduin, and it seems formless, vague, dark, drear. "The sun that lay on Lothlórien had no power to enlighten the shadow of that distant height" (351). Lothlórien is an Edenic realm, but it is surrounded by a darkness which is closing in; it is a besieged island of light in a dark sea. Galadriel uses Nenya to preserve the world of Lothlórien, and therefore the Elves as well, for their lives are connected with the life of Arda, and, if it fails, so do they. But her power has the limited range of Lothlórien, which stands in the wider world as an enclave (like Tom Bombadil's Withywindle Valley), "the heart of Elvendom on earth" (352).

Galadriel's First Gift: Reconciliation

Celeborn and Galadriel, the Lord and Lady of Lothlórien, greet each member of the Company by name, as they enter "a cham-

5 The list is Marjorie Burns's, from *Perilous Realms*, 126.

ber of soft light," high in a mallorn tree. The news of Gandalf's death is given from the depths of Good Friday: "'[O]ur grief is great and our loss cannot be mended,' said Frodo. 'Gandalf was our guide, and he led us through Moria; and when our escape seemed beyond hope he saved us, and he fell'" (355). Hearing his devastating news, even the Elves of Lothlórien lose hope. "We have fought the long defeat," Galadriel says. For her, there is little doubt about the eventual outcome for the Elves; they are a failing race, and will fail, whether or not the Ring is destroyed. Her generosity and love are all the more remarkable for the hopelessness of her situation.

Galadriel's first gift is reconciliation between Elves and Dwarves, who have long had bad relations. Reconciliation of man with God is impossible without reconciliation between people. Trespasses are forgiven by God as people forgive other's trespasses against them. Legolas's and Gimli's distrust of each other is a weakness, and Gimli's racial distrust has been exacerbated by Haldir's demand he be led blindfolded into Lothlórien because he is a Dwarf. But the quest cannot succeed without reconciliation. In response to Gimli's newly stoked anger and distrust, Galadriel blesses him by giving him and his ancestors her approval, in one of the most moving passages in the novel:

'Dark is the water of Kheled-zâram, and cold are the springs of Kibil-nâla, and fair were the many-pillared halls of Khazad-dûm in Elder days before the fall of mighty kings beneath the stone.' She looked at Gimli, who sat glowering and sad, and she smiled. And the Dwarf, hearing the names given in his own ancient tongue, looked up and met her eyes; and it seemed to him that he looked suddenly into the heart of an enemy and saw there love and understanding. Wonder came into his face, and then he smiled in answer.

He rose clumsily and bowed in dwarf-fashion, saying: 'yet more fair is the living land of Lórien, and the Lady Galadriel is above all the jewels that lie beneath the earth!' (356)

Galadriel proclaims her sympathy, solidarity, and even admiration of the Dwarves and pierces Gimli's heart. Galadriel understands that the Dwarves as well as the Elves are an ancient and failing race, that despite their tangled history, they have both loved Middle-earth. Galadriel gives Gimli the gifts of understanding and love, and she blesses[6] him by confirming and approving who he already is, a Dwarf—even though her traditional enemy. Gimli is the first of several of the Fellowship who receive confirmation from Galadriel. Gimli falls in love with her, as one falls in love with beauty and goodness. He weeps openly when he leaves Lothlórien, receiving three of Galadriel's golden hairs as a parting gift, when he'd only asked for one. "I would not have come, had I known the danger of light and joy," he said, "Now I have taken my worst wound in this parting" (378). It is one of Tolkien's rare accomplishments that he can make goodness exciting and intensely desirable. He creates characters who have a numinous aura, and Galadriel is one.

Every reconciliation is a relinquishment of the dark energy that flows from anger and the desire for revenge. That Galadriel replaces hate with love is a signal to the Company that they must do so too. Coming from Galadriel, who has spent much of her long life in quest for power and revenge, this renunciation and reconciliation are especially powerful, and an eloquent declaration of how the Fellowship must reject the Ring and bear with each other.

Nowhere is the invisible lamp that Tolkien's reader identified shining more brightly than in the Lady of Lothlórien and Caras Galadhon, the center of her realm. Tolkien revised his idea of Galadriel until his death. Many readers and critics have noticed her Marian quality, which Tolkien acknowledged in his letter of January 25, 1971 to Ruth Austin:

> I was particularly interested in your remarks about Galadriel. . . . I think it is true that I owe much of this character to Christian and Catholic teaching and imagination about Mary, but actually Galadriel was a penitent: in her youth a leader in the rebellion against the Valar (the angelic guardians). At the end of the First Age she proudly refused forgiveness or

6 "A blessing, (also used to refer to bestowing of such) is the infusion of something with holiness, spiritual redemption, divine will, or *one's hope or approval*," *Wikipedia*, http://en.wikipedia.org/wiki/Blessing, accessed December 9, 2012 (my emphasis).

permission to return. She was pardoned because of her resistance to the final and overwhelming temptation to take Ring for herself.[7]

A little over a month before he died, however, Tolkien seems to be reconceiving Galadriel along more purely Marian lines. Perhaps his readers have convinced him to take another look, or perhaps this is one of his own continuing discoveries. Here is what Tolkien says of Galadriel in a letter to Lord Halsbury on August 4, 1973:

> Galadriel was 'unstained': she had committed no evil deeds. She was an enemy of Fëanor. She did not reach Middle-earth with the other Noldor, but independently. Her reasons for desiring to go to Middle-earth were legitimate, and she would have been permitted to depart, but for the misfortune that before she set out the revolt of Fëanor broke out, and she became involved in the desperate measure of Manwë, and the ban on all emigration.[8]

Had Tolkien lived to revise *The Silmarillion*, it is hard to tell where all of this would have come out. He is clearly proposing a major revision with a much bigger part for Galadriel, whose story has grown in his mind. As for me, I am glad the revision did not occur. To me, Galadriel is more interesting as a Marian figure with a fiery past—one who must pass through trial and tribulation before she can say, "Be it done unto me according to thy word." But, in either version, the Marian aspects of Galadriel are clearly in Tolkien's mind.[9] Gimli is forever changed by his encounter with Galadriel, and he becomes fast friends with Legolas, who,

---

7 *Letters*, 407.

8 Ibid., 431.

9 Cate Blanchett's film portrayals of Galadriel in both *The Lord of the Rings* and *The Hobbit* pick up Marian aspects, although they are far more pronounced in *The Hobbit*, in which Jackson frames her in an arch, wearing a blue gown, against the night sky with moon to her right and moonlit clouds. In that scene, she is visually the traditional Mary, Queen of Heaven, and, later, her lines promise intercessory help to Gandalf, which is also Marian in quality. Blanchett's portrayal in *The Lord of the Rings* picks up Galadriel's darker, Celtic side, and, in contrast, makes her renunciation of the Ring dramatically effective.

while in Lothlórien, "took Gimli with him when he went abroad in the land, and the others wondered at this change" (359).

galaðriel as a mirror of conscience

Galadriel's second gift is to act as a mirror to the minds of the Company, each one in turn. She reflects to them their own minds, revealing their deepest temptations and failings. It is a grace to know one's own weaknesses and sins, knowledge hard to come by without help, and often as invisible and close to us as the back of our heads. For some of the Fellowship, Galadriel's examination is harrowing, but it is all in service of one practical question: are any of them tempted by the Ring?

> '[T]his I will say to you: your quest stands upon the edge of a knife. Stray but a little and it will fail, to the ruin of all. Yet hope remains while all the Company is true.'
>
> And with that word she held them with her eyes, and in silence looked searchingly at each of them in turn. None save Legolas and Aragorn could long endure her glance. Sam quickly blushed and hung his head.
>
> At length the Lady Galadriel released them from her eyes, and she smiled. 'Do not let your hearts be troubled,' she said. 'Tonight you shall sleep in peace.' Then they sighed and felt suddenly weary, as those who have been questioned long and deeply, though no words had been spoken openly. (357)

Each of the members of the Company reacts differently to this probing. Pippin teases Sam for breaking down so fast, but Sam is in no mood to be teased:

> 'If you want to know, I felt as if I hadn't got nothing on. . . . She seemed to be looking inside me and asking me what I would do if she gave me the chance of flying back home to the Shire to a nice little hole with—with a bit of garden of my own.' (357-8)

Merry admits to feeling "almost exactly" the same way, but refuses to elaborate. Pippin divulges nothing. Gimli says what he felt will remain secret. While the honest Hobbits and Gimli feel shame, Boromir reacts with anger—but neither will he say what the Lady offered him. Anger is the screen he uses to block his own shame, which, if honestly faced, might have saved him from his mistake on Amon Hen.

The Sacrament of Penance and Reconciliation is at the base of this episode, within the specific context of confirming the fitness of the Fellowship for the quest. Following Gandalf's death, Galadriel takes on a task that would more naturally have been his responsibility—functioning as priest. What has just happened may not seem like the usual way a sinner confesses his sins to a priest and receives absolution, but Galadriel shares two of the main concerns of the priest, whose responsibility is not just to the sinner, but to the health of the Church. People need help in recognizing their sins, and a strong Church requires this confrontation. The Fellowship has to face its internal demons, so it has the unity to fight external ones.

The first and most important sacrament is the Church itself, whose quest is to spread the gospel for the purpose of the salvation of mankind. To perform its mission, it has to deal with the sins of its own members. Otherwise it would be like an army going to war with walking wounded. (And one might say it is much like that under the best of circumstances.) The sacrament of penance, derived from Matthew 16 and 18, is the Church's method for dealing with sin within itself. Karl Rahner explains the necessity of the sacrament:

> These passages concern the way Christ's holy community is to deal with a sinful member. If such a member of that sacred society, which by her life is to announce the victory of grace and the coming of the kingdom of God, sins contumaciously, grievously, this cannot be a matter of indifference to Christ's Church, for otherwise, of course, she would belie her nature. She must react against such a sin, through which the member of the community not only puts himself in contradiction to God, but also to the Church of Christ, for the Church is her members and by their holiness must be the primal sacramental sign of the victorious grace of God.[10]

10 Karl Rahner, *The Church and the Sacraments* (London: Burns and Oates, 1963), 93.

The Church cannot complete its mission without being a sacrament to the world, and thus it is grievously injured by sin within the ranks of its members. But, most importantly, in forgiving sin, the Church manifests its fundamental nature as a vehicle of God's grace. Likewise, Galadriel needs the Fellowship to succeed in its quest, and that depends on the spiritual strength of its members.

The Fellowship's mission will be threatened from within its own ranks. Galadriel knows the corrupting power of the Ring, which is clearly working on Boromir. Sam is tempted to go home—but not so much that he would ever leave Frodo. Pippin, Merry, and Gimli are all clearly embarrassed by the weaknesses that Galadriel has turned up within them, but now they know their weaknesses. Legolas and Aragorn hold her gaze the longest, the implication being that they are the least temptable of any, except Frodo. But Boromir's reaction is revealing—forced to face himself, he interprets it as an attack and throws his guilt back upon Galadriel: "I do not feel too sure of this Elvish Lady and her purposes" (358). Aragorn, however, directs Boromir's attention back to himself: "You know not what you say. There is in her and in this land no evil, *unless a man bring it hither himself.* Then let him beware!" (emphasis added; 358). Galadriel only confronts the Fellowship with the evil they have brought with them, forcing to consciousness their potentially evil desires and whatever threatens to undermine their will to further the quest.

Although she cannot give absolution, Galadriel does give consolation, and she later confirms the charism of each member with a parting gift. Mainly, she imparts grace: love, hope, and the forgiveness of weakness. The Fellowship will be stronger if it can admit—even if only privately—its weaknesses and potential failures. The seal of confession is maintained. Galadriel tells no one what she has found, and all but Sam are closed-mouthed. But all know that something has been found, in themselves and the others, requiring a necessary humility and watchfulness. Galadriel succeeds with all but Boromir, who will eventually sin, but also find redemption and forgiveness.

galaдriel's prophetic mirror

Tolkien tells us nothing about Frodo's examination. Frodo's important moment comes when he looks into the second of Galadriel's mirrors. Near the end of the Company's convalescence in Lothlórien, Galadriel approaches Frodo and Sam and beckons them to follow. They come to an enclosed garden, open to the sky. "The evening star had risen and was shining with white fire above the western wood." This is the star Eärendil, most beloved of the Elves, associated with the goddess/angel they most venerate, Varda, whose name in Elvish is Elbereth, another powerful Marian figure and mediator of grace. Thus, two Marian figures are at the center of this scene.

Galadriel's Mirror is a silver basin, which she fills from the water of a stream, using a silver ewer. She invites Frodo and Sam to look into it, but does not counsel them to do so. She merely tells them they have the strength and courage to look, or she would not have afforded them the chance. The Mirror is ambiguous in what it shows: things in the past, present, and possible futures (362).

Why look in the Mirror then? How might it help Frodo and Sam? The question is implied and left to the consideration of the reader. I offer this reading: Frodo and Sam are shown the worst of what might happen, if the quest fails, and the worst they may have to confront, even if it succeeds. This is why looking requires strength and courage. The Mirror gives them a brutally realistic picture of the current situation and how much worse it *could* get. It increases the Hobbits' sense of the necessity of destroying the Ring.

Sam, who goes first, sees a vision of the future, Frodo's pale face "lying fast asleep under a great cliff." Sam will remember Galadriel's mirror, when he sees this vision come to pass on Cirith Ungol: he will look at Frodo, stung by Shelob, and believe that he is dead (731). Then Sam sees himself going up the stairs of what will turn out to be the Tower of Cirith Ungol, though he doesn't understand this either—it lies in the future. Finally, he has a vision of the Shire, industrialized, enslaved, and destroyed. He immediately wants to go home, but it doesn't take him long to realize that his way home is "by the long road with Mr. Frodo, or not at all" (363). This is Sam's third confirmation.[11] Though he wants to go home, he sees, if only vaguely, the horror that Frodo is heading toward, and this ties him even more strongly to Frodo.

Frodo has a vision of a man who might be Gandalf, but, oddly, in white rather than grey. He sees a powerful vision of "many great scenes of the history in which he had become involved." He sees the Sea, which he has never seen before, and a great storm; a tall black ship with torn sails, riding out of the west; Osgiliath with the Anduin flowing through it; the white towers of Minas Tirith; smoke, fire, and battle; and the ship once again, sailing west, bearing a banner with of the White Tree of Gondor. Finally, he sees the Eye of Sauron, rimmed with fire, searching for him. While having this vision, the Ring, on the chain about Frodo's neck, grows heavier and pulls him toward the water, which begins to steam. The vision is broken, when Galadriel warns him not to let the Ring touch the water. What would happen if it did? Again, we are left to speculate. Would Sauron then see what Frodo was seeing in the Mirror? Would the Mirror be polluted beyond use? What Frodo understands clearly is the threat of engulfment by the Eye and the Ring, which drag him toward the water. Frodo gets his clearest understanding yet of what he is up against, and it prepares him for facing the Eye again on Amon Hen.

Through Galadriel's mirror, Frodo and Sam begin to understand they are involved in an immense story, affecting their entire world, going back centuries. They have been given a glimpse of Providence—of the Music of Ilúvatar—and they find that, despite their small stature and humble origins, they have been given critical parts to play, if they will accept. As Gandalf told Frodo at the beginning, "All we have to decide is what to do with the time that is given us" (51). Frodo's path is clear even before he looks in the mirror, but the wider consequences of failure are now powerfully brought home.

Then Galadriel reveals something else to Frodo—that she has a

---

11 Preceded by Gildor Inglorion's directions to Sam to stick with Frodo and Elrond's acknowledgement at the Council that they are meant to be together.

part to play and her own story to close. In a reverse benediction, "She lifted up her white arms, and spread out her hands towards the East in a gesture of rejection and denial." The light of Eärendil glances upon a ring on her finger, which "glittered like polished gold overlaid with silver light, and a white stone in it twinkled as if the Even-star had come down to rest upon her hand" (365). She identifies the ring as Nenya, the Ring of Adamant, and herself as its keeper. The power of Nenya is to preserve Lothlórien, but its power will diminish, if the one Ring is destroyed. For the Elves, there is no victory: slow diminishment, if Nenya loses its power, or else quick destruction by Sauron are the alternatives. But they are willing to "diminish" and go into the West, to Valinor, if that is what it takes to defeat Sauron. By lifting her arms in rejection, Galadriel, in effect, has said a prayer of rejection. But this isn't the conclusion of her struggle.

What started as a test of Frodo now becomes Galadriel's greatest test. Frodo offers to give up the Ring for the third and last time: "You are wise and fearless and fair, Lady Galadriel. . . . I will give you the One Ring, if you ask for it. It is too great a matter for me." She replies that Frodo is "gently revenged" for her testing of him at their first meeting. Now she is the one being taken to "confession," and she is sorely tempted. We see her dark side, the rebellious Elf who wanted a kingdom of her own to rule, who defied the Valar to join Fëanor and even refused their pardon. For an instant she becomes a Queen, great in stature, "beautiful and terrible," whom all shall love—and then despair. Galadriel's last test is between her potential to be a demonic version of herself, a ruthless and beautiful Elf-Queen, or the Marian figure that finally triumphs:

> She lifted up her hand and from the ring that she wore there issued a great light that illumined her alone and left all else dark. She stood before Frodo seeming now tall beyond measurement, and beautiful beyond enduring, terrible and worshipful. Then she let her hand fall, and the light faded, and suddenly she laughed again, and lo! She was shrunken: a slender elf-woman, clad in simple white, whose gentle voice was soft and sad.
>
> 'I pass the test,' she said. 'I will diminish, and go into the West, and remain Galadriel.' (366)

Galadriel is confirmed as Galadriel, though, to become Galadriel, she has worked for centuries. What does it mean to "remain" Galadriel, who, for so much of her life, has hungered for power? It means to find and settle for a more real, if more limited, self—a self unintoxicated by dreams of dominance. Galadriel's relief comes almost as a sigh, with "s" sounds: "soft and sad. 'I pass the test,' she said." Tolkien's original conception of her as a penitent seems exactly right. The call to conversion and penance is not a call for outward transformation, from Lady of Lothlórien to World Dominatrix, but to transformation of the heart[12] and radical reorientation of life.[13] Galadriel has been purged of her vengeful pursuit of the Silmarils with Fëanor, but it has taken countless smaller acts of renunciation and all her will to avoid the same mistake with the Ring. Her Marian quality, as a conveyor of grace, has been achieved through pain and contrition—she is not "full of grace" from the start, but "full of grace" by the end.

Having found Gandalf, Aragorn, and now Galadriel unwilling to take the Ring, Frodo accepts his role, which he humbly confirms: "I am permitted to wear the One Ring" (366). Frodo does not say by whom he is permitted, but he understands that his permission is not to use it, as others might, but merely to destroy it. The fault he implicitly confesses is his fear, not just for himself, but of failing the quest. The matter is too great for him. He wants to pass it off. But this is not up to him. He has been chosen: *permitted* and *ordained*. No one else has that commission. In nothing is Tolkien's Christian synthesis of Celtic and Norse material more obvious than in the confirmation of Frodo as Ringbearer, rather than the three most powerful characters on the side of the good, who all refuse the Ring. The recognition of great strength in weakness and humility is not a pagan notion.

Che gifts of galadriel

When the Fellowship leaves Lothlórien, its path is along the frontier of war, the River Anduin. East of the River is the land of the

---

12 *Catechism*, no. 1430, 359.
13 Ibid., no. 1431, 360.

Enemy; west is the land that men tenuously hold. That narrow way is the edge of choice. "Which shore will you now take?" Celeborn asks, as the Company prepares to depart.

Aragorn senses that the message of Faramir's and Boromir's dreams is also a summons to *him*. He gets a confirmation from Elrond at the Council—he is Isildur's heir, the rightful king of Gondor, and Bilbo adds his verse to Elrond's judgment, "Renewed shall be blade that was broken: The crownless again shall be king." Aragorn believes his call is toward Minas Tirith. Frodo knows that his is in the other direction, probably alone, to Mt. Doom.

Those in the Fellowship are given many gifts by the Elves, practical gifts, which they will need to defeat "the Enemy," but these are spiritual gifts as well. In addition to boats, which will get them down the river, they are given *lembas*, Elvish waybread, "more strengthening than any food made by Men" (369). One cake can propel an Elf on a day's march. Gimli comments that it tastes better than the honey-cakes of the Beornings, the best bakers he knows of. The Elves say, "Eat a little at a time, and only at need. For these things are given to serve you when all else fails" (370). Many of Tolkien's readers have made the connection between *lembas*, described as "very thin cakes," and communion wafers, and it is valid; Tolkien suggests it himself in the letter to Carole Batten-Phelps, previously quoted. There is clearly more to *lembas* than calories: "One will keep a traveler on his feet for a day of long labour, even if he be one of the tall men of Minas Tirith" (370). Gollum, deep in mortal sin, cannot taste *lembas* without choking.

The Fellowship is given cloaks that take on the color of their surroundings, which Tolkien describes in a beautiful passage:

> It was hard to say what colour they were: grey with the hue of twilight under the trees they seemed to be; and yet if they were moved, or set in another light, they were green as shadowed leaves, or brown as fallow fields by night, dusk-silver as water under the stars. (370)

Pippin wants to know if these are "magic cloaks," but the Elves are baffled by the word "magic." They explain that they merely

TOLKIEN'S SACRAMENTAL VISION

"put the thought of all that we love into all that we make." Since the Elves love the world and are virtually at one with it, the cloaks reflect the world, like water. Most importantly, these cloaks were woven by Galadriel and her maidens—it is their love that is woven in. (The great spider Shelob, Galadriel's feminine opposite, weaves darkness visible for the purpose of feeding her appetite.) The cloaks are an anti-type of the One Ring. Like a ring, they surround a wearer, and make him "disappear"; however, the cloaks don't effect a complete disappearance, but rather, a blending in with what is loved. The disappearance the Ring produces is a direct spiritual attack on the substance of the person wearing it, causing the wearer to vanish as opposed to blending with his surroundings. The difference is between negativity and oneness. The cloaks are also an anti-type of Saruman's cloak of many colors. By its instability, Saruman's cloak separates him from everything; the Elvish cloaks enact the stable relationship of Elves to the natural world.

Sam is happy with the very practical gift of Elvish rope—he has been wanting rope since he left Hobbiton. Sam will find that this rope does not get itself in knots and comes undone when he wants it to. The rope is obedient to the will of its master. Anyone who has handled a garden hose or fishing line knows how handy such reliable cooperation would be. The rope, like the cloaks, has a harmonious relationship with both its surroundings and its handler.

Galadriel meets the Fellowship on the river with individual gifts, but, first, she offers Celeborn, then each of the members of the Fellowship, a drink of "white mead" from a common cup, "the cup of parting." This completes the Eucharistic motif begun with the giving of the *lembas* bread. By drinking from the same cup, the Company's unity is celebrated, unity within itself and with the Elves of Lothlórien. This models one function of the sacrament of communion, which is to affirm the unity of the Church as one body in Christ.

✠

Galadriel's individual gifts to the members of the Fellowship affirm and enable their *charismata*—divinely conferred gifts or talents. In her discussion of character complexity in Tolkien,

Marjorie Burns recognizes that the members of the Fellowship, and Tolkien's other heroes, stand out as independent and self-sufficient, but willing to subordinate themselves to a group.[14] She suggests that this contradiction or conflict indicates complexity of character, but from a traditional Catholic view, like Tolkien's, there is no necessary conflict here, the issue having been addressed early in the Church's history by Paul in 1 Corinthians 12:4–31, in which the variously gifted members of the Church come together in one body.[15] The sacrament of confirmation provides both an organizing pattern for Galadriel's gift-giving and a key to understanding several of the gifts. The specific talents and dispositions of each member of the Fellowship are recognized and supported by Galadriel's gifts, the ceremony of gift-giving serving to organize the members as a group—like a church—in which individual talent is pooled to form a whole, with no conflict between individuality and membership. Membership in a group magnifies the effect of individual talent, as, for instance, Legolas's farsighted vision informs Aragorn's wise decision-making.

Galadriel gives Aragorn a sheath for his sword and, most significantly, "a great stone of a clear green, set in a silver brooch that was wrought in the likeness of an eagle with outspread wings" (375). This gift is a confirmation of Aragorn's vocation as the king of prophecy, and she bestows a confirmatory name on him:

> 'This stone I gave to Celebrían my daughter, and she to hers [Arwen]; and now it comes to you as a token of hope. In this hour take the name that was foretold for you, Elessar, the Elfstone of the House of Elendil!'
>
> Then Aragorn took the stone and pinned the brooch upon his breast, and those who saw him wondered; for they had not marked before how tall and kingly he stood, and it seemed to them that many years of toil had fallen from his shoulders. (375)

---

14 Burns, *Perilous Realms*, 31–32.

15 For an excellent short summation of *charismata*, see the Wikipedia article, http://en.wikipedia.org/wiki/Charismata, accessed Dec. 11, 2012.

The gift of the brooch from Galadriel is not only a confirmation of Aragorn's vocation as king, but of his love for Arwen, Galadriel's granddaughter,[16] to whom the brooch had been passed. She is giving it to Aragorn on Arwen's behalf and blessing their relationship. Since the marriage of Elves and Men is an extremely rare event (Beren and Luthien, Tuor and Idril being the only earlier examples), this blessing is especially welcome to Aragorn.[17] Aragorn receives the gift of Arwen's love, mediated by Galadriel, but, as we saw in the previous chapter, "right judgment" is one of Aragorn's gifts as well, and the special charism of leadership grows in him and also that of healing, both kingly talents.

Legolas gets a Galadhrim bow and quiver of arrows to support his charism as an archer, Merry and Pippin silver belts, Boromir a belt of gold. Sam's and Frodo's gifts, like Aragorn's, specially coincide with their vocations. Sam is given a little box of plain wood with the letter "G" for Galadriel on the lid. It is earth from Lothlórien, which Sam can use as a gardener, should he ever return to the Shire. Though Sam does not know it, the box contains life for the Shire and will help him perform his vocation as its chief steward when he returns.

The gifts Gimli received from Galadriel, when he first met her, were "love and understanding" (356), but, in addition, he is given joy and beauty: "I have looked last upon that which was fairest. . . . I would not have come, had I known the danger of

---

16 Galadriel's daughter Celebrían married Elrond. Celebrían was captured and tortured by orcs on the Redhorn Pass of Caradhras. Though rescued by her sons, she could no longer find happiness in Middle-earth and left from the Grey Havens to Valinor.

17 Although Peter Jackson's movie version makes much out of Elrond's opposition to the marriage and Aragorn's concerns for Arwen, there is little of this in the novel, although Elrond's conditions to Aragorn do appear in Appendix A. I don't fault Jackson, however. Tolkien puts forward the problems of Elf and Human marriage quite explicitly in the story of Beren and Luthien and the opposition of Luthien's father, the powerful Elf King Thingol. He also deals with it in the dialogue between Finrod and the Wisewoman Andreth in the *Athrabeth Finrod ah Andreth*. Jackson finds a dramatically effective way to convey the difficulties that the characters of *The Lord of the Rings* would understand, yet accept.

light and joy" (378). She asks Gimli what he would have, and he replies just one of her golden hairs. She gives him three. Legolas tells him, "I count you blessed, Gimli, son of Glóin."

Che phial of galadriel

Frodo is given the most wonderful gift of all, the Phial of Galadriel. She tells Frodo that in it is "the light of Eärendil's star. . . . It will shine still brighter when night is about you. May it be a light to you in dark places, when all other lights go out" (376). In this Johannine passage, the history of Eärendil is important.

Eärendil, the father of Elrond, was a product of the second of two marriages between Elves and Men, his mother being the Elf, Idril, and his father, the man Tuor. Eärendil marries an Elf also, Elwing, making his son, Elrond Halfelven, actually Elrond Three-quarters Elven. Eärendil is one of the clearest "Christ-figures" in Tolkien's legendarium. Eärendil and Elwing, after many adventures and Elwing's transformation into a bird and then back into a woman, bear the last of the three Silmarils back to Valinor, the home of the Valar and the unfallen Elves of Middle-earth, where they plead for reconciliation between the angelic guardians and the Elves who followed Fëanor into war against Morgoth. Manwë, the leader of the Valar (an analog of Michael, the Archangel and with similarities to Odin as well)[18] hears Eärendil's plea and goes to war against Morgoth, whom he captures and thrusts into the Void. During the battle (The War of Wrath) Eärendil fights the great dragon Ancalagon and defeats him. Eärendil is given the Silmaril, which he wears on his brow, as his ship, transformed, voyages the skies of Middle-earth as the Evening Star. The light of Eärendil is the light of the original trees of Valinor. It is not a fractured light, but original and complete.

Thus, Eärendil plays the Christ-like parts of mediator to the Valar, slayer of Satanic dragons, and bearer of light. His light is instrumental in kindling Galadriel's mirror ("Remember Galad-

---

18 Marjorie Burns, "Spiders and Evil Red Eyes: The Shadow Sides of Gandalf and Galadriel," in *Perilous Realms: Celtic and Norse in Tolkien's Middle-earth* (Toronto: University of Toronto Press, 2005), 97.

riel and her Mirror!" Galadriel tells Frodo, when she gives him the Phial), and it will save Frodo and Sam on Cirith Ungol. Tolkien draws connections between Frodo and Galadriel and the Phial, the receiver and giver: Frodo himself, Gandalf says in Rivendell, may become "like a glass filled with a clear light for eyes to see that can," and Galadriel is finally pictured in this scene, as the Fellowship, paddling downstream, sees her in the distance, "like a window of glass upon a far hill in the westering sun, or as a remote lake seen from a mountain: a crystal fallen in the lap of the land" (377). Frodo and Galadriel are grace-filled characters, bearers of light, and the Fellowship last hears Galadriel singing a hymn to Varda (Elbereth), "Kindler, Queen of the Stars" (378).

Although, after Amon Hen, Gimli wishes he had the Phial to use like a flashlight, we find that Galadriel's Phial does far more than cast illumination. The Phial is a source of spiritual light, and its effect on the demonic Shelob, when Frodo holds it up to her, is like a spray of acid. Shelob's Lair has the spiritual darkness associated with her great ancestor Ungoliant. It is not just utterly and impenetrably dark, but has a darkness "deeper and darker" than the lightless passages of Moria. Sound falls dead. The air is stagnant, heavy, and saturated with stench. Shelob's darkness penetrates to the soul, when Sam and Frodo enter her lair:

> They walked as it were in a black vapour wrought of veritable darkness itself that, as it was breathed, brought blindness not only to the eyes but to the mind, so that even the memory of colours and of forms and of any light faded out of thought. Night always had been, and always would be, and night was all. (718)

As the Hobbits grope their way through, their senses grow dull, and they get on "mainly by the force of the will," which begins to fail. Hope falls dead in Shelob's Lair, for even the promise of light is abolished, and this is why Frodo forgets that he even has the Phial of Galadriel. The hope of salvation is dying in him, and his mind is going dark, incapable of thought, when the grace of Galadriel saves him. At the moment when Shelob moves in, Frodo's mind clears and he is given a vision of Galadriel, on the grass, giving him the Phial.

Tolkien employs a fundamentally Catholic understanding about grace and individual will in this scene. Frodo cannot accomplish anything without grace; without the Phial and the vision, Frodo and Sam would both be devoured. But although Frodo's will is not enough, once it is revived, Frodo has the responsibility to engage it. He must seize the opportunity given by grace.

When Frodo holds up the Phial, it slowly kindles and then bursts into light, as it empowers and is empowered by Frodo's rising courage. The light becomes dazzling, and Frodo's hand sparkles with white fire. When Frodo sees Shelob, and his heart falters, the Phial droops. He and Sam run, but, when Frodo realizes they cannot outrace Shelob, he turns for a last stand, and once again, as his courage rises, the light comes up, even more potently than before:

> 'Galadriel!' he called, and gathering his courage he lifted up the Phial once more. . . . Then Frodo's heart flamed within him, and without thinking what he did, whether it was folly or despair or courage, he took the Phial in his left hand, and with right hand drew his sword . . . then holding the star aloft and the bright sword advanced, Frodo, hobbit of the Shire, walked steadily down to meet the eyes. (721)

"Afflicted" by the light, Shelob quails and retreats.

Grace and will are partners, as Frodo's heart and the Phial flame together. In the final battle between Sam and Shelob, after Frodo has been stung and Sam has put out one of Shelob's eyes, Sam's "indomitable spirit" sets the Phial blazing with "intolerable light," and the effect on Shelob is devastating: "No such terror out of heaven had ever burned in Shelob's face before. The beams of it entered into her wounded head and scored it with unbearable pain, and the dreadful infection of light spread from eye to eye" (730). Shelob runs. Undamaged by the Ring, Sam's will is even stronger than Frodo's, and the Phial responds: "And the light shineth in the darkness, and the darkness did not overcome it" (John 1:5).

The Christological light of John's Gospel is incorporated into Catholic ritual and sacrament in many ways, including lit candles of all kinds. But the most important Catholic symbol in connec-

213

tion with the Phial of Galadriel is the monstrance, an ornate vessel used to display the Eucharistic host. Elaborate in design, made of silver and gold, the monstrance signifies a sunburst, light coming from the Son of God, whose actual presence is in the consecrated host.

The monstrance is used in Eucharistic adoration and also in processions, where it is held up by the priest. This way of communicating "the light of the world" would have been very familiar to Tolkien, and its use has been long and regular over the centuries.

Frodo and Sam's attacks on Shelob with the Phial held aloft are suggestive of a monstrance held aloft by a priest in procession, in which Christ as the light of the world is pitted against spiritual darkness. This is the Eucharistic message at the basis of the Logos-centric reality of the world and possibly an inspiration to Tolkien for the combat between light and dark on Cirith Ungol, where both Frodo and Sam hold up the Phial of Galadriel, as they march on Shelob, weaver of darkness.

9

PENANCE, RECONCILIATION, AND THEIR REFUSAL

Adam lay ybounden
Ybounden in a bond[1]

"The damned are, in one sense, successful, rebels to the end; . . . the doors of hell are locked on the inside." C. S. LEWIS[2]

"Why . . . you're one of my own children!" She reached and touched him on the shoulder. The Misfit sprang back as if a snake had bitten him and shot her three times through the chest.[3]

For TOLKIEN, evil is something by which we are *caught*. Tom Bombadil, as Goldberry says, is Master, because he has never been caught, and Tolkien suggests that, within the boundaries of his realm, Tom cannot *be* caught. But everyone else can; and positioning Tom at the beginning of the book provides a foil against which the weakness of everyone else is measured. Throughout *The Lord of the Rings,* Tolkien portrays the process of temptation, fall, and entrapment. The Ring is the nexus for most of this, but disordered desire can take anything for an object: Pippin becomes

---

1 Anonymous English lyric, dating from the reign of Henry V.

2 C. S. Lewis, *The Problem of Pain* (San Francisco: Harper, 1996; 1941), 130.

3 Flannery O'Connor, "A Good Man is Hard to Find," in *The Complete Short Stories of Flannery O'Connor* (NY: Farrar, Straus and Giroux, 1971), 132.

fixated with the palantír, Éowyn with Aragorn and the achievement of "renown," Denethor with the hereditary status of his
family, and, on a smaller scale, Lobelia Sackville-Baggins with
Bilbo's spoons. There is a strong element of addiction in all those
who are "caught," even if they are only addicted to an idea of
themselves or what they want.

To be caught by evil is, in some way, to be ensnared by death.
God's first and only warning to Adam is that eating of the tree of
knowledge will bring death into the world, and the life/death
opposition is the spiritual axis upon which the biblical world
turns. When Moses invites people into covenant with God, he
invites them to life if they keep it and warns of death if they
don't: "I call heaven and earth to witness this day, that I have set
before you life and death, blessing and cursing. Choose therefore
life, that both thou and thy seed may live" (Deut. 30:19). Centuries later, John the Evangelist is saying much the same thing: "We
know that we have passed from death to life, because we love the
brethren. He that loveth not, abideth in death" (1 John 3:14). The
word "abideth" is important. Death is not just an event but a condition that people enter while alive, and they *abide* in it; they
accept it without objection or struggle, and their consciences go
numb, as deathly living becomes habit.

The purest example in Tolkien's fiction of a character possessed by possessing is not Fëanor or Gollum, but Smaug, the
dragon of *The Hobbit*. Like the dragon of *Beowulf*, he sits on his
immense treasure hoard, never leaving it, knowing what he has
down to the last coin. He has the treasure, once he drives the
Dwarves from the Lonely Mountain, but the treasure has him as
well, literally grounded, lest someone should steal even the least
bit of it. Then rage and revenge take over, and the dragon flies
from his hoard to wreak destruction. The dragon is an image of
Satan, and Smaug is an image of living death, voluntarily
entombing himself with treasure, a reptilian Barrow-wight.

Tolkien's concern throughout *The Silmarillion* is that Men mis-
understand the nature of physical death, failing to recognize it as
the gateway into new life. In rejecting death, Men enter into a
deeper, spiritual death. The characters in *The Lord of the Rings*
who abide most deeply in death—excepting Orcs, Balrogs, and

other demonic forms—are all offered a way of escape. Some take it and some do not. Escape from the trap is "salvation," and, for a Roman Catholic like Tolkien, this means "a process of healing whereby God's forgiveness, grace, and loving attention"[4] are extended to human beings through Jesus Christ, so that unity among men and with God is possible. Grace is the help that God gives people to become his children. Salvation is not just an eschatological result, but a path which begins in this life. In Middle-earth, there are salvific moments and damning ones, and the acceptance or rejection of grace, which is the help to do what is necessary and right, is always a determining factor. Tolkien's sacramental vision illuminates the way of escape from death, incorporating many of the elements in the Catholic Rite of Penance and Reconciliation into scenes requiring characters to make the choice Moses offered his people.

What is it like, in *The Lord of the Rings*, to "abide in death"? Tolkien shows that one of evil's main properties is to isolate and split the individual from himself and the community. *Gaudium et Spes* describes this condition as follows: "Man is divided in himself. As a result, the whole life of men, both individual and social, shows itself to be a struggle, and a dramatic one, between good and evil, between light and darkness."[5]

Tolkien shows isolation and division throughout *The Silmaril-*

---

4 Michael Pennock, *This is Our Faith: A Catholic Catechism for Adults* (Notre Dame, IN: Ave Maria Press, 2007), 351.

5 *Gaudium et Spes* [Joy and Hope], *the Pastoral Constitution on the Church in the Modern World* is one of the four Apostolic Constitutions that came out of the Second Vatican Council. This quotation is from the *Catechism*, no. 1707, 425. It is suggestive that *Gaudium* uses the word "drama" to describe the struggle, with all that implies about a story unfolding in time with multiple characters. Understanding the struggle between good and evil seems to require, at bottom, thinking through narrative rather than argument, a very congenial notion for Tolkien, the novelist and mythographer. We perhaps do not give narrative enough evidential weight, because we do not take conscience seriously enough. A narrative immediately convinces if it arouses our sense of right and wrong—Peter and John do not give arguments about Jesus in Acts 3 and 4 when preaching to the crowd and the Sadducees. They give a narrative account, with the expectation that it will arouse the right response in those who have ears to hear.

lion, and its results occur at every level of *The Lord of the Rings.*
Fëanor's fall divides the Elves and leads to Elves killing Elves. The
lone person in the tower—Saruman, Denethor, or Sauron as disembodied Eye—is the image of isolation, split from the community in the attempt to stand over it and order it. Sauron is even
split from himself, so that only a piece of him takes physical
form. Gollum is shunned by his own kin, and his mind is schizoid; Boromir breaks the Fellowship, though he dies trying to
defend it; Théoden leaves his people leaderless, sitting alone on
his throne, as Wormtongue feeds his despair and self-indulgence.
Tolkien duplicates this image with Denethor, whom we first see
through the eyes of Pippin, alone in his steward's chair, the
throne empty, and no one else in the vast hall.

Division is exemplified in the mutual distrust that the major
races—Elves, Dwarves, and Men—have for each other. Tolkien
dramatizes the divisions between Elves and Dwarves, as the Fellowship enters Lothlórien, when Haldir, leading the Elvish border guards, demands that Gimli the dwarf be blindfolded before
he is allowed to enter the kingdom. Even Haldir doesn't like this
order, but he must enforce the law. Aragorn solves the problem
by requesting that *all* the members of the Fellowship be blindfolded. The folly of such division especially strikes the Elf, Legolas, who has longed to see Lothlórien:

> 'Alas for the folly of these days!' said Legolas. 'Here all are ene-
> mies of the one Enemy, and yet I must walk blind, while the
> sun is merry in the woodland under leaves of gold!'
> 'Folly it may seem,' said Haldir. 'Indeed in nothing is the
> power of the Dark Lord more clearly shown than in the
> estrangement that divides all those who still oppose him.' (348)

Evil tends to spread. Division begets more division and distrust
more distrust. Division is most virulent among the worst. Orcs
are often more inclined to kill each other than anyone else. As
Frodo says, "that is the spirit of Mordor" (926).

Another aspect of evil is perversion—transformation of an
individual by subtraction of the good: the taking away of something that goes to the essence of the creature's being. When evil
subtracts rationality from man, raising the will above reason, it
reduces him to the animal. The loss of rationality is the loss of

connection to reality and to the ultimate reality, the love of God. The elimination of imagination, intuition, or feeling has equally devastating consequences. The race of Orcs came from Elves who were tortured by Morgoth into the form of Orcs. Trolls came from Ents, and Balrogs from Maiar. Frodo makes an educated guess about the Orcs from his own observation, when he tells Sam: "The Shadow that bred them can only mock, it cannot make: not real new things of its own. I don't think it gave life to the orcs, it only ruined them and twisted them" (914). Frodo's assumption is consistent with Genesis: everything in the beginning was good—and later warped.

Evil not only divides and isolates individuals from each other, but from all the good things in life. Tolkien frequently uses a word we seldom hear today: "merry." To be captured by evil is to lose joy, merriness, gaiety—whatever gives light and exuberance to life. Tolkien dramatizes this effect in the despair of Théoden, Denethor, and Eówyn. Gollum is his most frightening case: "a crouching shape, scarcely more than the shadow of a living thing, a creature . . . wholly ruined and defeated, yet filled with a hideous lust and rage" (944). Almost everything human has been subtracted from Gollum. Having turned into a kind of frog-man with an awful stench, his degeneration is captured in his preference for fish, "raw and wriggling," to Sam's offer of "fish and chips."

Once caught in evil, escape is hard; one sin begets another, as one continues farther down the path. Dante portrays himself, at the beginning of *The Inferno*, as unable to ascend the hills he has come down, and he must go to the lowest level of hell to get back up, only making it with the help of his heaven-sent guide, Virgil, and the divine Beatrice.

> Sin creates a proclivity to sin; it engenders vice by repetition of the same acts. This results in perverse inclinations which cloud conscience and corrupt the concrete judgment of good and evil. Thus sin tends to reproduce itself and reinforce itself. . . . [6]

Sin is inherently addictive. The Ring captures this aspect of being bound most powerfully, and, as Gandalf says, it is "wholly evil."

---

6 *Catechism*, no. 1865, 457.

Tolkien's Ring is a powerful symbol, because we usually associate rings with the good. The exchange of rings at marriage symbolizes love and commitment, as people bind themselves to each other and become "one flesh." Hrothgar, the king of the Spear Danes in *Beowulf*, as do other Teutonic kings, gives out rings and torques to his retainers as a symbol of his love for them, and they accept them in the same spirit. The giving and acceptance of rings in the mead hall is a pledge of loyalty and solidarity, as is drinking from the common cup.[7] The ring links the king to his retainers and symbolizes a virtually familial relationship. It is not hard to see how the ring, as a piece of jewelry, acquired this symbolism, for rings encircle and enclose: they "bounden in a bond," and the enclosure of the finger metonymically signifies the enclosure of the entire person in a bond of trust.[8] But the One Ring is almost never given freely; it is stolen or taken through murder or conquest. Its possession is achieved through the application of power, not generosity, and it is a symbol of entrapment, enclosure, and possession. The encirclement of the finger by the One Ring is the encirclement of slavery and subtraction. One literally disappears when it is worn. This subtraction of visibility is but the physical representation of spiritual subtraction. The relationship it creates with Sauron, whose spirit is part of the Ring, is a perversion both of marriage and the giving of rings by the king to his retainers. To wear the One Ring is to swear fealty to a demon, to be married to evil. It is also a demonic parody of the relationship of Christ to his Church: Sauron becomes the demonic bridegroom to his own demonic disciples, the Ring Wraiths.

7 For this naturally Eucharistic practice in pagan northern Europe, see the cup scenes in *Beowulf*, for example, lines 1167–1250, which include the giving of rings and torques. All of this unifies the community. Tolkien echoes *Beowulf* in the scene of Éowyn serving the cup in Meduseld (522).

8 Someone once told me that people who join the military ought to be let out, if they want, because "they don't know what they are getting into." Does anyone ever know what he or she is getting into? The whole point of taking a loyalty oath or exchanging rings at marriage is to make a commitment without knowing what one is getting into—to be committed whatever happens. This is what Frodo does at the Council of Elrond, when he agrees to take the Ring to Mordor, even though he doesn't know the way.

The Ring has two functions. It tempts people to take it, because it promises them the power to acquire anything else they might want, and it imprisons them. Since what people want varies from person to person, how the Ring affects people goes "according to their stature" (53), as Gandalf says, the best having the potential to become the worst.

Those who continue to wear the rings which the One Ring controls are committed against their wills to another will that masters them. When the Elves wearing the three rings become aware of Sauron, who wears the One Ring, they immediately take them off and do not put them on, until Sauron loses his. The Dwarves, who have tough wills, keep their rings, and, although they cannot be utterly controlled, their hearts are perverted by greed for gold. But Men are so susceptible that they became the slaves of Sauron—the Ring Wraiths. This progression, from failed to complete domination, suggests that the Ring could have been resisted, but only by refusing the rings which it controlled. Only the Elves have the will to do this. Refusing the One Ring itself is even harder.

Even Saruman, who cannot get the One Ring, is entrapped by it. In the middle of the walled circle of Isengard, the tower of Orthanc juts like a finger. Within that ring, Saruman has created his own military-industrial complex to enslave others. But, when the Ents attack, he is trapped, encircled, isolated within his own walls, as if he himself has inhabited the Ring; for Isengard, like the Ring, has merely become a technology for the control of other wills, and Saruman's little round kingdom is destroyed, when nature rebels, just as Sauron's is, when the Ring is destroyed. Even as the giant Eye of Sauron collapses in defeat, Saruman loses his eye, the palantír, when Wormtongue tries to brain either him or Gandalf—Aragorn is not quite sure—by hurling it down.

Boromir's Repentance

Boromir displays the full range of temptation, fall, entrapment, and recovery within a short narrative. His story (one could take Pippin's experience with the palantír as well) introduces the more complex cases of Théoden, Denethor, and Saruman. When examined by Galadriel, Boromir doesn't interpret her action as a revelation of what he is tempted by, but rather that she herself is the temptress:

> '[A]lmost I should have said that she was tempting us, and offering what she pretended to have the power to give. It need not be said that I refused to listen. The Men of Minas Tirith are true to their word.' But what he thought the Lady had offered him *Boromir did not tell.* (my emphasis; 358)

Boromir's defensiveness and unwillingness to acknowledge his own weakness makes him all the more vulnerable. The man with a secret is already isolated. Confession would have been good for his soul, would have helped him meet the temptation ahead. But Boromir's lack of humility undermines him, as Gandalf later acknowledges: "It was a sore trial for such a man: a warrior, and a lord of men" (496). Later, when Denethor bitterly complains to Gandalf that Boromir would have brought him the Ring, if he could, Gandalf replies, "He would have stretched out his hand to this thing, and taking it he would have fallen. He would have kept it for his own, and when he returned you would not have known your son" (813).

In his desire, one part of Boromir, the desire to be a great commander, overcomes all the rest. At Amon Hen, his imagination runs away with him.[9]

> Boromir strode up and down, speaking ever more loudly. Almost he seemed to have forgotten Frodo, while his talk dwelt on walls and weapons, and the mustering of men; and he drew plans for great alliances and glorious victories to be; and he cast down Mordor, and became himself a mighty king, benevolent and wise. (398)

Boromir's fantasy powers his desire for the Ring, and self-control disappears. Tolkien writes, "a raging fire was in his eyes," connecting Boromir to the fiery single eye of Sauron and the way fire leaps out of control and assumes a life of its own.

---

9 Boromir is very much, in this scene, like Shakespeare's Hotspur; see *Henry IV, Part 1*, Act 1, Scene 3 for Hotspur's wild flight of martial fantasy. As his father Northumberland dryly comments, "Imagination of some great exploit / Drives him beyond the bounds of patience" (lines 197–8).

Once Frodo escapes, Boromir immediately returns to himself, as people often do, when the damage is done: "'What have I said,' he cried, 'What have I done? Frodo, Frodo!' he called. 'Come back! A madness took me, but it has passed. Come back!'" (400). Truly, Boromir has been "taken," momentarily overcome by that part of himself fed by the ring. The devil overthrows reason by inflaming desire, as is implied in the Greek word *diaballo*, whose meanings all have diabolical reference: to throw over, to set at variance or make a quarrel between, to traduce, slander, calumniate.[10] Boromir allows his will to be overthrown by desire, setting him at variance with Frodo and the rest of the Fellowship.

Boromir is unable to admit to Aragorn that he tried to take the Ring from Frodo. He is split, fighting a battle within himself. Nevertheless, Boromir's anguish is the first stage of repentance, and, when the Uruk-hai attack, he gives his life protecting Merry and Pippin. At the end, he confesses to Aragorn, who finds him sword in hand, pierced with many arrows and surrounded by slain Orcs: "I tried to take the Ring from Frodo. . . . I am sorry. I have paid. . . . I have failed" (414).

With his great pride, it may be that Boromir could only have admitted his sin after atoning for it with his own death. Aragorn serves as Boromir's confessor by comforting him—essentially assuring Boromir that he is loved: "You have conquered. Few have gained such a victory. Be at peace!" (414). Boromir has conquered, as Gandalf later acknowledges, when Aragorn tells him of Boromir's death: "He escaped in the end. I am glad. *It was not in vain that the young hobbits came with us, if only for Boromir's sake*" (my emphasis; 496). Gandalf declares that Merry and Pippin, seemingly superfluous members of the Fellowship, were providentially present, if only to provide Boromir with the opportunity for repentance and redemption. A warrior and nobleman, Boromir could best express his sorrow for his sin against Frodo by giving his life for the other Hobbits, the weakest members of the Fellowship—it was the course of penance most suited to his nature.

Herbert McCabe calls penance a "sacrament of return." Sin cuts off the sinner from his relationship with Christ and with his

10 Liddell and Scott, *An Intermediate Greek Lexicon* (Oxford, 1888).

fellow man. The Rite of Penance is meant to put the sinner back in union with Christ and the Church and is ideally accomplished by a perfect act of contrition, real sorrow for what one has done. But McCabe argues that "perfect contrition is sufficient for the forgiveness of sin even without the sacrament of penance itself. . . . Perfect contrition just is the forgiveness of sins; it is the grace of this sacrament."[11]

The sacraments all tend back toward baptism, a death and a resurrection, and the Rite of Penance is no different. Penance comes down to abandonment of our selves and acceptance of the dissolution of "all that self has meant to us." It is the work of grace,

> yet it is required of us that we make it personally our own. It is this personal appropriation of our death that is achieved by mortification in this life, by purgatory in the next.
>
> One effect of sin is that it becomes harder for us to die. Sin, besides turning us from God, binds us closer to ourselves, so that the abandonment of self becomes more difficult. This tendency to self-centredness is something that may remain even when our sin is forgiven; it is eradicated only by deliberate self-denial.[12]

The self-centered delusion that caught Boromir and sundered the Fellowship is dramatically healed by his self-sacrifice: he appropriates his own death by giving himself away. Boromir, though caught, has, as Gandalf says, "escaped in the end."

Đenethor's hands and Théoden's horn

Catholic theology holds that free will is a fact,[13] and Tolkien assumes it throughout *The Lord of the Rings*. Tolkien's story is based on the idea of freely-willed resistance to the Ring. Tolkien does not say the will cannot be overcome; Frodo's is in the end,

---

11 Herbert McCabe, *The New Creation* (London: Continuum, 1964), 71.

12 Ibid., 77.

13 *Catechism*, nos. 1730 and 1731, 430: "God created man a rational being, conferring on him the dignity of a person who can initiate and control his own actions. 'God willed that man should be "left in the hand of his own counsel," so that he might of his own accord seek his Creator and freely attain his full

but it is there as an obstacle evil must defeat. To have free will is not to be utterly determined by either circumstances or one's desires, but, rather, to have a zone of mental space in which it is possible to make difficult decisions and act on them. Free will starts as a gift, but continues and ends as an achievement, for the will is like a muscle that needs development.[14] Hundreds of small acts of self-discipline may be required to strengthen the will to do really difficult things and to resist temptation. On the other hand, one who lives a life of license has made hundreds of choices against resistance to whatever beckons. The capacity to marshal the will can be diminished by habit, disease, depression, grief, and crushing responsibility. Both the man who has let his will atrophy and the one whose will has been crushed need help. They need to be returned to a position in which their weakened wills are once again capable of deciding and acting.

In *The Lord of the Rings,* a good person is one who freely wills to do the good, but to have such a will is not just the achievement of the individual. It requires a supporting fellowship and, sometimes, divine intervention. One of Tolkien's major interests in *The Lord of the Rings* is the offer of grace and its acceptance or

and blessed perfection by cleaving to him,'" and "Freedom is the power, rooted in reason and will, to act or not to act, to do this or that, and so to perform deliberate actions on one's own responsibility. By free will one shapes one's own life. Human freedom is a force for growth and maturity in truth and goodness; it attains its perfection when directed toward God, our beatitude."

14 For the classical roots of this idea, see Helen North, *Sophrosyne: Self-Knowledge and Self-Restraint in Greek Literature* (Ithaca: Cornell University Press, 1966); for the Catholic roots, see *Catechism*, nos. 1804 and 1810: "Human virtues are firm attitudes, stable dispositions, habitual perfections of intellect and will that govern our actions, order our passions, and guide our conduct according to reason and faith. They make possible ease, self-mastery, and joy in leading a morally good life. The virtuous man is he who freely practices the good. The moral virtues are acquired by human effort. They are the fruit and seed of morally good acts; they dispose all the powers of the human being for communion with divine love," and "Human virtues acquired by education, by deliberate acts and by a perseverance ever-renewed in repeated efforts are purified and elevated by divine grace. With God's help, they forge character and give facility in the practice of the good."

refusal. Characters who refuse it have essentially exercised an option for damnation, and it begins by excluding oneself from the fellowship or community and relying on one's own powers. This is what Melkor does, when he goes off, alone, into the void and returns, unable to join the heavenly chorus except as an isolated individual, trying to drown it out.

The acceptance or refusal of help is at the heart of the stories of Théoden and Denethor, who, though placed in remarkably similar circumstances, make radically different choices and come to their ends with far different moral statures. We have a functionally contrasting pair in Théoden and Denethor, and Tolkien gives us a clue with their names, which almost form a syllabic palindrome. We might guess these characters are mirror images of each other, or perhaps similar, but, in some important way, opposites. Théoden is a king, and Denethor, though a steward, is steward to a kingdom that has been without a king for nearly a thousand years. Denethor has come to see himself as king.

Tolkien tightens the comparison by introducing the characters in startlingly similar ways, emphasizing their isolation. Gandalf's reception by both is an elaborate affair. To see Théoden, he must get through an outer screen of guards and the Doorward, Hama.[15] In both cases, Gandalf is received more cordially by the guards than the men he is coming to counsel. In Tolkien's first scenes of Théoden and Denethor, both are pictured at the far end of a throne room, where they sit, solitary and decrepit. Théoden is seated on his throne upon a dais with three steps, so "bent with age that he seemed almost a dwarf." His white beard flows onto his lap. Before him is his wizened counselor, Gríma Wormtongue, and, behind him, his beautiful niece Éowyn, slender and tall, steely

15 Tolkien adapts the language of Beowulf's reception by the Spear Dane's coastguard and the decision of the coastguard to rely on his own judgment to let in the outsider. See *The Lord of the Rings*, ca. 508 and contrast it with *Beowulf*, trans. Seamus Heaney (NY: Farrar, Straus, Giroux, 2000), lines 237–289. Tom Shippey, *The Road to Middle-earth: How Tolkien Created a New Mythology* (NY: Houghton Mifflin, 2003), 124–25, is, I believe, the first to have noted that *Beowulf* and the chapter, "The King of Golden Hall," agree "down to minute detail" on the procedure for approaching kings and the initiative of individual guards.

and cold (515). Although Théoden has men around him, suggesting a community that would like to help, his counselor, Wormtongue, is a barrier to that community, and Théoden's physical and mental condition put him out of reach of those who love him.

We first see Denethor alone, at the end of a much grander and longer hall, full of pillars and statues. At the far end, there is a dais of many steps on which stands an empty throne and, at the bottom of the stairs, a black, unadorned stone chair in which Denethor sits, "an old man gazing at his lap" (754). Of the two, Denethor's isolation seems the stronger, as no one is with him, and he is in a vast, cold hall in comparison with the homey, if shabby, Meduseld. Théoden's depressive isolation is deeper than Denethor's, however; he is virtually possessed by the evil spirit of Wormtongue's counsel. These men share another isolating factor: they have both recently lost their sons to war, Denethor his eldest, Boromir, and Théoden his only son, Théodred. Denethor sits, holding Boromir's great horn, which has been recovered from the River Anduin; it is split in half. No breath will ever move through that horn again. (That image of breathlessness, signifying lack of spirit, will become very important in contrast to the horn imagery associated with Théoden.)

Both men elicit our sympathy. They are embroiled in war, under immense stress, suffering personal loss. Théoden is bedeviled by self-doubt, considering himself a lesser son of great ancestors. Denethor has self-doubts as well, but he is also plagued by pride and the worry that finally a legitimate king—Aragorn—may claim the throne of Gondor. Gandalf draws a broad distinction between the two men, as he and Pippin enter the Citadel of Minas Tirith: "Théoden is a kindly old man. Denethor is of another sort, proud and subtle, a man of far greater lineage and power, though he is not called a king" (753).

Another important parallel scene, illustrating the difference between the two men and the cultures they represent, occurs when Pippin swears fealty to Denethor and Merry to Théoden. Pippin's oath is to a great king of a great empire; it is impersonal and frightening. Merry's oath, typical of the mead hall of *Beowulf*, is familial.

Here is Pippin's:

'Here do I swear fealty and service to Gondor, and to the Lord and Steward of the realm, to speak and to be silent, to do and to let be, to come and to go, in need or plenty, in peace or war, in living or dying, from this hour henceforth, until my lord release me, or death take me, or the world end. So say I, Peregrin son of Paladin of the Shire of the Halflings.' (756)

Pippin repeats this oath, phrase by phrase, after Denethor says it. Solidified sometime in the past, this oath is official, impersonal, all-encompassing, and subordinates Pippin's will to Denethor's in ways reminiscent of the Ring. (And later, when Beregond saves Faramir from Denethor's funeral pyre, we find that such oaths must be broken, when loyalty comes into conflict with what is right.) Denethor's response to Pippin's oath is revealing: fealty will be repaid with love, valor with honor, and oath-breaking with vengeance. There is something evil in the imperial will of Gondor and the way Denethor wields it: pride, implacability, and a lack of forgiveness reduce the promise of love for fealty to a mere contract.

Merry's oath is different at the start, because it is not to a kingdom, Rohan, but to its king, personally, and it is motivated by love. It does not proceed by formula, but spontaneously, on both sides. Also, it occurs after Théoden, unlike Denethor, has been freed from his spiritual imprisonment:

Filled suddenly with love for this old man, he knelt on one knee, and took his hand and kissed it. 'May I lay the sword of Meriadoc of the Shire on your lap, Théoden King?' he cried. 'Receive my service, if you will!'

'Gladly will I take it,' said the king; and laying his long old hands on the brown hair of the hobbit, he blessed him. 'Rise now, Meriadoc, esquire of Rohan of the household of Meduseld!' he said. 'Take your sword and bear it unto good fortune!'

'As a father you shall be to me,' said Merry.

'For a little while,' said Théoden. (777)

Théoden blesses Merry, accepting him not just as a retainer, but as a son, and Merry takes Théoden as a father. The Germanic king in his mead hall was the father of his people, and that relationship formed the metaphorical basis for loyalty, which was personal and based on love. In Merry's ceremony, love isn't split off from fealty as its reward. Fealty on both sides *is* love. The core of faith is fidelity. Théoden has begun the necessary process of dying to himself. He tells Merry he will be his father "for a little while," and, as his story proceeds, we see him giving up more authority to his sister-son nephew, Éomer.

Gandalf uses drastic measures with Théoden and is able to help him very quickly. In the Peter Jackson film, Théoden is portrayed as possessed and under the control of Saruman, whom Gandalf casts out. As an interpretation for the visually dependent medium of cinema, this works well. In the book, however, Théoden is more possessed by the bad counsel of Gríma, who is an agent of Saruman, than he is by sorcery. In the book, Théoden has moral culpability for his depression, and it gives rise to Éowyn's profound loss of honor. Gríma, like a demonic tempter, has insinuated despair into Théoden. Under Wormtongue's influence and like Denethor, Théoden greets Gandalf merely as the perpetual bearer of bad news, "Gandalf Stormcrow." In response, Gandalf brings the best news he can by gently singing a song of light and hope. It is a balm to Théoden's grief, his "consolation": "Seldom have walked the feet of Men, / Few mortal eyes have seen the light / That lies there ever, long and bright. / Galadriel! Galadriel / Clear is the water of your well" (514). Holy light is what Gandalf wants to bring to Théoden's vision, the light of Eärendil's star and the water of life. Then Gandalf virtually blasts Théoden with light:

> He raised his staff. There was a roll of thunder. The sunlight was blotted out from the eastern windows; the whole hall became suddenly dark as night. The fire faded to sullen embers. Only Gandalf could be seen, standing white and tall before the blackened hearth. . . . There was a flash as if lightning had cloven the roof. (514)

This breaks Gríma's lock on Théoden and gives him the chance to exercise his will; however weak, he has a genuine opportunity. Gandalf is not overbearing his will to make him choose rightly, but giving him a choice of his own and offering hope:

> 'Do you ask for help?' he lifted his staff and pointed to a high window. There the darkness seemed to clear, and through the

opening could be seen, high and far, a patch of shining sky. 'Not all is dark. Take courage, Lord of the Mark; for better help you will not find. No counsel have I to give to those that despair. Yet counsel I could give, and words I could speak to you.' (514)

Victory for Gandalf is to give Théoden the chance to call up his own courage, to reject despair on his own. This is how grace and free will work together. Gandalf never imposes help on anyone. Rather, he makes it possible for them, once again, to choose. If Gandalf were to force the good choice, he would not be offering help or love, but acting as a tyrant, another Sauron. Gandalf is the great forcer of decisions, but not the great decider. The old king must still take up the reins, and he does. This is the critical fact. Théoden is not too proud to take help. Tolkien uses the Johannine imagery of light throughout the next several pages that describe Théoden's awakening, as Gandalf takes him outside the mead-hall. "Suddenly through a rent in the clouds behind them a shaft of sun stabbed down. The falling showers gleamed like silver, and far away the river glittered like a shimmering glass" (515).

The similarity of this vision to Frodo's last dream in the house of Tom Bombadil is striking. Frodo had dreamt of "a pale light behind a grey rain-curtain . . . growing stronger to turn the veil all to glass and silver." Théoden, led outside the mead hall by Gandalf, is brought to see the world in a new way. Like Frodo in his dream vision, Théoden sees the glory of God shining through the translucent world. They both receive grace, and Théoden recognizes the gift: "Dark have been my dreams of late . . . but I feel as one new-awakened. I would now that you had come before, Gandalf" (515–6). This imagery is not only Johannine. Given the wakening of Théoden and the imagery of dark passing to light, Tolkien also may have built this scene—and Théoden's speech—on two verses from Romans: "It is now the hour for us to rise from sleep. For now our salvation is nearer than when we believed. The night is passed, and the day is at hand. Let us therefore cast off the works of darkness, and put on the armour of light" (Rom. 13:11–12).

When Théoden then clutches the sword that Éomer lays before him, the years drop away, and he becomes once again a king, crying:

Arise now, arise, Riders of Théoden!
Dire deeds awake, dark is it eastward.
Let horse be bridled, horn be sounded!
  Forth Eorlingas! (517)

His men look at him in amazement and cry, "Command us!"

Gandalf counsels the king with advice that goes back in Christianity at least as far as Boethius, "To cast aside regret and fear. To do the deed at hand." Gandalf is both stern and kind, sometimes by turns and sometimes all at once: stern, when he needs to get someone's attention, kind, when people open themselves to the spirit that it is his job to impart. Tolkien's model for Gandalf is certainly Jesus, whose sternness is often overlooked in Christian sentimentality, but whose kindness has an iron backbone: "Behold, thou art made whole: sin no more, lest a worse thing come unto thee" (John 5:14).

Denethor is the member of the pair who refuses help, torn between fear that his kingdom will fall and that Gandalf is helping Aragorn to the throne. At his first meeting with Gandalf, Denethor pointedly ignores him, only questioning Pippin, in a deliberate snub that asserts his authority over Gandalf's. He refers to himself as the Lord of Gondor who "is not to be made the tool of other men's purposes" (758). The generic application of "man" to Gandalf is wholly inadequate and a subtle insult. Pippin understands the difference between Gandalf and Denethor instinctively:

> Denethor looked . . . much more like a great wizard than Gandalf did, more kingly, beautiful, and powerful; and older. Yet by a sense other than sight Pippin perceived that Gandalf had the greater power and the deeper wisdom, and a majesty that was veiled. And he was older, far older. 'How much older?' he wondered, and then he thought how odd it was that he had never thought about it before. . . . What was Gandalf? In what far time and place did he come into the world, and when would he leave it? (757)

Denethor, who prides himself on his wisdom and vision, has become deranged by his use of a palantír, a seeing stone, having made the decision to confront Sauron himself and to wrest information from him. As brave (and desperate) as this is, Denethor does not seem to understand that he has over-estimated his own capabilities. He is no match for a demon who feeds him misleading information and encourages his despair and his fear of Aragorn. Full of bitterness over the loss of Boromir, Denethor sends his only remaining son, Faramir, on a suicide mission, and, when Faramir returns on the point of death, Denethor is crushed by guilt and bitter disappointment and thwarted pride:

> 'I sent my son forth, unthanked, unblessed, out into needless peril, and here he lies with poison in his veins. Nay, nay, whatever may now betide in war, my line too is ending, even the House of the Stewards has failed. Mean folk shall rule the last remnant of the Kings of Men, lurking in the hills until all are hounded out.' (824)

Denethor becomes another man isolated in a tower, cut off from everything but illusion. After Faramir is brought home, Denethor "himself went up alone into the secret room under the summit of the Tower; and many who looked up thither at that time saw a pale light that gleamed and flickered from the narrow windows of a while, and then flashed and went out" (821).

The light is from the palantír, a false light, and even that goes out. Denethor decides to burn himself and Faramir to ashes. He wants to own his and his son's bodies to the last, denying them to the Orcs by incinerating them. It is a mean death, motivated by spite. Gandalf arrives in time to save Faramir and tries to free Denethor from the trap he is caught in. He reminds Denethor of his duty, tells him there is much that he can do still to help Gondor, that a steward who faithfully surrenders his charge is not diminished in love or honor, and that "Authority is not given to you, Steward of Gondor, to order the hour of your death." None of this helps, and Denethor lights his funeral pyre.

Tolkien summarizes with a defining image. Denethor dies, holding the palantír that was instrumental in his despair. Recovered from the fire with no physical damage, it is unusable, because anyone who looks into it sees only Denethor's grasping, burned hands clutching the stone globe—Denethor is not freed like Frodo by the loss of a digit; he grasps himself to the very end. The parallel opposite image is certainly that of Théoden, resting his hands in blessing on the head of Meriadoc Brandybuck. One man refuses love, refuses to place his hands on his son's head in blessing, and dies in despair, clutching the instrument of his own death; the other blesses a Hobbit and a stranger, who becomes his son for a while, and then he dies in grace and with honor.

Théoden, who is meeting his death in battle at the time of Denethor's suicide, has successfully let go of himself, becoming the servant of the moment. As burned, grasping hands capture the truth of Denethor's end, a great horn blast is what Tolkien associates with Théoden's, and this is as deeply symbolic as the burned hands. It is the giving in and out of breath in a living body, and especially in the spoken word, that signifies Life and the Holy Spirit throughout the Bible and makes the connection of spirit to breath, wind, and word. Life and breath (ruach in Hebrew), Word and creation, all fit together in a symbolic complex. In Genesis 1, God speaks the universe into being and order through language, and the words of Jesus newly create and order his disciples. In John 20:22, Jesus breathes on his disciples and says, "Receive ye the Holy Ghost." The shofar, the Hebrew ram's horn, is directly associated with the presence of God on Mount Sinai (Ex. 19:16, 19; Ex. 20:18) and victory at Jericho, when the Spirit of the Lord, through the blasting of the horns, brings down the structure of evil.

In contrast with the broken horn of Boromir, which Denethor cradles in his lap, Théoden's horn is whole, and, with a great horn blast, Théoden leads the charge of the Rohirrim that will raise the siege of Minas Tirith: "and he blew such a blast upon it that it burst asunder. And straightway all the horns in the host were lifted up in music, and the lowing of the horn of Rohan in that hour was like a storm upon the plain and a thunder in the mountains" (838). Théoden's blast is a great giving of spirit, and it begets more horns, more breath, and more spirit, as the Rohirrim charge the Orcs.

Tolkien is making an important point about grace. When Merry first sees the agony of Minas Tirith, he almost loses hope: "They were too late! Too late was worse than never!" But the Rohirrim get help once more, this time directly from heaven rather than in the person of Gandalf, as light begins to penetrate the dark clouds covering the battlefield. It is a reiteration of the light that Gandalf brought into Meduseld, when he brought Théoden out of his trance:

> Then suddenly Merry felt it at last, beyond doubt: a change. Wind was in his face! Light was glimmering. Far, far away, in the South the clouds could be dimly seen as remote grey shapes, rolling up, drifting: morning lay beyond them.
>
> But at that same moment there was a flash, as if lightning had sprung from the earth beneath the City. For a searing second it stood dazzling far off in black and white, its topmost tower like a glittering needle; and then as the darkness closed again there came rolling over the fields a great *boom*. (837)

This is not an instance of the pathetic fallacy. It is not nature that mimics the despair that once again threatens Théoden, but the grace coming through nature that alleviates it, for, when this cosmic change occurs, Théoden rouses himself to battle, and his horn blast raises the combined blasts of the Rohirrim. Grace begets grace, and breath breath. Théoden gives his life away and gets it back: "Fey he seemed, or the battle-fury of his fathers ran like new fire in his veins, and he was borne up on Snowmane like a god of old, even as Oromë the great in the battle of the Valar when the world was young" (838). For Pippin, the horns of the Rohirrim echo through time. When he hears them, he feels that a great weight has been lifted, "and he stood listening to the horns, and it seemed to him that they would break his heart with joy. And never in after years could he hear a horn blown in the distance without tears starting in his eyes" (850).

The difference between Théoden and Denethor is that between humility and pride. Humility puts Théoden in contact with reality, which allows him to trumpet the breath of life into the charge of the Rohirrim and to put life-giving hands on the head of Merry, who, adopted as a son, will save the life of his niece. But Denethor has no breath of life; Boromir's horn lies shattered on his lap, and he cannot sound it. His hands, rather than resting on Pippin's head in benediction, when he receives Pippin's oath of fealty, only remain as images, grasping at the life-destroying palantír. Théoden accepts Gandalf's help, acknowledges his past mistakes, and receives grace; Denethor rejects Gandalf's help, regards himself as a king, and fails as a steward, dying in a state of rejected grace.

Saruman's Cloak

Saruman is the most extreme example of one who is offered life time after time and yet chooses death. Of all Tolkien's characters, he is most representative of a modernity that must constantly reinvent itself, because it has parted company with any stabilizing truth. Tolkien uses four potent symbols to convey the spiritual condition of Saruman: his cloak of shifting colors; his mesmerizing voice; the tower of Orthanc, surrounded by water and wreckage; and his last identity as "Sharkey," a bum on the road. What we see in Saruman's story is the collapse of modernity under its own weight, a tower of Babel, built on illusion.

Saruman was sent by the Valar to save Middle-earth from Morgoth's lieutenant, Sauron, and, as the chief of the Istari, the "wizards," the function of Saruman is to apply wisdom to the problem of Sauron. But Saruman becomes a one-man Enlightenment project, and in the Enlightenment and modernity Tolkien sees the technological overthrow of the most valuable wisdom: freedom through self-restraint, the classical virtues, the primacy of Christian love.

The shifting colors of Saruman's cloak are the first symbol that Tolkien employs to give visual reality to Saruman's character and agenda. When Gandalf seeks Saruman's counsel at Orthanc, he is surprised by the change in Saruman's cloak from white to what he finally perceives as a constant change of color. Gandalf testifies at the Counsel of Elrond:

> 'I looked then and saw that his robes, which had seemed white, were not so, but were woven of all colours, and if he

moved they shimmered and changed hue so that the eye was bewildered.

"'I liked white better,' I said.

"'White!' he sneered. 'It serves for a beginning. White cloth may be dyed. The white page can be overwritten; and the white light can be broken.'

"'In which case it is no longer white,' said I. 'And he that breaks a thing to find out what it is has left the path of wisdom.'" (259)

What does the change of color imply, and why does Gandalf distrust it? First, it refers to the analytic way of understanding something by breaking it into its constituent pieces. This approach to knowledge is not only a secure part of scientific inquiry, but of logical positivism as well. It is has proven to be both powerful and inadequate. Its most basic flaw is the lack of perception that the whole of something may be greater than the sum of the parts; the moral flaw is that knowledge comes from destruction: "He that breaks a thing to find out what it is has left the path of wisdom." Saruman has engaged in an act of destruction that yields some wisdom, but obscures a great deal as well. It leads to Saruman's downfall with the Ents, who represent nature holistically. As Pippin says, "He did not understand them; and he made the great mistake of leaving them out of his calculations. He had no plan for them" (567).

Paul J. Griffiths makes the key distinction between *curiositas* and *studiositas,* which distinguishes Saruman's way of knowing from Gandalf's.[16] *Curiositas* is the "deformed kissing cousin" of *studiositas. Curiositas* is an appetite and ordering of the affections whose object is new knowledge, with which it seeks control and domination. It wants to make a *possession* of the knowledge. (Here we have the Edenic appropriation of the fruit of the tree of knowledge, and, as we have seen with Tolkien, possession is nine tenths of what goes wrong in life. Francis Bacon, at the beginning of the modern scientific enterprise, exemplified Sarumanic *curiositas,*

---

16 Paul J. Griffiths, *Intellectual Appetite* (Washington, DC: Catholic University Press, 2009), 19–22.

when he said, "My only earthly wish is . . . to stretch the deplorably narrow limits of man's dominion over the universe to their promised bounds . . . [nature will be] bound into service, hounded in her wanderings and put on the rack and tortured for her secrets.")[17] *Studiositas*, on the other hand, is a particular kind of love. It also has knowledge as its object, but does not seek to possess or dominate what it hopes to know. Rather, it participates in the object of study as a gift of love. (For examples of knowing something this way, see any number of Gerard Manley Hopkins' poems, especially "The Windhover.") To engage the world with *studiositas* is to engage it sacramentally. To engage it with *curiositias* is to break it apart, dominate it, and exploit it.

Griffiths points out that both of these form the intellectual appetite, but that *curiositas* is concerned with novelty for its own sake. This itch is captured in the image of Saruman's shimmering cloak: "White . . . it serves for a beginning," but only a beginning promoting continual change. Modernity promises constant change, in every fashion, from petticoats to the intellect, an "ism" for every appetite, all billed as progress, but progress measured by what yardstick? Saruman would have no idea, for it is power in pursuit of constant change that has him enthralled. Saruman's cloak is an emblem of the instability of *curiositas* and the cultures that take it as a foundation.

Another implication of the passage is that Saruman, deep down, hates himself. His dissatisfaction with the world as it is grows out of deep dissatisfaction with himself and his limitations. To be a "creature," a creation of another, is to be limited. Saruman gives up being the white wizard to become the rainbow wizard, because he wants to be everything all at once. But, as Gandalf says, he has lost the white to get it, refusing his God-given identity to create his own. Among philosophers, in this respect he most resembles Sartre, having declared that existence precedes essence: he will remake himself however he wants. But, as Saruman moves to grab one thing, another will elude his grasp: white or colors,

17 Francis Bacon, *The Great Instauration and New Atlantis* (Arlington Heights, IL: Harlan Davidson, 1980), viii.

but not both at the same time, in the same place and manner. Saruman would out-god God, making square circles if he could.

Saruman's cloak of many colors links him directly to the Eye of Sauron. The Eye, at the top of the Tower of Barad-Dur, is depicted as a giant search-light. To be in its gaze is to be under the most severe analysis—to be broken to pieces in the Eye's desire to discover whatever it needs to know. The Eye tortures and interrogates. It is the fully demonized scientific gaze that rejects the sacramental nature of the world and unrepentantly destroys to know, the dehumanizing gaze that Eliot's Prufrock says fixes you in a formulated phrase and then pins you to the wall.

If Saruman were brought into a 20th century novel, he would be the perfect leader of C.S. Lewis's N.I.C.E. (National Institute for Coordinated Experiments), a group of evil academics, government bureaucrats, and NGO operatives who mix dreams of world domination and a re-engineered humanity with applied science and diabolism. Saruman is the striving Baconian magus, in his lonely tower of Orthanc, ringed by an industrial park and research complex, laying waste to the countryside to feed it, and genetically engineering a half-human, half-Orc army, the Uruk-hai. (In light of Tolkien's and Lewis's concerns about technocrats, Michael Moorcock's criticism of them as establishment apologists who "don't ask any questions of white men in grey clothing who somehow have a handle on what's best of us"[18] is impossible to fathom.)

When nature, in the form of Treebeard's Ent counter-attack, leaves Saruman stranded in Orthanc, amidst flood and wreckage, Tolkien brings the biblical imagery of the Flood and the Tower of Babel into his story. The flood unleashed by Treebeard and the Ents washes away the industrial evil of Orthanc and allows the Ents to begin its ecological recovery. Stranded in the tower, Saruman is left with his voice, which he projects from the tower to Théoden, Gandalf, and the rest of the company below. Though meaningless, what he says is hypnotic and dangerous:

---

18 Michael Moorcock, "Epic Pooh," in *Bloom's Modern Critical Interpretations: J.R.R. Tolkien's 'The Lord of the Rings'*, ed. Harold Bloom (NY: Infobase, 2008), 6.

> Those who listened unwarily to that voice could seldom report the words that they heard; and if they did, they wondered, for little power remained in them. Mostly they remembered only that it was a delight to hear the voice speaking, all that it said seemed wise and reasonable, *and desire awoke in them by swift agreement to seem wise themselves.* When others spoke they seemed harsh and uncouth by contrast; and if they gainsaid the voice, anger was kindled in the hearts of those under the spell. (578)

In this passage, Tolkien has at least two targets in mind. The most obvious is the hypnotic voice of Adolph Hitler, whose persuasive power with the German people seemed diabolical. The second target is academic discourse, especially in the humanities and social sciences, which progressively excluded God as a reality, resulting in: naturalism, materialism, American pragmatism, existentialism, behaviorism, Nietzschean liberation and relativism, Marxism, Freudianism—the list goes on, like the mesmerizing colors of Saruman's cloak. All of these belief systems rejected a foundation to reality or an objective moral order. Man was the author of man. Tolkien lived long enough to watch this endless parade take possession of people and, had he lived longer, would have seen the full panoply of "post" modernisms and post-structuralisms that followed.

Hearing Saruman again is Théoden's most difficult, dangerous moment, even more so than when he meets his death in the Battle of Pelennor Field. Both he and the Rohirrim are once again drawn into a spell. Gandalf, as Théoden's spiritual teacher, allows him to confront the danger himself and sits quietly, while Théoden fights off this last demonic attack. Gandalf's priestly mission is to help Théoden grow, not protect him (579). Théoden does get help from Gimli, however, and this is not an interruption of Gandalf's educational program, for it is a community, committed to mutual aid, that Gandalf wants to nurture. Gimli's gift to the community is his stubborn, hard-to-fool practicality, and he is the first to speak: "'The words of this wizard stand on their heads,' he growled gripping the handle of his axe. 'In the language of Orthanc help means ruin, and saving means slaying'" (579). Théoden, with the additional counsel of Éomer, pulls himself out of the trance: "You are a liar, Saruman, and a corrupter of men's hearts. . . . I fear your voice has lost its charm" (580). That Théoden cannot stand up to Saruman alone is not a weakness—that he relies on help from the community is a strength.

Théoden is able to assert his will, to avoid making the same mistake twice, which is far from easy.[19] Tolkien's point is simply that people can be captured repeatedly by evil through an intellectual attack—or one that seemingly appeals to the intellect—and be led into the greatest stupidities and crimes. The Church's word for this is "heresy," a word associated with a crushing authoritarianism, but which refers to the obvious historical fact that enough of the people can be fooled enough of the time to cause immense damage, politically and spiritually. Théoden escapes from the trap of modern propaganda and wishful thinking and receives one of the principal gifts of the sacrament of penance—not getting caught again.

Only after Théoden speaks up, does Gandalf confront Saruman on his own account, and the scene shifts in a remarkable and unexpected way, as Gandalf attempts to minister to Saruman by offering him a chance to repent. Despite everything, Gandalf does not want to punish Saruman, but to save him. Gandalf does not excommunicate Saruman (by breaking his staff), until Saruman decisively rejects repeated invitations to rejoin the community. Altogether, Saruman will be given the chance to repent no less than six times: four times by Gandalf, once by Galadriel, and once by Frodo. He will refuse it each time. Saruman's refusals form Tolkien's most detailed account of how hard a soul must work to achieve damnation. (I would also note that the repeated offer of forgiveness to a deadly enemy is a decisively Christian imperative, detached from utilitarian concerns. It is one of the elements of Christian morality that defines it in contrast to classical morality and Nordic belief.)

---

19 In *The Tempest*, Prospero, whose initial mistake is the absence of mind that loses him his dukedom of Milan, nearly makes the same mistake by forgetting the conspiracy of Caliban, Trinculo, and Stephano. Shakespeare's point is that natural tendencies of character can trip us up again and again, no matter how badly they've burned us before.

When Saruman tries to cast his rhetorical spell on Gandalf, he merely replies, "Perhaps you have things to unsay" (Offer #1). When Saruman pretends puzzlement and launches into another speech, Gandalf just laughs: "Saruman, Saruman . . . you missed your path in life. You should have been the king's jester" (582). Saruman's rhetoric has run dry. Gandalf is both stern and generous. He wants to make Saruman face reality, which would be the first step toward penance and reconciliation:

> 'Listen, Saruman, for the last time! Will you not come down? Isengard has proved less strong than your hope and fancy made it. So may other things in which you still have trust. Would it not be well to leave it for a while? To turn to new things, perhaps? Think well, Saruman! Will you not come down?' (Offer #2; 582)

The tower of Orthanc becomes the visual likeness of Saruman's ego. He can either "get off it" or remain a prisoner within it. Gandalf's repeated offer to "come down" is an invitation for Saruman to make some gesture of humility to heal himself. Despite all the bloodshed that he has caused, Gandalf can still see the value in his soul, as he does in Gollum's. Tolkien highlights the moment in which Saruman could choose: "For a second he hesitated, and no one breathed." This is the mental space, given to him by grace, through Gandalf, in which Saruman can exercise free will. "Then he spoke, and his voice was shrill and cold. Pride and hate were conquering him" (582). He refuses. Gandalf asks him one more time: "I am giving you a last chance. You can leave Orthanc, free—if you choose" (Offer #3). This time, when Saruman mocks Gandalf, Gandalf reveals himself in his full authority: "Behold, I am not Gandalf the Grey, whom you betrayed. I am Gandalf the White, who has returned from death. You have no colour now, and I cast you from the order and from the Council" (583). With this, Gandalf breaks Saruman's staff asunder. But excommunication is not final; the excommunicated can return. Tolkien wants to make the point that love never quits trying to bring the sinner to life—that it takes a real *will* to hold out against it. Saruman will be offered forgiveness three more times.

In "Many Partings," Gandalf, Elrond, Galadriel, and the four Hobbits meet Saruman, as they travel toward the Shire, an old

man leaning on a staff, clothed in rags of grey and dirty white.
Saruman has become a bum on the road—and a petty dictator in
the Shire. He is like T.S. Eliot's "bankrupt millionaire"[20]: his
outer poverty and homelessness reflect his spiritual condition.

Gandalf is the first to recognize him and once again offers him
help, but Saruman rejects it. He is leaving the realm: "'Then once
more you are going the wrong way,' said Gandalf, 'and I see no
hope in your journey. But will you scorn our help? For we offer it
to you'" (Offer #4; 983). To leave the realm, like leaving the
Church behind, is to put oneself beyond help. Saruman needs to
face himself and then die to himself; to flee is to avoid the necessary rite of penance and reconciliation, to reject grace decisively.
Galadriel also urges him to accept help: "Say you are overtaken
by good fortune; for now you have a last chance" (Offer #5; 983).
But Saruman says he hopes it *is* the last chance, so he will not be
troubled anymore with refusing. They urge Gríma Wormtongue, slouching behind Sauron, to leave him, but he cannot.

The sixth and last offer comes in "The Scouring of the Shire,"
in which Saruman, whose name has been animalized to "Sharkey," is wrecking the Shire for spite and picking on those half his
size. After he attempts to knife Frodo, as Sam raises his bow to
kill him, Frodo intervenes:

> 'No, Sam!' said Frodo. 'Do not kill him even now. For he has
> not hurt me. And in any case I do not wish him to be slain in
> this evil mood. He was great once, of a noble kind that we
> should not dare to raise our hands against. He is fallen, and his
> cure is beyond us; but I would still spare him, in the hope that
> he may find it.' (1019)

John the Evangelist writes that "God is love" (1 John 4:8). Tolkien
demonstrates this love by showing it being offered again and
again to even the worst. But Saruman sees Frodo's kindness as
the final blow: "You have robbed my revenge of sweetness, and

---

20 Eliot's reference to Adam and original sin in "East Coker": "The whole
earth is our hospital / Endowed by the ruined millionaire / Wherein, if we do
well, we shall / Die of the absolute paternal care / That will not leave us, but
prevents us everywhere." That "absolute paternal care" is Eliot's ironic description of original sin.

now I must go hence in bitterness, in debt to your mercy" (1019). This is the essence of damnation—the refusal of love, perversely characterized as the incursion of a debt, clinging to impossible self-sufficiency despite facts, logic, and charity. When Wormtongue kills Saruman almost immediately thereafter, Saruman's soul is blown away, much as the black, soaring darkness of Sauron is finally blown away:

> To the dismay of those that stood by, about the body of Saruman a grey mist gathered, and rising slowly to a great height like smoke from a fire, as a pale shrouded figure is loomed over the Hill. For a moment it wavered, looking to the West; but out of the West came a cold wind, and it bent away, and with a sigh dissolved into nothing. (1020)

In *The Lord of the Rings*, the most important battle is always the inner struggle against temptation or, when caught, in overcoming it. Comparing the sheer amount of time Tolkien spends on this, in contrast to the battle scenes, one realizes that he gives the interior struggle far more attention. The greatest battle for anyone turning to God is genuine confession—the removal of the barriers that human beings put between themselves and divine love. Baptism is a sacrament that Christians only receive once, but the sacrament of penance and reconciliation, which is the ongoing extension of baptism, can be repeated as many times as needed. As baptism takes one through death to new life, so does confession.

For Saruman, the greatest self-sacrifice would be to admit that he is wrong—to confess and repent. He cannot make this sacrifice—he cannot die to himself and so he cannot live.[21] Herbert McCabe describes this as the state of damnation:

> The fire of hell is God. God is terrible and no man can look upon him and live, he is a consuming fire. To be safe in the presence of God you must be yourself sacred, you must share in God's power and life. To have come into the presence of God without this protection is damnation. That is one picture of hell, the fundamental biblical one. . . .

---

21 *Hamlet*'s Claudius and Marlowe's Dr. Faustus are famous precursors of characters who would like to repent, but cannot achieve the necessary self-sacrifice. Faustus, another scientific sorcerer, is a close ancestor of Saruman.

But hell is also the inability to accept death. The damned man is he who does not die in Christ, for whom death is therefore not a means of resurrection to new life. He is not able to make the act of self-sacrifice required of him. He is unable to see why he should. I picture the damned as spending their time continually justifying themselves to themselves, constantly showing how right they were and why they have no need to repent. . . .

All the souls in hell, I think, are quite convinced that they have been damned unjustly. The analogy I find most useful is that of the child who has lost his temper and is sulking. He wants, of course, to return to the affection of his friends, but he is blowed if he is going to apologize, his pride keeps him out even though he wants very much to return. Everybody is fully prepared to receive him back if only he will make the gesture of returning, but this he finds himself unable to do. He cannot perform the self-abandonment required. He is unable to die.

Anyone in hell who was sorry for his sin would of course instantly be in heaven; the point of hell is that this does not happen.[22]

Although there are and have been Catholic universalists, those who believe that every human being will be saved, even the worst, because the love of God will be irresistible, neither Tolkien nor C. S. Lewis[23] fall into this category. They see a genuine possibility that, rather than make the sacrifice necessary, some souls will refuse the self-abandonment required to have a self at all, and they will refuse it for all eternity. "For whosoever will save his life shall lose it; for he that shall lose his life for my sake, shall save it" (Luke 9:24). The function of the sacrament of confession is to help the sinner achieve that necessary dying to self which real repentance requires. The Roman Catholic Church has long held that people need help with this, and so priests hear confessions and grant absolution, as does Aragorn with Boromir, Gandalf with Pippin (after his theft of the palantír) and Théoden, and as Gandalf tries to do with Denethor and Saruman, who would rather abide in death than acknowledge a less than exalted reality about themselves.

22 McCabe, 135–6.
23 See Lewis's treatment of this issue in his novel, *The Great Divorce.*

10

TOLKIEN'S EUCHARISTIC MESSENGERS

"Friendship functions as the fundamental life activity in which men and women live now, however incompletely, the wholeness human life is given to achieve." PAUL J. WADELL[1]

Greater love than this no man hath, that a man lay down his life for his friends. JOHN 15:13

No longer do I call you servants . . . but I have called you friends. JOHN 15:15

TOLKIEN SAID that the main subject of *The Lord of the Rings* was death, which is to say that he was concerned with the world of time, in which all passes away. To sharpen the issue, he examines it from two perspectives, that of Elves and Men:

> The real theme for me is about something much more permanent and difficult [than Power]: Death and Immortality: the mystery of the love of the world in the hearts of a race 'doomed' to leave and seemingly lose it; the anguish in the heart of a race 'doomed' not to leave it, until its whole-evil aroused story is complete.[2]

In another letter he comments, "It is about Death and the desire for deathlessness. Which is hardly more than to say it is a tale written by a Man!"[3]

---

1 Paul J. Wadell, *Friendship and Moral Life* (Notre Dame, IN: Notre Dame University Press, 1989), xvi.

2 *Letters*, 246.

3 Ibid., 262.

"Its whole evil-aroused story" was never far from Tolkien's mind when he thought about history, whether in the primary or his own secondary world. At the heart of *The Lord of the Rings*, Tolkien pits the "mystery of love" against the "doom" of loss, which affects every character in the book.

Although Elves have the lifespan of Middle-earth itself, they must live to watch Middle-earth itself pass away. Their doom, unlike men's, is an eventual living death and then death itself, when the world dies. Their future is to "diminish," as the world diminishes. They live facing the past and, like a hard-pressed army, are pushed back into the future. Elves can die of grief or in combat or by accident, but, if they do, they go to the Halls of Mandos in Valinor, where they await reincarnation,[4] to continue for the lifespan of the world. "The Elves were sufficiently longeval to be called by Man 'immortal.' But they were not unageing or unwearying,"[5] and many choose to leave Middle-earth, taking ships from the Grey Havens to Valinor.

Men, who are not bound to the fate of the world, also go to the Halls of Mandos after death, and, from there, no one knows. Unlike the Elves, their exit is permanent, their life span short. So both face nonexistence, *seemingly,* Tolkien says. That important word suggests the Music of Ilúvatar may have eucatastrophic surprises for both Elves and Men and once again harkens to the New Testament as a subtext of *The Lord of the Rings*.

In a world that Men and Elves are doomed to leave and which passes away itself, inevitable sacrifice can either be futilely denied or actively embraced, and, rightly seen, death is both enemy and friend, "a release from the weariness of time."[6] The world of *The Lord of the Rings* teaches that, paradoxically, we must love the things of this earth and also let go of them. Yet it is the evil things, however damaging, that are often the hardest to give up.

---

4 Ibid., 246 and 204–5; *Morgoth's Ring*, 365; Glorfindel, who helps Aragorn and Frodo at the Ford of Bruinen, is a reincarnated Elf who had died fighting a Balrog; see J. R. R. Tolkien, *The Peoples of Middle-earth*, ed. Christopher Tolkien (NY: Houghton Mifflin, 2000), 380.

5 *Letters*, 325.

6 Ibid., 205.

Time as a School of Sacrifice

The dominant tone of *The Lord of the Rings* is elegiac. It begins in a birthday party for a very old Hobbit, passing out of the Shire for good, leaving his property to the nephew who will sorely miss him, and ends with that same Hobbit and nephew, leaving Middle-earth for good, on a healing voyage toward death. In between, the passing away of things—people, kingdoms, species, ages of history—crowd the book with a sense of sublime loss. St. Bede compared the duration of a man's life to the time it takes a sparrow to fly in one window of a mead hall and out the other.[7] The constant bass thrum of desolation in *Beowulf* and its portrayal in "The Wanderer" provide Tolkien with a pervasive counter-melody to hope:

> So this middle-earth each day fails and falls. No man may indeed become wise before he has had his share of winters in this world's kingdom. . . . The wise warrior must consider how ghostly it will be when all the wealth of his world stands waste, just as now here and there through this middle-earth wind-blown walls stand covered with frost-fall, storm-beaten dwellings. . . . Where has the horse gone? Where the young warrior? Where is the giver of treasure? What has become of the feasting seats? Where are the joys of the hall? Alas, the bright cup! Alas, the mailed warrior! Alas, the prince's

---

7 Bede records in *Ecclesiastical History of the English People* that the young king Edwin, before accepting the Christian faith, was advised by one of his councilors: "The present life of man upon earth, O King, seems to me in comparison with that time which is unknown to us like the swift flight of a sparrow through the mead-hall where you sit at supper in winter, with your Ealdormen and thanes, while the fire blazes in the midst and the hall is warmed, but the wintry storms of rain or snow are raging abroad. The sparrow, flying in at one door and immediately out at another, whilst he is within, is safe from the wintry tempest, but after a short space of fair weather, he immediately vanishes out of your sight, passing from winter to winter again. So this life of man appears for a little while, but of what is to follow or what went before we know nothing at all." (Book 2, Chapter 13), trans. A.M. Sellar (London: George Bell and Sons, 1907), Christian Classical Ethereal Library, http://www.ccel.org/ccel/bede/history.v.ii.xiii.html (accessed March 10, 2014).

glory! . . . Here wealth is fleeting, here friend is fleeting, here man is fleeting, here woman is fleeting—all this earthly habitation shall be emptied.[8]

So speaks the Anglo-Saxon poet, like Qoheleth of Ecclesiastes. Tolkien makes a gift of horses to his Anglo-Saxon Rohirrim and adapts the poetry of "The Wanderer" as the song of a "long forgotten" poet of Rohan:

> Where now the horse and the rider? Where is the horn that was
> blowing?
> Where is the helm and the hauberk, and the bright hair flowing?
> Where is the hand on the harpstring and the red fire glowing?
> Where is the spring and the harvest and the tall corn growing?
> They have passed like rain on the mountain, like a wind in the
> meadow;
> The days have gone down in the West behind the hills into shadow.
> Who shall gather the smoke of the dead wood burning,
> Or behold the flowing years from the Sea returning? (508)

Different poets and philosophers have proposed different solutions to the problem of time: slowing it down, stopping it, speeding it up. Tolkien considers all of them in *The Lord of the Rings*. But it is clear that his solution, enacted through the book again and again, is submission to time. Time pries our fingers loose from whatever we want to grasp; it is the very school of sacrifice; time itself is a lesson, forced upon us, until we accept the letting go. Since we cannot hold onto our lives, no matter how tightly we clutch them, pouring ourselves out and into the world is the only answer.

For Tolkien, this solution was reaffirmed daily in sacramental Communion. The Eucharist does not just memorialize Christ's death and resurrection, although it does that. It breaks the barriers of time and space and makes each communicant a participant in those events; the Eucharist anchors time in eternity. As Tolkien said, the Eucharist is always itself. By taking the body of Christ into himself, Tolkien took Christ's time-transcending sacrifice into himself. Christ's death and resurrection enacted a solution to

---

8 "The Wanderer," *Norton Anthology of English Literature*, 6th ed. Gen. ed. M.H. Abrams Vol. 1 (NY: W.W. Norton & Company, 2012), 69–70.

the problem of time: the sacrificial giving out of what human beings could not keep. For Tolkien, the Eucharist was the other side of the darkness expressed by the Anglo-Saxon poets and Qoheleth, the side of Johannine light.

✠

Since time itself is also a creation of the Logos, the attempt to evade its imperatives is almost always sinful. The Ring in part is a technology for evading time, because it gives its wearer unnaturally long life. Its side effect, however, is to destroy the soul. Bilbo, aged III when the book begins, tells Gandalf that he is not "well-preserved" at all, but badly preserved: "I feel all thin, sort of *stretched,* if you know what I mean: like butter that has been scraped over too much bread" (32). Bilbo struggles to let go of the Ring despite its attraction, because, deep down, he realizes the Ring is "thinning" him, stretching him out on the rack of time, beyond the span he was meant to live. Those who deny the sacrificial aspect of time, as manifested in aging, begin to lose their souls and become wraiths.

Giving up the Ring is hard, because it seems to become an essential part of the bearer. The Ring makes its keeper "special," more individual, superior. It gives long life, the ability to become invisible, and perhaps deeper insight into the difference between good and evil, like the Edenic apple. But the paradox is that the eventual fate of the keeper is to lose all specialness or individuality and be subsumed into the will of Sauron as a wraith and a slave. Bilbo's difficulty in giving up the ring comes from the artificial sense of being superior, on top of the world, even while he knows the Ring is his enemy. Giving up the Ring is a sacrifice, a psychic disempowering of himself. Bilbo's renunciation of all his goods, his home, Hobbiton, is only a means toward getting enough momentum to also renounce the Ring. Yet, Tolkien's greater point is that, as our lives draw to a close, divestiture of home and possessions, gradual or sudden, is not just inevitable, but an indispensable preparation.

Bilbo ages very rapidly once he gives up the Ring, because he hasn't been significantly damaged by it, but Gollum doesn't age at all. His soul, which wasn't healthy when he got the Ring, has been so stretched that it is rent in two, the necessary sacrifice of aging having been refused. Gollum becomes schizophrenic, so wretched that he hates the Ring as much as he loves it and wants to die even as he grasps for it.

☩

Galadriel faces a more complex moral problem with regard to time. As the bearer of the Ring, Nenya, with whose power she preserves Lothlórien, she must decide about time for an entire civilization. Lothlórien is a realm apart. It is ringed by a darkness that it has been able to exclude, and, inside it, time seems to move differently than in the larger world.[9] Using Nenya, Galadriel encloses Lothlórien in a time capsule to preserve it from the evil outside: "on the land of Lórien no shadow lay" (349). Frodo feels the temporal change as he crosses the border: "as he set foot upon the far bank of Silverlode a strange feeling had come upon him . . . it seemed to him that he had stepped over a bridge of time into a corner of the Elder Days, and was now walking in a world that was no more" (349). Tolkien sets forth the moral flaw in Galadriel's action:

> [T]he Elvish weakness is . . . to regret the past, and to become unwilling to face change. . . . Hence they fell into a measure to Sauron's deceits: they desired some 'power' over things as they are . . . to make their particular will to preservation effective: to arrest change, and keep things always fresh and fair.[10]

When the Fellowship leaves Lothlórien, Sam notices the moon has barely changed; either they have been there at least a month, which seems too long, or only a few days, which seems too short. Puzzled, he says, "Anyone would think that time did not count in there!" (388). Frodo and Aragorn understand the truth: the hours in Lothlórien are rich and seem short, shorter than they were, and, seemingly, time flowed in the outer world at a faster pace.

9 See Verlyn Flieger, *A Question of Time* (Kent, Ohio: Kent State University Press, 1997), 90–115.

10 *Letters*, 236.

But time in Lothlórien is mysterious. It turns out that the Fellowship has spent a month in Lothlórien (from January 17 to February 16 according to Tolkien's chronology in Appendix B, page 1092). Although time moves there, it is a world which does not decay. It is not utterly static, but frighteningly close to being so: we see no Elf children. Second, it is closer to eternity than the rest of the world—it is "unstained." The usual reminders of the passage of time are absent in Lothlórien. "Time doesn't count," because Galadriel's kingdom is virtually impervious to the destruction we associate with time's passage.

Galadriel's erection of a temporal barricade is understandable, under the circumstances, but it is dangerous, for the nature of the world is change: death and decay are necessary for birth and growth, and the Elves have excluded themselves from regenerative forces as well as destructive ones. Galadriel, in her own way, has committed the sin of Melkor, although he tried to disrupt the Music and Galadriel has tried to insert a giant "rest." Legolas speaks wisely, like the preacher of Ecclesiastes, when he says, "beneath the Sun all things must wear to an end at last" (388). The Elves would like to dodge this reality, but they are more aware of it than anyone. They know they do not have the capacity to adapt to what is coming. Even if the Ring is destroyed, they will have to either leave Middle-earth or dwindle into a much-diminished race, as the world slowly passes. Galadriel's refusal of the Ring is a double sacrifice: that of the personal power the Ring would give her and of Nenya's power to perpetuate Lothlórien. When she sacrifices Lothlórien, "the heart of Elvendom on earth" (352), she sacrifices her own heart and the hearts of her people. It is the greatest sacrifice in *The Lord of the Rings* and finally achieves Galadriel's penance for pursuing the Silmarils with Fëanor. In making this sacrifice, Galadriel realigns herself with time, and, although she doesn't age like Bilbo, since she is an Elf, she begins to become a relic of the past. When Frodo meets her on the river, as the Fellowship leaves Lórien, she sinks into time, fading into a dream: "Already she seemed to him, as by men of late days Elves still at times are seen: present and yet remote, a living vision of that which has already been *left far behind by the flowing streams of Time*" (373).

Yet, the refusal of the Ring sets her free; she can return to Valinor. At the end of the book, in the chapter "Many Partings" (the parallel opposite of the early chapter "Many Meetings"), Tolkien returns to this elegiac image in describing Gandalf, Galadriel, Celeborn and Elrond, talking late into the night after the Hobbits have gone to sleep:

> If any wanderer had chanced to pass, little would he have seen or heard, and it would have seemed to him only that he saw grey figures, carved in stone, memorials of forgotten things now lost in unpeopled lands. For they did not move or speak with mouth, looking from mind to mind; and only their shining eyes stirred and kindled as their thoughts went to and fro. (985)

Time has already turned this group of heroes to monuments; their thoughts, outside the range of human comprehension, are silent and inaccessible. Finally, the grey-cloaked Elves leave Gandalf and the Hobbits and ride into the mountains and gathering mist with a lightning flash: "Frodo knew that Galadriel had held aloft her ring in token of farewell." The flash from Nenya, whose power is dying, puts a period on the Elves' chapter in Middle-earth. Grey is the least assertive color, a color for the acceptance of loss and for blending in. The Elves have accepted sacrifice and blended in, once more, with time. At this very moment, perhaps, the third age ends, and the fourth begins, the age of Men.

☩

Gondor has much the same problem as Lothlórien—it has grown decadent by falling in love with the past. It sees no future for itself and would like to make time stand still, or even retreat. The people of Gondor are descendants of the survivors of Númenor; they seem to have once again caught the Númenorean desire to live forever, which Tolkien describes in *The Silmarillion*:

> The fear of death grew ever darker upon them, and they delayed it by all means that they could; and they began to build great houses for their dead, while their wise men labored incessantly to discover if they might learn the secret of recalling life, or at the least of prolonging men's days . . . yet they

achieved only the art of preserving incorrupt the dead flesh of men, and they filled all the land with silent tombs in which the thought of death was enshrined in the darkness. But those that lived turned the more eagerly to pleasure and revelry, desiring ever more goods and more riches. (266)

The Númenoreans are Tolkien's ancient Egyptians—and his moderns—all in denial of time and death. Many of the features of old Númenor, which the Dúnedain (Elvish for Númenorean) fled, are now part of Gondor. The visibly depopulated Minas Tirith, with its low birthrate, has lost half its population (752); yet the throne room is lined with great statues of former kings, and, as in Númenor, tombs are one of the city's most impressive features. The White Tree, the emblem of Minas Tirith, has died. There may be some despondency about the state of Britain in Tolkien's description; it was embroiled in the Second World War, clearly losing its empire, and its birth rate contracting. (The fertility rate of England and Wales had been in decline since 1900 and in the 1930s was 1.78.[11]) Gondor needs Aragon, the true king, who will take it into the future rather than mire it in the past.

Speeding up time is as much a refusal of its sacrificial nature as slowing it down. In English literature, John Donne and Andrew Marvell offer both as playful alternatives to the pressure of time. Donne's lovers would like to stop the sun in its tracks, while in "To His Coy Mistress," Marvell's lover suggests to his lady that, if they cannot slow time down, they can speed it up:

> And tear our pleasures with rough strife
> Through the iron gates of life
> Thus, though we cannot make our sun
> Stand still, yet we will make him run.

Tolkien rejects both alternatives. The trick, as Niggle learns in Purgatory, is to become the Master of Time, and the paradoxical

11 David Coleman, "The Road to Low Fertility," *Ageing Horizons,* Issue No. 7, 7–15. Oxford Institute on Aging, 2007. http://www.ageing.ox.ac.uk/files/ageing_horizons_7_coleman_fd.pdf, accessed February 4, 2013.

truth is that mastery comes through obedience and submission. Tom Bombadil is Master, as Goldberry says, because he has never been caught. All the traps of Time, whether Niggle's procrastination or Saruman's ambition to speed the future, come from the refusal of sacrifice. Niggle would rather paint pictures in his head than get down to work; Saruman would rather impose a technocratic future on the present than allow the world to develop at its natural pace.

Treebeard speaks for Tolkien's position: "Don't be hasty," he keeps telling Merry and Pippin, who come from a folk that are anything but hasty according to modern standards. Treebeard, the oldest living thing in Middle-earth,[12] is whom we trust for chronological advice. He sees that "young Saruman" is too fast and the Elves of Lothlórien artificially slow. Of Saruman he says, "He has a mind of metal and wheels; and he does not care for growing things, except as far as they serve him *for the moment*" (473). Of Lothlórien he says, "They are *rather behind the world in there*, I guess. . . . Neither this country, nor anything else outside the Golden Wood, is what it was when Celeborn was Young" (467). Saruman does not have the patience for natural growth. The slow things of the world, trees, are fodder for his dream of ever accelerating development. But trying to live outside the Logos-centric reality of time eventually catches up with him, as Tolkien believed it would catch up for the modern world, in ecological disaster. Treebeard's final assessment of Saruman: "He always was hasty. That was his ruin" (980). The Elves, on the other hand, having sealed themselves from time, will eventually feel its bite all the more sharply. Saruman and Lothlórien both resist the cosmic time scheme: a world of cyclical planting and harvest, of seasons, but also a linear progression of beginnings, middles, and endings. The Hobbits, in their staid agricultural existence and distributist economy come closest to mastering time in the cyclical sense. However, they are somewhat like the Elves. They have been protected for so long by the Rangers,

---

12 Earlier, Bombadil says he is "Eldest" (131), but Tom perhaps does not fall into the classification of a normal "living thing."

without knowing it, that they have forgotten history and are only reminded of it when Saruman, as "Sharkey," takes over the Shire.

Treebeard, part of a dying race in which Ent-wives and Ent-husbands have seemingly achieved a permanent divorce, feels the end is not far off and accepts it. In conversation with Galadriel, he says, "[T]he world is changing: I feel it in the water, I feel it in the earth, and I smell it in the air. I do not think we shall meet again." Although Celeborn hesitates to accept this, Galadriel's reply indicates that she has: "Not in Middle-earth, nor until the lands that lie under the wave are lifted up again. Then in the willow-meads of Tasarian we may meet in the Spring. Farewell!" (981).

✠

Among the most courageous of Tolkien's characters are the Elf-women who sacrifice their relative immortality to marry human men. In taking human husbands, they accept a short (by Elvish standards) life in return for love. In effect, they lay down their lives for the love of another, fulfilling the ideal of John 15:13. For love, Arwen goes out of sync with the time decreed for Elves, and although, as I've argued, working contrary to time is generally a very bad decision for Tolkien's characters, in these few instances Tolkien sees an exception: love was made to transcend time, so when they conflict, it is best to follow love. Here, Tolkien's faith forms the inscape of his story, as he shows Arwen's love informing her fidelity to Aragorn. The Elves who marry men demonstrate the boundary-crossing character of love, which exists at a higher level of reality than time. "For I am sure that neither death, nor life . . . nor things present, nor things to come . . . shall be able to separate us from the love of God, which is in Christ Jesus our Lord" (Rom. 8:38–9).

Aragorn is given the "grace to go" in keeping with his own will. He lives to the age of 210, after a 120 year reign as king, and then decides to die. But in consolation to Arwen, he prophesies before he dies, "Behold! We are not bound forever to the circles of the world, and beyond them is more than memory. Farewell!" (1063). It is a Christian promise, delivered in the timbre of Norse myth. But Aragorn's words are ratified by what happens next—

Tolkien describes the transformation of Aragorn's body to what it may be like after resurrection:

> Then a great beauty was revealed in him, so that all who after came there looked on him in wonder; for they saw that the grace of his youth, and the valour of his manhood, and the wisdom and majesty of his age were blended together. And long there he lay, an image of the splendour of the Kings of Men in glory undimmed before the breaking of the world. (1063)

Nothing is taken from Aragorn by time—all the good remains, together. Arwen dies that winter, in Lothlórien, "alone, under the fading trees," but with the prophecy of Aragorn that we are not "bound to the circles of this world." That she goes to Cerin Amroth to die, in the middle of Lothlórien, is very important, and we get a good hint that Aragorn meets her there in spirit, though this is given very subtly, far ahead of the event, in *The Fellowship of the Ring*. Frodo sees Aragorn upon Cerin Amroth in Lothlórien, "wrapped in some fair memory," and hears him say *"Arwen vanimedla, namárië!"* which means "Fair Arwen, farewell!" Aragorn is reliving a previous good-bye to Arwen, when they plighted their troth on the spot where he is standing (Appendix A, 1060). He smiles and tells Frodo: "'Here is the heart of Elvendom on earth . . . and where my heart dwells ever'. . . . And taking Frodo's hand in his, he left the hill of Cerin Amroth and came there never again *as a living man*" (my italics; 352). The hint is that he came there in another way and that he and Arwen departed from Middle-earth together.

Arwen's love of Aragorn is part of Tolkien's realized eschatology. Arwen's sacrifice connects her to Aragorn within time and, finally, in eternity. Love conquers time.

The Eucharistic Messengers

Gandalf does not at first refer to those sent with the Ring as a fellowship, but as "messengers" (270). A messenger is not only one who bears a message, but also one who has an errand. Though the errand of these messengers is to destroy the Ring in the Cracks of Doom, they are Eucharistic messengers, because they put their lives on the line to do it. For Frodo, both bearing the Ring and giving it up are an immense sacrifice. The willingness to make these sacrifices characterizes all members of the Fellowship and most of the people pulled into their orbit.

The principal Catholic mode of giving up evil attachments is to replace them with the body of Christ in the sacrament of Communion. Attachment to the self is replaced by attachment to Christ and to a community of friends. Shared meals are a universal way of human coming-together and community formation. The Eucharist binds the Church together as a "fellowship," a sacrificial community that becomes one, "in the unity of the Holy Spirit," as each member takes in Christ's sacrifice through his body and blood. Ideally, the community formed by the Eucharist fosters friendship with God and between its members, so that the virtues, and particularly kenotic love, can flourish.

This ideal is surprisingly like Aristotle's ideal of the *polis* as a seedbed of virtue based on friendship. The city-state could only flourish if it was virtuous, and individuals could not become virtuous without the support of a virtuous community. Aristotle himself had to recognize that this ideal had not been achieved, so he relied on groups of friends—fellowships—within the *polis* to be the nursery of virtue.

The sacraments all require the choice of one thing over another, a commitment to a quest that rejects other paths. Love cannot be imagined without sacrifice, and one cannot imagine love flourishing without friendship to nourish it. In a consumer society connected by "social media," where the intimacy of friendship is harder than ever to achieve, *The Lord of the Rings* is all the more poignant for its portrayal of what is essential to a good life: the deep friendship that leads to the cultivation of virtue and willingness to sacrifice for others.

The Lord of the Rings is built on self-sacrificial love. In the many Christian readings now available, the most explicated episodes are Gandalf's death and resurrection, Frodo's failed attempt to save Gollum, and Frodo and Sam's march up Mt. Doom to destroy the Ring. Sacrifice is a central concern in all three, Eucharistic self-sacrifice in the first and third, and sacrificing security for the sake of mercy in the second. The elements of comparison between Tolkien's myth and the account of Christ given in the gospels are obvious for biblically literate readers. Gandalf goes into Moria, a virtual tomb, knowing he may have to give his life to protect the rest of the Company. Aragorn warns him, "if you pass through the doors of Moria beware" (297) and tells the rest of the Fellowship, "He has led us in here against our fears, but he will lead us out again, at whatever cost to himself" (330). Gandalf pays the price, at the Bridge of Khazad-Dûm, where he plunges into the abyss with the Balrog, protecting the retreat of his friends. Later we find that Gandalf didn't die in the fall, but in his epic combat with the Balrog, which Gandalf fights in tunnels that go even deeper than Moria, "gnawed by nameless things" older than Sauron. In this darkness and despair, Gandalf can only escape by sticking to the heels of the monster, whom he kills on Mt. Celebil: "Then darkness took me, and I strayed out of thought and time, and I wandered far on roads that I will not tell. Naked I was sent back—for a brief time, until my task is done" (502). At first, when Aragorn, Gimli, and Legolas meet him in Fangorn Forest, they do not recognize Gandalf, whose death has been a voyage of transformation—he comes back as Gandalf the White, much changed, more powerful, and full of light.

Gandalf is resurrected, not resuscitated—he dies and comes back in something akin to Paul's description of a resurrection body; he is immensely more powerful than he was before. Also, like the transformed Jesus on Easter morning, Gandalf is not immediately recognized.[13] Tolkien, of course, is not portraying Christ in Gandalf, but is creating a character who acts in imitation of Christ, in fact, a particularly medieval version of the Christ who dies as a bloody but victorious combatant over the Enemy of mankind.[14]

The parallels between Christ's passion and Frodo's journey

---

13 In Luke 24:13–33, the difficulty in recognizing the resurrected Christ is captured in the Road to Emmaus story and in the account of his first appearance to the disciples in Jerusalem, 24:36–45; in John 20:15, Mary Magdalene takes him for the gardener.

14 Gustave Aulen, *Christus Victor: An Historical Study of the Three Main Types of the Idea of the Atonement* (Eugene, OR: Wipf and Stock, 2003; SPCK, 1931).

into Mordor and up Mt. Doom are many and obvious. Frodo's Via Dolorosa starts on Amon Hen, his Garden of Gethsemane, when he goes off by himself to find the courage to go alone into Mordor, the land of death, and struggles with the evil spirit, Sauron. He is stripped, scourged, and mocked by Orcs in the Tower of Cirith Ungol (910). He gives up violence once and for all after fending off Gollum's penultimate attack: "'I'll be an orc no more,' he cried, 'and I'll bear no weapon, fair or foul. Let them take me, if they will!'" (937). This scene recalls Jesus's statement to Peter in the Garden of Gethsemane, "all that take the sword shall perish with the sword" (Matthew 26:52). The Ring weighs more and more on Frodo, as he goes up Mt. Doom (literally, the "mountain of judgment"), becoming a symbol whose "applicability" includes the weight of the cross and sin endured by Christ; and, when Frodo can go no longer, Sam becomes his Simon of Cyrene, carrying him up the mountain. Frodo is a fictional character shown to be acting in imitation of a Christ unknown to him—except that he lives in a Logos-centric universe that is lit by its Creator. The Eucharistic nature of Frodo's trek is emphasized by the long passage about *lembas* in the chapter, "Mount Doom":

> The *lembas* had a virtue without which they would long ago have lain down to die. It did not satisfy desire, and at times Sam's mind was filled with the memories of food, and the longing for simple bread and meats. And yet this waybread of the Elves had a potency that increased as travelers relied on it alone and did not mingle is with other foods. It fed the will, and it gave strength to endure, and to master sinew and limb beyond the measure of mortal kind. (936)

Even the rationale for fasting before taking communion is implied here, as is the connection of "waybread," to "wayfarers," a traditional name for Christians, who see themselves on a lifetime quest. The potency it has for those who rely on it alone alludes to Jesus's many sayings about offering "living water," so that people will never thirst, and "the bread of life," so they will never hunger, and recalls God's provision of *manna* in the wilderness to the Hebrews. Frodo and Sam are empowered by this "communion bread," so they can commit the necessary Eucharistic act of sacrificing themselves, for the love of Middle-earth, to destroy the Ring. Tolkien shows us Holy Communion and the way it works by the usual technique of fairy story: defamiliarization in the service of *recovery*. By showing us Communion in the context of heroic quest, he restores our understanding of the heroic nature of the sacrament.

Like a regular communicant, Frodo eats *lembas* from Lothlórien to the Cracks of Doom. It is after eating the *lembas* in the Emyn Muil that Frodo begins to pity Gollum. He stops wishing for Gollum's death and hopes for his redemption. When Frodo looks at Gollum, he sees his own eventual corruptibility, which is realized at Mt. Doom, when he cannot give up the Ring. Finally Frodo can forgive Gollum, who bites off his finger and thus saves him. Peace comes into Frodo's eyes: "He felt only joy, great joy"; "Let us forgive him," he tells Sam. Tolkien gives us a literary representation of a communicant who doesn't know Communion, imitating a Christ he doesn't know, in a time before the Incarnation. Certainly, Tolkien believed with the Gospel of John and the Letter to the Hebrews that Christ was active in the world from the beginning.

fRiendship as a school of sacRifice

Like time, friendship is another school of sacrifice in *The Lord of the Rings*, because it fosters the love that makes one willing to die for others. Friendship starts with the Hobbits. Sam is hauled through the window by Gandalf to accompany Frodo, but he would never let Frodo leave without him anyway. Sam tells Frodo, after they meet Gildor Inglorion and his Elves, "*Don't you leave him!* They said to me. *Leave him!* I said. I never mean to. I am going with him, if he climbs to the Moon" (87). Out of love for Frodo, Sam says good-bye to the Shire and Rosie Cotton. Frodo's young friends Merry and Pippin are just as adamant about sticking to him: "You can trust us to stick to you through thick and thin. . . . You can trust us to keep any secret of yours. . . . But you cannot trust us to let you face trouble alone. . . . We are your friends, Frodo" (105). This friendship is set at the core of the Fellowship. Elrond does not create the Fellowship by requiring the members to swear an oath; he knows that love will hold it together or it won't. And although Boromir temporarily betrays the love of the Fellowship, he dies defending Pippin and Merry, whom Aragorn, Legolas, and Gimli pursue after their capture. It is the *love* of the Fellowship that is in metaphysical conflict with Sauron's hate. Gimli and Legolas become fast friends in Lothlorien; perhaps because of Gimli's love for Galadriel, Legolas begins to see Gimli as a person rather than a generic "Dwarf." Their friendship grows to such an extent that, after many years pass, they are allowed to leave the Grey Havens together to voyage to Valinor (1098).

The love of the Fellowship is not exclusive, but grows to universal proportions: *philia*, the love of friends, includes more and more people, until it becomes universal love, *agape*. The Fellowship is joined, in spirit, by Elrond, Galadriel, Celeborn, Théoden, Éomer, Éowyn, Faramir, Beregond, and, finally, all those who fight at the Black Gate. All offer themselves to almost certain death, out of friendship.

Τhε Ϝʀιεnδʃhιp οϝ (ΠεʀʀΥ αnδ ἘοωΥn Ͻεϝεατʃ Ͻεατh

In the Battle of Pelennor Fields, Merry and Éowyn, under the guiding hand of Providence, confront the Nazgûl King and destroy him. They are the only two people who could kill him, Éowyn being a woman and Merry having the right weapon. They have both disobeyed Théoden to be there, and Éowyn has gone to war for the wrong reasons; but in the end, the bond of love between Éowyn, Merry, and Théoden redeems disobedience and skewed motives. Éowyn goes from being a shieldmaiden of Rohan with the battle character of a valkyrie to being a Marian valkyrie, engaging the great dragon—the Nazgûl King and his dragon-like steed—to protect Théoden. Éowyn and Merry are, as Tolkien describes it, in a "sacrificial situation."

Tolkien's Nazgûl King is based in part on John Milton's character, "Death." In *Paradise Lost*, Book 2, as Satan is looking for a way out of Hell, he meets his daughter and paramour, Sin, with whom he has conceived a child, Death. Death in turn has raped his mother, who has given birth to a pack of Furies who gnaw at her guts. Sin, Death, and the Devil form Milton's demonic trinity. Death is described as follows:

> The other shape,
> If shape it might be call'd that shape had none
> Distinguishable in member, joint, or limb,
> Or substance might be call'd that shadow seem'd,
> For each seem'd either; black it stood as Night,
> Fierce as ten Furies, terrible as hell,
> And shook a dreadful Dart; what seem'd his head
> The likeness of a Kingly Crown had on. (lines 666–673)

Milton's piles up the word "seem'd," because Death is substance-less, nothing but a voracious black hole. The likeness to the Nazgûl King is obvious. A wraith, the former witch-king of Angmar no longer has a physical form, yet clothing fits him as if he were a man. He too wears a crown, which sits atop virtually nothing. In his confrontation with Gandalf at the destroyed gate of Gondor, the Nazgûl King describes himself as Death:

> In rode the Lord of the Nazgûl. A great black shape against the fires beyond he loomed up, grown to a vast menace of despair....
> The Black Rider flung back his hood, and behold! He had a kingly crown; and yet upon no head visible was it set. The red fires shone between it and the mantled shoulders vast and dark. From a mouth unseen there came a deadly laughter.
> ....'Old fool! This is my hour. Do you not know Death when you see it? Die now and curse in vain!' And with that he lifted high his sword and flames ran down the blade. (829)

Death arrives in person and claims the hour for his own. "Die now," he commands, and it isn't just a physical death that he desires, but a spiritual one as well: "curse in vain!" Even Death is distracted, however, when the horns of the arriving Rohirrim sound. The Wraith King leaves Gandalf and mounts another steed for the battlefield, a flying horror that has the characteristics of both a lizard and a bird; it is, essentially, a dragon. He descends from the sky on Théoden and his horse Snowmane, flinging the horse on top of its rider. Then he advances on

Théoden, so that his beast may devour him. Only "Dernhelm" stands in the way.

In this tableau, Éowyn is the primary sacrificial figure. Initially, her intention is to die in battle out of despair, to achieve "reknown" for herself and to redeem the injured glory of her people. Her objective is as bad as her reasons. She is broken-hearted, because Aragorn has refused her love. He is committed to Arwen and he recognizes that Éowyn is not in love with him but the idea of martial valor. Théoden has ordered her to stay home, with the women, children, and old men, whom she is to govern in his place and may have to die defending. Before he leaves to raise the army of the dead, Aragorn tells her that her duty is to her people:

> 'Too often have I heard of duty,' she cried. 'But am I not of the House of Eorl, a shieldmaiden and not a dry-nurse? I have waited on faltering feet long enough. Since they falter no longer, it seems, may I not now spend my life as I will?'
>
> 'Few may do that with honour. . . .'
>
> 'A time may come soon,' said he, 'when none will return. Then there will be need of valour without renown, for none shall remember the deeds that are done in the last defense of your homes. Yet the deeds will not be less valiant because they are unpraised.' (784)

Most of the good deeds in Tolkien's story do enter the collective memory and are rightfully praised. In *The Lord of the Rings*, self-sacrifice never goes wrong, is never in vain. When critics like Edmund Wilson complain that *The Lord of the Rings* is a boys' book, one of their reasons is that Tolkien is sentimental, blind to reality, as if the door to modernity had a sign on it saying, "Be fashionable and abandon hope, all ye sophisticates and intellectuals who enter here." However, it happens to be the Catholic belief that self-sacrifice *is* the highest form of love, that suffering *is* meaningful and redemptive, and that neither is in vain. Tolkien was a veteran of the Somme who lost two of his three best friends in battle[15] and was evacuated for trench fever, which

15 Rob Gilson and Geoffrey Smith, members of the "T.C.B.S," the "Tea Club and Barrovian Society" of Tolkien's youth. See John Garth's *Tolkien and*

required long hospitalizations. He was an orphan who lost his last parent at the age of 12. He knew the wounded of World War I, including his friend C.S. Lewis, who had had a succession of surgeries to remove shrapnel from an artillery shell. He was not naïve or inexperienced about war or suffering; he had seen far more, perhaps, than most of his critics. But he interpreted suffering and sacrifice with a belief in hope and hope's fulfillment.

In this short exchange between Éowyn and Aragorn, Tolkien offers consolation to the millions who died and went to mass graves and had no witnesses for their ending. He acknowledges the value of uncelebrated courage. It is the Christian consolation that good deeds do not go unnoticed by God, however unpraised by men, that what we do is meaningful, because God sees and remembers.

Tolkien tempers the Germanic mythos, in which great deeds that are unwitnessed lack reality. Even in *Beowulf*, written by a Christian poet sometime in the 8th century, courage motivated by pride is criticized, and, in the end, gets Beowulf killed. Early Christians made the same criticism of classical heroes like Achilles or Hercules. For them, it was the martyrs, however unsung, who truly defined courage, because their sacrifice was motivated by love. Referring to Wiglaf and Sir Gawain as heroes who display this Christian understanding of courage, Tolkien writes, "It is the heroism of obedience and love not of pride or willfulness that is the most heroic and most moving."[16]

Éowyn willfully rides off to battle, leaving her post with the women, children, and old men, disguised as Dernhelm. She takes Merry, whose desire also is to go to battle. Merry does not know her, until she takes her helmet off to face the Nazgûl King, and then he is struck with pity, when he recognizes Éowyn in the face of Dernhelm, "one without hope who goes in search of death" (803).

Merry's motives are purer than Éowyn's. Days before, he had

The Great War: The Threshold of Middle-earth (NY: Houghton Mifflin, 2003). On Tolkien's trench fever, see 200 and 207 et seq.

16 J.R.R. Tolkien, "The Homecoming of Beorhtnoth Beorhthelm's Son," *Essays and Studies* 6 (1953): 1–18; 13–16.

told Théoden, "I do not want to be parted from you like this, Théoden King. And as all my friends have gone to the battle, I should be ashamed to stay behind" (801). Merry truly loves Théoden, and he knows the great danger of Frodo, Sam, and Pippin. His courage arises from the love of his friends.

The battle with the Nazgûl King is described through the dazed consciousness of Merry, who has been thrown with Éowyn from their horse. Tolkien puts us into the viewpoint of the shocked Hobbit:

> Then out of the blackness in his mind he thought that he heard Dernhelm speaking; yet now the voice seemed strange, recalling some other voice that he had known.
> 'Begone, foul dwimmerlaik, lord of carrion! Leave the dead in peace!' (841)

The Nazgûl King tells "Dernhelm" that no man can kill him, but Éowyn takes off her helmet and discloses that she is a woman. It is one of the most piercing moments in *The Lord of the Rings;* Éowyn's love for Théoden and Merry's for both Éowyn and Théoden transfigure the two heroes:

> [T]he helm of her secrecy had fallen from her, and her bright hair, released from its bonds, gleamed with pale gold upon her shoulders. Her eyes grey as the sea were hard and fell, and yet tears were on her cheek. A sword was in her hand, and she raised her shield against the horror of her enemy's eyes.
> [I]nto Merry's mind flashed the face of one that goes seeking death, having no hope. Pity filled his heart and great wonder, and suddenly the slow-kindled courage of his race awoke. He clenched his hand. She should not die, so fair, so desperate! At least she should not die alone unaided. (841)

Significantly, Éowyn begins the fight by hacking off the head of the dragon ridden by the Nazgûl. "A light fell about her, and her hair shone in the sunrise." The King rises from the wreckage of his beast, smashes Éowyn's shield with a mace, and moves in to finish her, when Merry pierces him behind the "knee," allowing Éowyn to drive her sword through the Nazgûl's helmet, causing him to vanish or, stunningly, in the Peter Jackson movie, to implode.

There are several important sacramental aspects in this scene.

First, Tolkien portrays providence working with freely committed love to accomplish the good. The only two people on the battlefield capable of defeating the Nazgûl King are Éowyn and

Merry—Éowyn because she is a woman and Merry because he pierces the Nazgûl King with the only blade capable of cleaving his undead flesh, "breaking the spell that knit his unseen sinews to his will." It is the blade that Merry acquired, "by chance, so it may seem," in the Barrow-downs, when he and the Hobbits were rescued by Tom Bombadil, a blade with a spell on it. Although the two are on the battlefield against orders, and Éowyn is partly motivated by despair and the desire to die with glory, they both

offer themselves in sacrifice out of love and, for a moment, are transfigured by it.

In this scene, Éowyn becomes another of Tolkien's Marian women. There is a long Catholic iconographic tradition, based on Jerome's translation of Genesis 3:15, in which it is Eve who crushes the serpent's head. "I will put enmities between thee and the woman, and thy seed and her seed: she shall crush thy head, and thou shalt lie in wait for her heel." Mary is taken traditionally as the New Eve, the one who could defeat Satan in a way the first Eve could not, and she is often depicted with her heel on the serpent's head. Iconographic examples are the paintings Our Lady of Succor by Giovanni da Monte Rubiano and The Immaculate Conception by Giovanni Battista Tiepolo, above.

Both of these pictures capture an aspect of Éowyn in battle. In Rubiano's painting, she is a sword-wielder, going up against a satanic figure, a being close to Death itself. She is in the role of a protector—of children in these pictures (and Merry, as a Hobbit, has a child's stature). She is an intercessory figure; she puts herself between the children and Satan in the first picture, as Éowyn puts herself between Théoden and the Nazgûl. One of the meanings of *intercede* is "to interpose a veto," which is certainly what Éowyn does, when she interposes herself. Finally, Éowyn's action elevates her from an unhappy shieldmaiden looking for death and glory to a Marian self-sacrificer. Tolkien underscores this with the language of light and brilliancy, describing her "bright hair," which "gleamed with pale gold upon her shoulders": "A light fell about her, and her hair shone in the sunrise."

Revelations 12 is important here: A woman "clothed with the sun," wearing "a crown of twelve stars," confronts the great dragon Satan, and although she does not kill him, with divine help, she protects her son. The woman is Mary, the Queen of Heaven; her brilliancy, her function as a protecting figure, her confrontation with the dragon all link her to Éowyn. Tolkien is not asking us to see Éowyn as an allegory of Mary; rather, he is asking us to see that all women, in the courage of self-sacrifice, particularly when interceding for the helpless, become like Mary. He is asking us to see Mary again, to "recover" one aspect of her motherhood—her willingness to sacrifice, even in battle. Catholics are told to conform their lives to Christ—and to his great human reflector, Mary. Tolkien shows us how this happens for Éowyn. It happens throughout history, because people at their best do conform to the Marian potential the Logos has given them: "Let it be done unto me according to your will."

11

THE GOOD STEWARDS
OF MIDDLE-EARTH

*Let us glorify the Master Craftsman for all that has been done wisely
and skillfully; and from the beauty of the visible things let us form an
idea of Him who is more than beautiful; and from the greatness of
these perceptible and circumscribed bodies let us conceive of Him who
is infinite and immense and who surpasses all understanding in the
plentitude of His power.*   SAINT BASIL OF CAESAREA[1]

> *We shall not cease from exploration*
> *And the end of all our exploring*
> *Will be to arrive where we started*
> *And know the place for the first time.*
> T. S. ELIOT, "Little Gidding"

A SACRAMENTAL UNIVERSE, which figures forth the glory of
God, must be defended and preserved. In Genesis, the world
is given to Adam and Eve as a gift to use, but also as a realm of
intrinsic value to be contemplated. As tenders of the Garden of
Eden, the first couple has dominion not in the sense of domination but responsible care. They are not given *carte blanche* to plunder nature, but are the first stewards. Tolkien's appreciation of the
ethics of stewardship is evident throughout *The Lord of the Rings*.
Even before Sauron is vanquished, Tolkien starts to shift his

---

1 Saint Basil of Caesarea, *On the Hexaemeron*, in *Exegetic Homilies*, trans. Sister Agnes Clare Way, *Fathers of the Church* 46 (Washington, DC: Catholic University of American Press, 1963), homily 1.11, 19.

focus from military conflict to healing the wounds of war, as protecting the good gives way to nurturing it. The defenders of Middle-earth are stewards both as warriors and healers. Tolkien examines healing in application to three domains of woundedness: the individual, the social-political, and the natural.[2] Of the many stewards of Middle-earth, Aragorn takes center stage as the healer of the wounded people and the body politic of Gondor and Sam Gamgee as the healer of cultivated nature. Éowyn, the most wounded person in body and spirit, becomes the focal patient whose injuries and dislocation most represent those of Middle-earth. Her healing, more than anyone's, begins the healing of the war-ravaged world that will continue with her marriage to Faramir and their joint mission to restore Ithilien; it will extend to Sam's healing of the Shire. The specific sacrament behind the closing chapters of *The Lord of the Rings* is that of anointing the sick, and the theology is that of Catholic social thought, grounded in the sacramental understanding of Creation. Healing the body and healing the earth go hand in hand. Pope Benedict XVI could be stating a thesis for *The Lord of the Rings*, when he writes in *Caritas in Veritate*, "The environment is God's gift to everyone, and in our use of it we have a responsibility towards the poor, towards future generations, and towards humanity as a whole."[3]

Gandalf has the most encompassing mission as steward: the preservation and healing of all Middle-earth. He is not interested in "kicking the problem down the road," but in permanent and responsible solutions. Those alive now, at the time of crisis, have a duty to protect future generations by dealing with evil in the present; so he tells Elrond's Council the Ring must be disposed of once and for all: "[I]t is not our part here to take thought only for a season, or for a few lives of men, or for a passing age of the world. We should seek a final end of this menace, even if we do not hope to make one" (266).

---

2 See Matthew Dickerson and Jonathan Evans, *Ents, Elves, and Eriador: The Environmental Vision of J.R.R. Tolkien* (Lexington, KY: University Press of Kentucky, 2006).

3 Pope Benedict XVI, *Caritas in Veritate*, paragraph 48.

For Gandalf, everything in Middle-earth has intrinsic as well as instrumental value. The gifts of God are to be used wisely, with the understanding that, as part of a sacramental world, they mediate the presence of God and are part of the glory of Creation. In his confrontation with Denethor, a steward who has forgotten what stewardship means, Gandalf reminds him that it is servanthood:

> 'The rule of no realm is mine, neither of Gondor nor any other, great or small. But all worthy things that are in peril as the world now stands, those are my care. And for my part, I shall not wholly fail of my task, though Gondor should perish, if anything passes through this night that can still grow fair or bear fruit and flower again in days to come for I also am a steward. Did you not know?' (758)

As the book ends, however, Gandalf progressively turns over his stewardship duties to those around him. He will be leaving Middle-earth after Sauron's defeat; others who have followed him will have the responsibility for carrying on. Gandalf, at the end, is mainly a teacher whose task is nearly done and who has confidence in his pupils. His most accomplished student is Aragorn, who has worked at Gandalf's side for many years.

Aragorn Heals the Wounded

After the siege of Minas Tirith is lifted, the city must recover from the wreckage. Théoden's body is laid in state in the throne room; pits are dug for dead orcs and animals, graves for the dead of Minas Tirith and Rohan; the wounded are taken to the Houses of Healing. But the city has to deal with a "super-natural" malady as well, the Black Breath or Black Shadow that comes from prolonged exposure to the Nazgûl. Tolkien never explains the exact nature of the disease, but he provides clues. The Nazgûl are wraiths and they turn others into wraiths—their property is subtractive. "Living" black holes, they suck the spirit out of those around them and destroy the will to live. Gandalf is their natural enemy, for he *in*spires those around him. To be around the Nazgûl is to *ex*spire.

After the battle of Pelennor Fields, Aragorn, who does not know the political situation in Minas Tirith or that Denethor is dead, is careful not to enter the city for fear of creating political conflict over his claim to the throne. But, when he hears that Éowyn is dying, he comes to the Houses of Healing, hiding his face under an Elven cloak. If being around evil creatures causes the Black Breath, then being around good people—being restored to a community—is the cure; likewise, if evil breath/spirit is the problem, then the restoration of good breath is the cure. Aragorn, even as the unacknowledged king, represents the community and he treats the plague with an herb that provides good air, *athelas,* also known as kingsfoil.

Aragorn first treats Faramir, who is the closest to death, and it is the most theologically revealing of all Aragorn's healings. Faramir is like a man who has been gassed without knowing it. Aragorn says, "Slowly the dark must have crept on him, even as he fought and strove to hold his outpost" (864). Although Faramir has an arrow wound, Aragorn sees that what is killing him is "weariness, grief for his father's mood . . . and overall, the Black Breath." Aragorn, as spiritual doctor, goes on a search for Faramir's soul. He puts his hand on Faramir's brow: "And those that watched felt that some great struggle was going on. For Aragorn's face grew grey with weariness; and ever and anon he called the name of Faramir, but each time more faintly . . . as if Aragorn himself was removed from them, and walked afar in some dark vale, calling for one that was lost" (865). Aragorn returns to the land of the dead,[4] from which he led the Army of the Dead, as if looking for a lost sheep, and leads Faramir's soul out.

The second step of the healing process is the replacement of Black Breath with good through the crushing of kingsfoil into steaming water. This has a reviving effect on everyone in the room, filling the room with the sparkling freshness of spring (865).

---

4 Marjorie Burns notes that such passages to the land of the dead to rescue "a wandering soul" were part of the pagan beliefs of Northern Europe: "It is not an easy journey. In the process, likely enough, the shaman will have met an adversary and undergone a contest of strength or wit or will," *Perilous Realms,* 71. This accurately describes Aragorn's effort to bring Faramir back.

As with Frodo's dream at Tom Bombadil's house and Théoden's vision after he is released by Gandalf, this is a view of paradise, so fair that it is beyond the finest spring morning. This is part of calling the soul back, giving it a pleasant home among the living.

When Faramir awakes, his first words are, "My lord, you called me. I come. What does the king command?" which echoes Samuel's and Isaiah's response to God. Unlike his father, Denethor, Faramir is not jealous for rulership; his obedience to Aragorn is immediate, and this deference to just authority is crucial to his survival, for he follows Aragorn's call from the doors of death. His faith has made him whole in the most basic meaning of the word through his "fidelity" to the rightful king. Aragorn commands him to get better and be ready when he returns. This is the first step in healing the body-politic of Gondor and having a peaceful accession of Aragorn to the throne. He has healed the lineal steward himself, and Faramir, as the steward, has just recognized Aragorn as king (all of which is later formalized, for Faramir yields his stewardship to Aragorn, who then gives it back to him).

The healing of Gondor itself begins with the healing of wounded individuals. Ioreth, the nurse, recalls an old prophecy about the return of the king: *"The hands of the king are the hands of a healer, and so shall the rightful king be known"* (862). As Aragorn goes through the Houses of Healing, curing people, word spreads throughout the city "that the king was indeed come among them, and after the war he brought healing." The city begins to reconstitute itself as the capital of a monarchy.

The parallels with Christ's healings in the gospels, especially those in the gospel of John, are striking. Healing in all of the gospels contains an element of spiritual warfare. Christ's expulsion of demons is preliminary to his victory over death and the devil on the cross, but all his healings repair the damage of sin. Herbert McCabe recognized that sickness was a temptation toward despair. Misery, boredom, and pain work to Satan's benefit and degrade mankind unless resisted courageously. In fact, every sickness is a spiritual enemy with a spiritual component. The purpose of the sacrament of anointing the sick is return to a loving, Eucharistic community:

I want to suggest that sickness has somewhat the same relation to the realm of darkness that the sacraments have to the kingdom of the Son. Human infirmity, everything which tends of itself to degrade mankind, is a sign of the power of Satan, as the sacraments are signs of the power of Christ.... [Even when sickness does not degrade a man, it is because a man shows dignity in dealing with his sickness] precisely because it is his enemy.... Of itself the influence of Satan appears not in pleasure and vitality and joy of any kind, but in misery and boredom and pain. ...

.... I do not mean that sickness is brought about by the devil and *not* by the causes isolated by medical science. What I mean is that the fact that man is subject to disease is a result of his domination by the power of evil. It is because man deliberately placed himself under this power that he is liable to bodily infirmities; if he had not fallen he would have been preserved from such evils. Thus sickness shows forth the realm of Satan and every cure, quite apart from whether it works a moral improvement in the individual who is cured, represents a setback for that realm.[5]

Aragorn's healings are also a combat against spiritual evil, a palpable effect of demonism that diminishes and degrades the afflicted.

Christ's healings are, moreover, a sign that he is the Messiah, the King, in accordance with prophecies about how the Messiah will be known; this is especially true in the Gospel of John's "Book of Signs." So Aragorn's healings identify him as the prophesied king. In both cases, healing the sick announces the formation of a new polity: the City of God on the one hand and the kingdom of Gondor on the other. This has great, practical, political significance. The best leader is the one who heals the wounds and fissures in the body politic, not one who exacerbates them to fan civic strife. Good leaders bring healing that promotes harmony, just as good doctors promote harmony in the body. The comparison between Christ and Aragorn comes to an end with the one power that Tolkien would never grant Aragorn, the power to restore the soul and forgive sin, and we see this limitation explicitly in Aragorn's healing of Éowyn, which is only partial.

5 McCabe, *The New Creation*, 84–85.

Éowyn presents a harder case than Faramir for two reasons. She rode into battle seeking death out of despair and brought her own hopelessness with her. Also, by plunging her sword into the Nazgûl King, she has connected with the abyss in him, as if by electrocution. Of these two wounds, the first is the bigger problem. Gandalf tells her brother, Éomer, that, though born in the body of a maid, Éowyn had a courage and spirit to match his own (867). Yet, she had to watch Théoden, whom she loved as a father, fall into "a mean dishonoured dotage." In the process, she came to see herself as part of a dishonored and degraded house, described by Saruman as "a thatched barn where brigands drink in the reek, and their brats roll on the floor among their dogs." These thoughts were subtly insinuated by Wormtongue, who instilled in Éowyn a deep sense of dishonor on the part of her people (867).

Perhaps we have lost this deep sense of communal dishonor in the West, where consumerist individuality has done much to eclipse communal identity, but, as we have found, it exists very strongly in Islam and persists in our own military. Tolkien imagines a military honor culture in Rohan, and a high one, based on cavalry. The way honor is achieved and dishonor erased is through military victory. Éowyn is like Joan of Arc; she is a shieldmaiden of Rohan. As a woman she might remedy dishonor by attaching herself through marriage to an honorable man who can achieve the necessary military victory, and so she believes she loves Aragorn. Failing here, because Aragorn loves Arwen, Éowyn has no roads open to her. Disgrace leads to despair. She takes the desperate step of disguising herself as a man, so she can die in battle.

Aragorn brings Éowyn back, but, he says, if it is only to despair, she will die, unless her spirit can be healed (867). Éowyn must reconnect to joy and love; she must transcend the honor culture of her people and find deeper springs of life. So, although Éowyn awakes, the bigger part of her healing is yet to come and takes place when she discovers Faramir.

Éowyn Comes to Know Her Heart

When Aragorn leaves Minas Tirith to confront Sauron at the Black Gate, Éowyn is left to combat her own despair. Éowyn

comes to know her own heart, when she comes to know someone else's, when she falls in love with Faramir, who is also recovering in the Houses of Healing. The transfer of Éowyn's
affections to Faramir may seem fast and almost perfunctory,
unless we recognize a potential for love in Éowyn that goes
deeper than her love for "honor." We have to see her as more
than a Valkyrie. Tolkien suggests that potential in many ways.
Éowyn is mainly a dutiful servant of her people. She leads the
women and children on the march to Helm's Deep and in the
caves, as they wait out the siege. She loves her brother Éomer
and Théoden, and they love her back and wish her happiness.
She wants to serve, and her greatest dread is being caged so that
she cannot. In addition, she is clearly unsuited to Aragorn, who is
already 87 and, as one of the Dúnedain, can count on a lifespan,
unless he dies a violent death, of at least a hundred more years.
Aragorn, in comparison to the average human being, is almost
part Elf, most suited for a Dúnedain woman, if any were available, or even for Arwen, who has the option of giving up her relative immortality.

When Éowyn gets on her feet, she is a sad, lonely figure, who
tells the Warden that she is healed in body, except for her left
arm, but that she will sicken anew, if she can find nothing useful
to do (958). Faramir, who sees her with the Warden, sees her
hurt, sorrow, and unrest, and is moved with pity. Éowyn tells
Faramir her survival was a failure, for she looked for death in battle, and the battle continues without her (959). She doesn't desire
to be healed. She wants to go to war with her brother. But there
are two small steps toward healing in her first encounter with
Faramir. A warrior bred among warriors, she recognizes him
immediately as a man of great strength. She also sees "a grave
tenderness" in his eyes. Faramir counsels patience and gets her a
room with a window that faces east, so she can see the first sign
of a returning army.

The word that Tolkien uses repeatedly in this scene to describe
Faramir's feeling for Éowyn is "pity": "he was moved with pity,"
"being a man whom pity deeply stirred," "his heart was filled with
pity." It is the same word that Gandalf uses to describe Bilbo's feeling, when he spared Gollum. "Pity," which derives from the Latin

word "pietas," has no bad connotations in Tolkien's work. Rather, it is comes from the deepest Judeo-Christian understanding of God as one who feels sympathy, compassion, and loving kindness for humanity. Humans at their best emulate God's pity for humanity, and Tolkien the philologist reaches into the Middle Ages for the root meaning of the word. In a post-Nietzschean world, "pity" has come to assume connotations of superiority and condescension. It is wretched to be the object of pity, to be pitiful or pitiable. But even Éowyn does not feel demeaned by Faramir's pity; she recognizes it as love, and it begins to melt her "pride," the other word which occurs repeatedly: "Though her words were still proud, her heart faltered, and for the first time she doubted herself," "Her proud head drooped a little."

The linguistic import of the scene is that Faramir's compassion is dissolving Éowyn's pride, and again we have to leave aside the way we currently construe "pride," which makes it a trait we are proud to own. Tolkien, the medieval philologist, recognizes pride as the first of the deadly sins. Pride can serve a useful purpose, but it can also be a barrier between our will and fruitful love and compassion. It has become this for Éowyn, as it stands between her and her better nature.

Éowyn and Faramir look for seven days toward the east for the return of Aragorn and his men, wondering what the fate of the world will be, and it is there that Faramir's great capacity for hope is communicated to Éowyn. They are like the watchman on the tower of Isaiah 21:6–9:

> For thus hath the lord said to me: Go, and set a watchman: and whatsoever he shall see, let him tell.
>
> And he saw a chariot with two horsemen, a rider upon an ass, and a rider upon a camel: and he beheld them diligently with much heed. . . .
>
> Behold this man cometh, the rider upon the chariot with two horsemen, and he answered, and said: Babylon is fallen, she is fallen, and all the graven gods thereof are broken unto the ground.

In this case, the messenger is an Eagle, flying west, but Boromir senses the news about Sauron's defeat even before the Eagle arrives:

'The reason of my waking mind tells me that great evil has befallen and we stand at the end of days. But my heart says nay; and all my limbs are light, and a hope and joy are come to me that no reason can deny. Éowyn, Éowyn, White Lady of Rohan, in this hour I do not believe that any darkness will endure!' (963)

Tolkien's Eagle cries a psalm based on Psalm 23:7–10: "Lift up your gates, O ye princes, and be ye lifted up, O eternal gates: and the King of glory shall enter in." As the Psalm announced Babylon's fall, the Eagle's song announces Sauron's, incorporating part of Isaiah 21: "*Sing now ye people of the Tower of Anor, for the Realm of Sauron is ended for ever . . . Sing and rejoice, ye people of the Tower of Guard, for your watch hath not been in vain, . . . Sing and be glad, all ye children of the West, for your King shall come again*" (963). Tolkien writes, "And the people sang in all the ways of the City."

In the romance of Éowyn and Faramir, Tolkien writes one more scene where pity is replaced by a love in which Faramir values Éowyn as a whole human being. Though pity is not to be despised, marriage must be built on admiration. Tolkien provides a beautiful image of these two coming together and bringing their cultures into communion as well: "a great wind rose and blew, and their hair, raven and golden, streamed out mingling in the air. And the Shadow departed, and the Sun was unveiled" (963).

One of the miraculous properties of loving someone and being loved is that, seeing the qualities of the other person, we come to realize that we may have some of those qualities in ourselves, qualities that we come to value and develop in emulation of the person we love. What Éowyn finds in Faramir is gentleness and humility coexisting with strength and courage. It would be a great misreading of Tolkien to see Éowyn as just another heroine submitting stereotypically and with gratitude to a strong male. Rather, in Faramir, she finds herself by finding her complement, someone who brings out her gentleness with his own: "Then the heart of Éowyn changed, or else at last she understood it. And suddenly her winter passed, and the sun shone on her" (964). She finds her vocation: "I will be a shieldmaiden no longer, nor vie with the great Riders, nor take joy only in the songs of slaying. I

will be a healer, and love all things that grow and are not barren"
(965). Éowyn chooses creation over destruction.

Faramir and Éowyn will marry and "cross the River" to "dwell
in fair Ithilien and there make a garden." They become partners
in bringing back to life the land that bordered on Mordor. Thus
Tolkien brings us back to the basis of Christian stewardship in the
Garden of Eden.

healing the Body politic

The healing of Gondor requires the restoration of many broken
ties and a sacramental sign that community is being achieved. In
Christianity, the sign of unification is the Eucharist. In Gondor, it
is a tree. The White Tree of Gondor, which has grown by a fountain outside the throne room, has as its mythical ancestor the
world trees of both Hebrew Scripture and Norse mythology.
Yggdrasil, the world tree of Norse myth, has its source in the
Prose Edda. Its branches go far into the heavens and its roots deep
into the earth, symbolically joining all of creation as an organic
unity. (Interestingly, Odin sacrifices himself to himself by hanging
on this tree for nine days.) The Tree of Life and the Tree of
Knowledge of Good and Evil from Genesis are similar cosmic
trees, connecting man to God in ways that man is not yet ready
to assume, but which lie in the future. Jacob's ladder is much like
a world tree, connecting heaven to earth, and the Eucharist
achieves the organic unity of the church and heaven by organizing its members as the body of Christ in communion with God;
in Christianity, the cross is the world tree that connects man to
heaven through the Eucharist.

Tolkien's greatest world trees are from *The Silmarillion*, the
original light giving trees Laurelin and Telperion. The White
Tree of Gondor was a descendant of Telperion, but it gradually
died, while Gondor became more decadent and its birthrate
plummeted, as it lost hope in the future. Gondor lost contact
with heaven and earth, and the White Tree withered into an
emblem of spiritual alienation, fragmentation, disconnection,
and civic death. Aragorn must heal this wound.

For this spiritual task, he needs the help of a prophet, as David needed Samuel. This is Gandalf's role. But first, Aragorn must be crowned, and this ceremony begins the restoration to Gondor of social and cosmic harmony. Aragorn formally restores steward-ship to Faramir and his line. Although tradition has it that the new king receives the crown either from the hands of his living father or takes it from the hands of his father in the tomb where he is laid, neither of these options is available to Aragorn. But rather than crowning himself, Aragorn asks Faramir to give the crown to Frodo, who brings it to Gandalf, who then crowns Ara-gorn, for, as Aragorn says, he has come into his inheritance through the labor and valor of many (967–68). Aragorn's corona-tion involves all members of society, from the humblest Hobbits, represented by Frodo, to the guardian angel of the planet, Gan-dalf. When Aragorn rises after kneeling to receive the crown, he is transformed: "Tall as the sea-kings of old, he stood above all that were near; ancient of days he seemed and yet in the flower of manhood; and wisdom sat upon his brow, and strength and heal-ing were in his hands, and a light was about him" (968).

Several days after the coronation, Gandalf takes Aragorn from the city at night and they ascend Mount Mindolluin, which rises behind Minas Tirith and there, miraculously, they find an ances-tor of the tree Telperion. "Who shall say how it comes here in the appointed hour?" asks Gandalf. They transplant it to the court by the fountain in place of the old tree, which is not burned, but "laid to rest," and the new tree thrives. This tableau has much in common with the Mount Sinai experience, though it is translated into a Northern vernacular, for the tree represents the reconnec-tion of heaven to Gondor—it is a social covenant with the future, a functional equivalent of the Hebrew ark, much as is the Arken-stone of *The Hobbit*.[6]

---

6 Though developing this idea is tempting, it would take me beyond the scope of this book. I would suggest, however, that Thorin Oakenshield wants the Arkenstone so badly, because he sees it in very much the same way as Ara-gorn sees the sapling of Telperion—as a covenant that assures the future of his people. Losing these symbols provokes a crisis very similar to that of losing the Ark of the Covenant to the Philistines in 1 Samuel 4.

Frodo's Love for Gollum

It may seem strange to claim that Frodo loves Gollum, but if love is seeking the good of the other for the other, then Frodo does love him. Love is a matter of will—not a sensation. Although Frodo needs Gollum as a guide and has few illusions about how dangerous he might prove to be, Frodo also treats him with dignity, unlike Sam, whose least endearing trait is an often callous judgmentalism. Sam and Frodo both see the practical necessity of using Gollum and its dangers. They cannot find their way into Mordor without him, but he is a murderer who cannot be trusted. The difference is that Frodo holds hope Gollum can be saved, while Sam does not. Despite his evaluation of Sam as the main hero of *The Lord of the Rings*, Tolkien also notes that he is a representative Hobbit in possessing "a mental myopia" that has the faults of smugness, cocksureness, and "a readiness to measure and sum up all things from a limited experience."[7] Sam does not have the capacity of Frodo to understand Gollum or pity him. Yet, even Sam refrains from killing Gollum, after Gollum tries to kill him on Mount Doom.

Frodo's first moment of decision comes in "The Taming of Sméagol," when he and Sam capture Gollum. Frodo remembers Gandalf's words, "Be not too eager to deal out death in the name of justice, fearing for your own safety. Even the wise cannot see all ends" (615). Frodo tells Sam he will not hurt Gollum, for, once he sees him, he pities him (615). Sam recognizes that the two are "akin" somehow, that they can reach each other's minds (618), and this is certainly because of the mutual experience of having the Ring. Paradoxically, while the Ring damages Frodo, it makes him grow in love as well. Frodo gives Gollum his dignity by calling him Sméagol.

Though Frodo is tempted to let Faramir kill Gollum at the Forbidden Pool, he cannot do it. He realizes that Gollum, the servant, has a claim on his master and that Gandalf would not want Frodo to let him die. And even though, at the Pool, Gollum feels betrayed by Frodo, part of Gollum responds to the love of Frodo

7 *Letters*, 329.

with love in turn, so that on the Stairs of Cirith Ungol, Gollum almost changes: a poor, "pitiable," old Hobbit, he reaches out to touch the sleeping Frodo, but Sam awakes, demanding what he is up to, and the moment passes (714). Gollum's salvation is lost in this instant, but Frodo's course of kindness, pity, and forgiveness toward Gollum saves the world.[8]

Frodo's care for Gollum ultimately extends toward all Middle-earth. All of the other healings, of Gondor, Ithilien, and the Shire, could never occur without Frodo's "unsuccessful" attempt to heal Gollum. The pity of Frodo, like Bilbo's, has ruled the fate of many. Tolkien's universe runs according to a spiritual economy even the wisest cannot understand. Good has an objective life of its own and spreads. Tolkien re-inscribes the Parable of the Mustard Seed (Matthew 13:31–32, Mark 4:30–32, and Luke 13:18–19) in Middle-earth.

Che hoßßits heal the Shire

In the last two chapters of *The Lord of the Rings,* Tolkien's experience as a veteran of World War I and the Somme played a part. Tolkien must have been aware of many soldiers who, after the war, had trouble adjusting to civilian life or who could never recover psychologically or physically. After Gandalf leaves the four Hobbits near the border of the Shire, Merry comments that The War of the Ring "seems almost like a dream that has slowly faded." But Frodo says, to him, going back to the Shire "feels more like falling asleep again." As Ring-bearer, Frodo has been awakened to aspects of reality that Sam has glimpsed, but are unknown to Merry and Pippin.

When the Hobbits attempt to enter the Shire and find it blocked by a closed gate, they discover the War of the Ring is not yet over and, on a reduced scale, must be fought within the Shire. As Tolkien hinted in the chapter "Flotsam and Jetsam," when Merry and Pippin discover food stores and Longbottom Leaf from the Shire in the wreck of Isengard, Saruman has been plundering outlying districts to feed his armies, and he has enslaved

---

8 See *Letters,* 234.

the Shire to this end. There, he has created his own bureaucratic paradise of impoverishment and devastation, turning the Shire into an over-regulated, economically non-functioning police-state, in which the intimidated Hobbits cooperate in their own destruction. The Hobbits are cowed by the men that Saruman has brought in, and some have become collaborators. Those who resist are thrown in "lock-holes." He has destroyed traditional Hobbit holes, introduced shoddy "government housing," and regulated or forbidden everything that gives Hobbits joy—like pipeweed and ale. He has worked an environmental disaster.[9]

Saruman hates the Shire for the part the Hobbits have played in denying him the Ring and wants to destroy it, for spite, because Gandalf values it. His dictatorship and environmental destruction are gratuitously mean and rendered emblematic by his cutting down the Party Tree, the "world tree" of the Shire. Saruman exemplifies the "banality of evil" more than ten years before Hannah Arendt applied the phrase to Eichmann.

Tolkien is politically canny about the first step of resistance to modern totalitarianism: to refuse its view of the world. Many of the Hobbits have, under threat, swallowed Saruman's political economics, despite its effect on the Shire. The first thing the returning Hobbits do to overthrow the oppressors of the Shire is to laugh at Sharkey's arrangements. No one has ever been bossed around by Shirriffs before or been stopped by border gates. No one accumulated property beyond what was reasonably manageable or useful. Having been arrested, Merry, Pippin, and Sam are "at their ease laughing and talking and singing," while the dour and worried Shirriffs stump along in front of them, "trying to look stern and important." The four Hobbits go where they want to and do what they want, as in the days before they left the Shire, without heed to warnings. This alone is a revolution. But it

---

9 "The Scouring of the Shire" has striking parallels with the development and "restoration" of New Wanley in George Gissing's novel *Demos: A Story of English Socialism*, though Gissing presents a more complex picture of the economic consequences of undoing industrialism. Suburbanization and destruction of the countryside occupied many writers of Tolkien's generation and the one before, including H.G. Wells.

is not enough. Tolkien has taken the Hobbits far out into the world, but finally their freedom comes down to protecting their homes and their own front doors, and, for this, neither bloodshed nor the willingness to die can be avoided. The second step is unity under good leadership. Pippin rides to rouse the Tooks, Sam gets the Cottons to raise Hobbiton, and, most important of all, Merry winds the horn of Rohan. That blast reminds the Hobbits who they are and gives them courage.

Merry and Pippin become the military leaders in the uprising, and they get most of the glory in the annals of Hobbit history. In the final battle, The Battle of Bywater, seventy "ruffians" are killed against nineteen Hobbits killed and thirty wounded. Saruman is killed by the hand of Wormtongue at Frodo's doorstep, and Wormtongue dies with three Hobbit arrows in him. Frodo sighs, "The very last stroke. But to think that it should fall here, at the very door of Bag End! Among all my hopes and fears at least I never expected that" (1020).

Throughout the conflict, Frodo gives the Shire a great gift that few either perceive or appreciate: he does all he can to keep the bloodletting and hatred to a minimum. When Frodo, Sam, Merry, and Pippin are initially "arrested" by a group of Shirriff Hobbits, they give their arrestors some anxiety by not taking the idea seriously. Since they are on the way to Bag End anyway, they tell the Shirrifs they will go with them: "'Very well, Mr. Baggins,' said the leader, pushing the barrier aside. 'But don't forget I've arrested you.' 'I won't,' said Frodo. 'Never. But I may forgive you'" (1001). Thus begins Frodo's campaign to heal the Shire, even before battle is joined. Frodo addresses the situation of the collaborative Lotho Sackville-Baggins, whom Pippin wants to "destroy": "I don't think you quite understand things, Pippin. . . . Lotho never meant things to come to this pass. He has been a wicked fool, but he's caught now" (1006).[10] Frodo can see this, and Pippin cannot, because Frodo has been inside evil in a way no one else has, and Frodo recognizes his initial desire that Gollum should die in Pip-

10 Frodo is being a good Jesuit, extending to Lotho the Ignatian "Presupposition" of giving our neighbor the benefit of the doubt. See James Martin, S.J., *The Jesuit Guide to (Almost) Everything* (NY: Harper Collins, 2012), 234–236.

pin's thought about Lotho. Before the Hobbits move to oust their oppressors, Frodo sets a ground rule that is crucial for the future good of the Shire: no Hobbit has ever killed another Hobbit in the Shire on purpose, and it is not to begin now (1006). Immediately after Saruman attempts to knife him, Frodo seeks to prevent Sam's vengeance. Saved by his chain mail, Frodo stops Sam from putting an arrow into Saruman and says, "It is useless to meet revenge with revenge: it will heal nothing" (1019). To offer forgiveness so quickly after attempted murder demonstrates Frodo's stature as a saint. He becomes a means of grace himself, someone who points to God and the ways of God.

Frodo's great insight on Mount Doom, when he declares that he will be an Orc no more, is that revenge causes profound spiritual damage to the revenger. It wounds the capacity to both give and receive love. It destroys society by leading to an unending reaction of revenge, and ends in Mordor, the last link in the chain begun by Morgoth, when he attempted to sabotage the chorus of the Ainur. Frodo has seen this reality from the inside, while carrying the Ring, and on the outside, surrounding him, as he and Sam walked over Cirith Ungol and into Mordor. In "The Scouring of the Shire," Frodo is the only Hobbit who recognizes the Shire must be saved from a spiritual death as well as an occupation. The end of Frodo's quest is to finally understand what Gandalf told him at the beginning: "The pity of Bilbo may rule the fate of many." The same can be said of Frodo's pity for Gollum, and it now rules the fate of many in the Shire.

It is instructive to compare Tolkien's attitude toward Germany with that of Frodo's toward Saruman. In a letter to his son Christopher, serving at the time in the RAF, Tolkien writes of the German people as the Russians invade:

> I have just heard the news.... Russians 60 miles from Berlin ... people gloat to hear of the endless lines, 40 miles long, of miserable refugees, women and children pouring West, dying on the way. There seem no bowels of mercy or compassion, no imagination, left in this dark diabolic hour. By which I do not mean that it may not all, in the present situation, mainly (not solely) created by Germany, be necessary and inevitable. But why gloat? ... The destruction of Germany, be

it 100 times merited, is one of the most appalling world-catastrophes.[11]

Frodo's desire to put hate aside, avoid killing, and forgive is motivated by his native love for his people and a deep understanding of evil that comes from his own wounds in carrying the Ring.[12] As he and Sam survey the wreckage of the Shire, Sam says that it is worse than Mordor: "it comes home to you, as they say; because it is home, and you remember it before it was all ruined" (1018). Frodo replies, "Yes, this is Mordor. . . . Just one of its works." Frodo has come to see Mordor not as a place, but a spiritual condition that must be fought with more resources than swords.

It takes Merry, Pippin, Frodo and Sam only a few days to rouse the Shire and overthrow Saruman. All the Hobbits have lacked is courageous leadership to mobilize them. The chapter is the necessary ending of the Hobbits' journey. It shows how much they have grown and expresses Tolkien's belief in the Catholic idea of "subsidiarity"—that, if left to their own devices, localities have the resources in tradition and custom to take care of themselves better than a centralized government. Gandalf knows what has happened in the Shire, but he lets the Hobbits sort it out for themselves. His last lesson is to let his four pupils stand on their own to discover how far they have come.

✠

When Sam remembers the box which Galadriel had given him, he consults Frodo, Merry, and Pippin about how to use it. Inside, there is grey dust, "soft and fine" and, in the middle, a small, silver nut. Pippin advises throwing the entire contents into the air in Sam's garden and letting it do its work. This is the typical Pippin approach to most things, but Sam is justifiably wary of this

11 *Letters*, 111.

12 Christine Chism, in "Myth, the Middle Ages, and the Aryan Nation," in *Tolkien the Medievalist*, argues that, after the Ring's destruction, Frodo is left "crippled and will-less," 86. Crippled, yes, "will-less," no. Frodo asserts his will quite strongly and effectively in "The Scouring of the Shire," but as a peacemaker, not as a warrior.

advice. No matter what gifts or assistance have been given to the Hobbits in the past, effort has always been required to use them well. Sam is sure Galadriel wasn't making a personal gift to him, after "so many folk have suffered." Frodo advises Sam to use all of his own wits and knowledge as a gardener, and this is what Sam does, travelling all over the Shire, planting new trees, and using just one grain of dust to fertilize each, though he pays special attention to Hobbiton and Bywater. He plants the silver nut where the Party Tree used to stand and, when he has only a little dust left, he tries to find the exact middle of the Shire and throws the remainder into the air.

Galadriel's gift supports and enhances Sam's charism. The result in the year 1420 is a gardening miracle, with each sapling growing at many times its normal rate. The nut turns out to be the seed of a *mallorn* tree, the tree of Lothlórien, sequoia-like in stature, with silver bark and golden flowers. Tolkien describes the total effect on the Shire in two luxurious paragraphs. "Not only was there wonderful sunshine and delicious rain, in due times and perfect measure, but there seemed something more: an air of richness and growth, and a gleam of a beauty beyond that of mortal summers that flicker and pass upon this Middle-earth" (1023). Crops fill the barns to bursting; fruit is so plentiful that young Hobbits "very nearly bathed in strawberries and cream," and the "leaf" and barley are so fine that they set the standard for smoking and beer thereafter.

In his description of the restoration of the Shire, "beyond mortal summer," Tolkien gives us a glimpse of the *sacrum convivium,* the sacred banquet of the Eucharist, which, as Thomas Aquinas wrote, is a pledge of future glory given to us. This sacred feast, which brings together all people and unites them, is envisioned in Isaiah 25:6 as taking place in the location usually thought to be closest to God in the Old Testament, a mountain: "And the Lord of hosts shall make unto all people in this mountain, a feast of fat things, a feast of wine, of fat things full of marrow, of wine purified from the lees." In Hobbiton, a good smoke and ale will do.

The point of the *sacrum convivium* is to reunite all people in joy, and this is what has happened in the Shire due to the providential efforts of the four Hobbits, the citizens of the Shire, and people far away, such as Aragorn, Galadriel and Gandalf—and even Gollum, without whom the Ring would not have entered the fire. It is impossible without the military effort to fight the intruders, led by Merry and Pippin, as well as Frodo's peace-making, or Sam's use of Galadriel's gift, in which a little of Lothlórien persists in the Shire.

✠

Three marriages occur as *The Lord of the Rings* draws to a close: Arwen to Aragorn; Éowyn to Faramir; and Sam to Rosie Cotton. They signify many of the same things as the multiple marriages at the end of Shakespeare's romantic comedies. Love between members of the opposite sex finds fulfillment in the total commitment of marriage, mirroring the Trinitarian understanding that God is a community of Love flowing between the Father and the Son. Married love, therefore, has its grounding in the most fundamental reality of the Logos-centric universe; it is so much part of the Music of reality that even the Valar paired off almost immediately. The community finds fulfillment in these marriages as well, for it is sustained by marriages that produce children and in wedding festivities where the community unites to celebrate its own continuity and identity.

The Arwen-Aragorn marriage unites Elf to Human and promises an heir to a kingdom long bereft of kings and a stable future. Éowyn and Faramir unite Gondor to Rohan and, in addition to children, their union promises the future restoration of Ithilien. Sam and Rosie have thirteen children, Elanor being the first, named after the star-shaped flower of Lothlórien. Sam becomes mayor of Hobbiton for many years and is later known as Samwise Gardener. Human fecundity is part of the spring that Sam brings to the Shire: "All children born or begotten in that year, and there were many, were fair to see and strong, and most of them had a rich golden hair that had before been rare among hobbits" (1023). (The Lady of Lórien's dust affected more than plant life!)

Only Frodo is left out. He cannot find healing in Middle-earth. The Ring has eaten a hole in him, and he fingers the white jewel given to him by Arwen as a substitute, which he wears on a chain around his neck. Finally, he must leave on the ship for Valinor, with Bilbo, Gandalf, Galadriel, and Elrond. Tolkien was consistent in saying that the main subject of *The Lord of the Rings* was death, and Frodo's deliverance, by sailing into the West, does start that journey. Without complete sanctification, long life eventually becomes a burden and then a torture. Death is God's gift in Tolkien's world; rather than a punishment for sin, it is an exit to communion with God. Frodo is Everyman in the sense that Everyman is damaged and in need of healing. As Frodo sails into the west, a more complete healing begins:

> And the ship went out into the High Sea and passed on into the West, until at last on a night of rain Frodo smelled a sweet fragrance on the air and heard the sound of singing that came over the water. And then it seemed to him that as in his dream in the house of Bombadil, the grey rain-curtain turned all to silver glass and was rolled back, and he beheld white shores and beyond them a far green country under a swift sunrise. (1030)

I said at the beginning of this book that my students love Tolkien for reasons they do not completely understand, and I can say the same for myself. That is the way with all great books. To read Tolkien is to be included in one man's vision of the holy, a vision that he himself understood only in part, like a fascinated explorer from a new found land returning with his journal.

To read and reread Tolkien with pleasure, to experience the world with Tolkien's sense of wonder and holiness, is to be Christianized, perhaps without knowing it, to be invited into the presence of a "beauty beyond the circles of the world." It is to fall in love with a meaningful universe that has a beginning and end, where good and bad are not subjective choices but objective realities, a world which is full of grace, though damaged by sin, in which friendship is the seedbed of the virtues, and hard-earned virtue culminating in self-sacrificing love is recognized as the highest human achievement. It is a world where the worst are forgiven, again and again, even if they do not accept that forgiveness, and where the humble of spirit find within themselves great resources and do great things. It is a world invested in the providential care of the One Creator, who brings goodness and beauty out of evil, in which eucatastrophe does not always happen, but can happen, and where the greatest warriors finally become the greatest healers. The world of Tolkien's secondary creation is God's story, reinscribed as a history before our records of history, reflecting the Logos as does the universe and all that is in it, including history, myth, fairy-tale, and secondary myth, since everything in existence, even Tolkien's sub-creation, bears the Primary Artist's inscription.

INDEX